The Promise of the Revolution

The Promise of the Revolution

Stories of Fulfillment and Struggle in China's Hinterland

Daniel B. Wright

ROWMAN & LITTLEFIELD PUBLISHERS, INC.
Lanham • Boulder • New York • Oxford

On the cover: The painting, "Qinggang Charcoal" (*Qinggang Meitan,* 165 x 150 cm, 1997), was created by Long Kanghua, a painter from a rural county in southern Guizhou Province. Long Kanghua, like this book, intends to reflect through his work the perspective of local Guizhou citizens. According to Long Kanghua, "Qinggang Charcoal" portrays migrant laborers who have carried homemade charcoal on their bicycles to the nearby county town. Though they stand in the city, the benefits and pleasures of urban life, represented by the karaoke and stomach medicine advertisements painted on the wall behind them, remain a distant reality.

The poster reproduced on page 101 belongs to the International Institute of Social History Stefan R. Landsberger Collection.

ROWMAN & LITTLEFIELD PUBLISHERS, INC.
Published in the United States of America
by Rowman & Littlefield Publishers, Inc.
A Member of the Rowman & Littlefield Publishing Group
4501 Forbes Boulevard, Suite 200, Lanham, Maryland 20706
www.rowmanlittlefield.com

P.O. Box 317, Oxford OX2 9RU, United Kingdom

British Library Cataloguing in Publication Information Available

Library of Congress Cataloging-in-Publication Data

Wright, Daniel B., 1962–
    The promise of the revolution : stories of fulfillment and struggle in China's hinterland / Daniel B. Wright.
        p.   cm.
    Includes bibliographical references and index.
    ISBN 0-7425-1915-5 (alk. paper)—ISBN 0-7425-1916-3 (pbk. : alk. paper)
        1. Wright, Daniel B., 1962—Journeys—China. 2. China—Description and travel. I. Title. II. Title: Stories of fulfillment and struggle in China's hinterland.
DS712 .W75   2003
951'.3405—dc21   2002154388

Printed in the United States of America

♾ ™ The paper used in this publication meets the minimum requirements of American National Standard for Information Sciences—Permanence of Paper for Printed Library Materials, ANSI/NISO Z39.48-1992.

to
Guowei, Margaret, and Jon
fellow travelers on the journey

Contents

Maps and Figures

MAPS

FIGURES

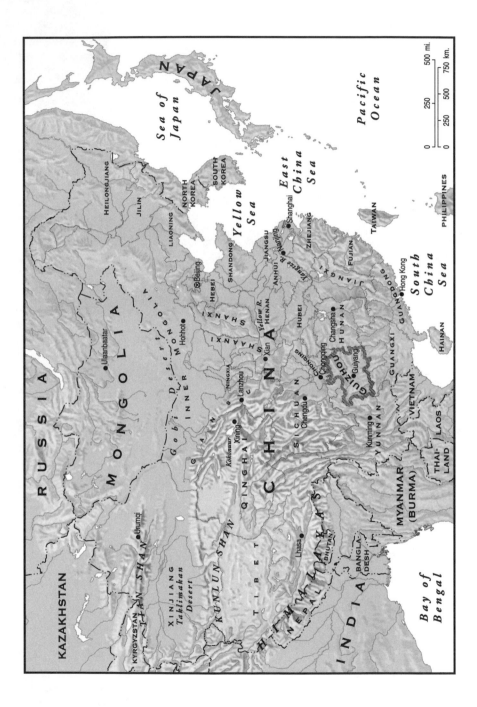

Foreword

In this volume's introduction, Daniel B. Wright approvingly quotes former U.S. ambassador to China Stapleton Roy, who observed that "Knowledge does not equal understanding." This terrific volume not only imparts knowledge, it also provides the reader with great understanding of what Wright calls China's "search to find itself."

The author accomplishes this by viewing China from the bottom up and from the inside out. He brings the reader along with him on his journey to understand contemporary China from the perspective of China's poorest province, Guizhou—both "the inside" and "the bottom." In so doing, *The Promise of the Revolution: Stories of Fulfillment and Struggle in China's Hinterland* makes its contributions to the tradition of rural and hinterland studies undertaken by the likes of Sidney Gamble, John L. Buck, and China's own Fei Hsiao Tung. Moreover, this examination of the hinterland's struggle to overcome the dead hand of tradition and circumstance contrasts with, and adds to, the work of a fellow grantee of the Institute of Current World Affairs (ICWA), Cheng Li. In *Rediscovering China,* Li wrote about the dynamic transformation of China's lower Yangtzi River Valley—one of China's wealthiest regions. These two volumes stand together as bookends on the shelf of works about social, economic, and political change in China during the era of reform.

Wright, along with his wife and children, had the opportunity to spend about two years in the small city of Duyun in southeastern Guizhou; he was a fellow in the prestigious Institute of Current World Affairs (more on ICWA later in this section), formerly known as the American University Field Staff. He did not let grass grow under his feet, relaxing in the relative ease of life in Duyun, a prefectural capital. Rather, among a great number of other activities, he chose to retrace 150 miles of the Long March on foot through some of the most rugged terrain traversed on that epic trek by the Chinese Communists more than fifty years earlier. Similarly, he examined the circumstances and aspirations of inland migrants heading for China's coast by taking a grueling, nearly two-day train ride to Guangzhou in a third-class rail car packed cheek to jowl with what became his "informants," in the antiseptic jargon of social science—that train was anything but antiseptic! And he spent time living with his local friend Jianhua in the mountainous, dirt-poor Splendid Village (annual per capita income U.S. $56), learning about life in an isolated rural area inhabited by "minority peoples." This elegant study is a mixture of systematic data and intimate reportage.

The chapters in this volume are, for the most part, Wright's ICWA Letters, the periodic reports he was to write as the primary obligation of his two years (1997–1999) in the Institute's program. Wright's seven predecessors as ICWA China fellows span the last seventy-five years. They include A. Doak Barnett in 1947–1949 (the period in China that resulted in his classic *China on the Eve of Communist Take-over*), as well as Cheng Li, who was a fellow from 1993 to 1995. The Fellows Program has provided exceptional young people who have analytic ability, perception, and advanced writing skills with the opportunity to live in China and all over the world, picking a vantage point from which to try understand the society, and to convey what they learn to a broader audience through monthly "letters."

Wright brought a unique background and set of skills to this task, not the least exceptional language ability, as reflected by his prior experience as a translator at the Chinese Literature Press in China. Prior to that, he studied at Beijing University, Beijing Foreign Languages Institute, Beijing Languages Institute, and Shanghai Foreign Languages Institute. Along the way, he received a Masters in Divinity from Fuller Theological Seminary, part of the preparation that made it possible for him to write one of the book's most powerful chapters—"Matters of the Heart . . . The Rebirth of Religion." Beyond his further preparation through a Masters Degree at Johns Hopkins-SAIS, not to mention his abilities in the observation and writing domains, this book reflects his ability to connect with those he met in China in a way that enabled him to penetrate to the deeper levels of human anxiety and aspiration.

And it is here, at this intersection of individual and collective anxiety and aspiration, that this book makes its major contributions to our understanding of contemporary China. Chapter by chapter, it does so by taking events in daily life and probing their meaning with respect to larger issues. So, for example, he gives meaning to the discussion of corruption in China, a theme that courses through much of the book, by showing how the work of one dedicated village teacher at Big Nest Elementary School—Chen Dongfang—in getting village students enrolled was undone by "a government-corruption-induced tobacco-price debacle." He gives new depth and detail to our understanding of the economic idiocy of the late–Mao Zedong period by examining the effect of the "Third Front" industrial relocation policy of the 1964–1971 period—we get a tour of Factory "321," which was relocated outside of Duyun in a muddy mountain fastness designed to protect and isolate the manufacturing plant and its community of three thousand persons. Mao tried to protect factories from attack by the West and the Soviet Union, while his successor, Deng Xiaoping, subsequently tried to connect these very same plants to the West. Locating China's industry up the muddy byways of China's hinterland may have accomplished the first purpose, but it made impossible achievement of the second.

One of the most powerful themes in the book deals with inequality. Wright correctly observes that while the coastal–inland and interprovincial divides are large, it is the rural–urban gap that is truly cavernous. When one is confronted in this book with the differences in life opportunity that accrue to anyone in a Chinese city, as opposed to almost any peasant in Guizhou, the gaps are enormous and almost compel the reader to believe, as one Chinese peasant put it to Wright, "It's time for the dynasty to change"—*Chaodai yao bianle!* And yet, Wright eschews the inevitability of this conclusion, observing that "most who have come out on the short end of Deng's economic miracle . . . are more eager to take advantage of the income gap than to despise it." And herein lies the force behind the floodtide of impoverished peasants seeking temporary work in both far-off (from Guizhou) coastal cities, as well as any urban place closer to home.

Capping off the entire discussion of inequality, one will find chapter 16 ("Golfing in Guiyang") particularly illuminating, not the least because of the vignette of the peasant girl golf caddie telling the author to use a six-iron rather than a seven-iron on the approach shot to the Guiyang Golf Club's final green. One cannot help but be struck by the fact that the Club membership fee was 200,000 yuan, about 145 times the average net peasant income in the province at the time—not to mention the 250 yuan monthly fee, more than five times the province's figure for average net peasant monthly income.[1] Wright, however, avoids the facile impulse to simply be aghast, instead concluding that "Reason, however, suggests that if a market-driven real estate investment company from coastal Guangdong is willing to put up the money, there is no rationale why the course should not be here. And if the course makes Guizhou a more attractive location for business executives, more power to them and the province. Shared prosperity is not guaranteed by simply maintaining the lowest common denominator."

Nonetheless, the author also knows that the story of inequality and its implications does not end here, with free-market logic. Every regime needs legitimacy, of some sort, and this was a regime whose founding myth had to do with urban–rural equality, peasant prosperity, and the unworthiness of the urban bourgeoisie's wealth and power. "Every government," Wright tells us, "needs a story to tell." Given current reality in China, what is the new story that China's leaders can tell to spur future progress and maintain tolerable social peace along the way—what is to be the legitimating myth of the Communist Party in a capitalist society? Citing two 1994 surveys by China's innovative and fearless economist Professor Hu Angang, Wright reports that about 90 percent of polled provincial and county leaders "believed that regional disparity had reached extreme proportions, violating socialism's 'shared prosperity' principle."

In a particularly perceptive section of the book (chapter 18), its conclusion, the author discusses China's new fourth generation of leaders just settling into positions of power throughout the Chinese political system. Appropriately for this book, the new general secretary succeeding Jiang Zemin, Hu Jintao, spent part of his career in Guizhou, as well as in Tibet and Gansu. Wright seems to have hope that Hu's experiences, and those of many of his elite colleagues, of having been posted to rural areas during the Cultural Revolution and throughout their careers will give them both the skills and the compassion to begin to reconstruct a new legitimating myth and a more equitable economic and social order. He hopes that this new generation will give birth to "A policy environment created by top-down legislation and support, met by a bottom-up response of increased civic participation by the people." In short, he hopes, without being naive, that China's new generation of leaders will care about the parts of China left behind, that they will construct a framework of law and policy to address these challenges, and that they will unleash the creative potential of civil society to address them. Wright, like the rest of us, will be watching closely to see if this occurs. These are among the principal challenges that confront China's new elite.

David M. Lampton

Acknowledgments

The night before my family and I left southwest China's Guizhou Province to return to the United States, a high school principal we had come to know gave me a present. He handed me the small package with a smile. I opened the red velvet box to find three keys mounted inside. "Those two keys are to my school; the other one is to my home," Principal Di said as he pointed. "I'd like you to have a set." Like his gift, scores of Guizhou residents, many of whose stories are in this book, opened for me all kinds of new understanding about China. I wish to first acknowledge the people of Guizhou whom I encountered during my two-year stay in the province—poor and rich, rural and urban, illiterate and well educated, young and old, insignificant and powerful—too many to name, but each of whom provided me with valuable keys of insight into China's hinterland.

My purpose in researching and writing from a base in southwest China was straightforward: to pursue wisdom and understanding about China from the perspective of the country's interior—from the bottom looking up and from the inside looking back out to the coast. Few studies of China choose the country's poorest regions as their point of departure. From this vantage point, this book attempts to contribute to our understanding of China by addressing the following question: What do the lives of people in China's hinterland tell us about the country fifty years since the Communist takeover and twenty-five years since Deng Xiaoping initiated reform? I am deeply indebted to the Institute of Current World Affairs, which made this opportunity for study possible and which has granted me permission to publish this material in book form. I am indebted to ICWA's executive director Peter Bird Martin as well, whose profound insights into the problems of studying and understanding contemporary international affairs have had an enormous impact upon all those who have been privileged to be Institute fellows under him.

I would also like to express my appreciation for other ICWA members and trustees who provided companionship and guidance, albeit from a distance, throughout the fellowship. The late Doak Barnett, Joseph Battat, Richard Dudman, Cheng Li, and Peter Geithner, in particular, provided encouragement throughout and beyond. I treasure the memory of several pre-departure planning sessions at the home of Doak and Jeanne Barnett, together discussing issues to look for during the adventure we were about to launch in southwest China. ICWA program administrator Gary Hansen and publications manager Ellen Kozak provided me with enthusiastic logistics and publications help throughout the fellowship.

Few pursuits of understanding occur in isolation. One's community shapes one's study. I am especially grateful for the encouragement of Doak Barnett, David Lampton, and Carol Lee Hamrin, each of whom has influenced my view and approach to the study of China. Barnett taught me to ground my analysis in study, observation, and experience at the grassroots level. Lampton, my colleague at Johns Hopkins University-SAIS, has provided an example in exercising the obligation of speaking the truth to power. And Hamrin, a friend for many years now and an accomplished China scholar, is a constant reminder that we need not allow the head and the heart to become divided in our pursuit to understand and relate to China.

Throughout the preparation of this manuscript I benefited from the generous input and advice from the following friends, colleagues, and China specialists: Halsey Beemer, Kam Wing Chan, Kang Xiaoguang, Murray Hiebert, Hu Angang, Scott Kennedy, Ching Kwan Lee, Jing Lin, Sheila Melvin, Minxin Pei, Alan Piazza, Stapleton Roy, Anne Thurston, Kellee Tsai, Ezra Vogel, Peter Wonacott, and Tim Vinzani, among many others. My special thanks go to Joseph Fewsmith, Cheng Li, and Martin King Whyte, who read the entire manuscript and provided comment. I also want to thank Nicholas Sheets, who worked with me for several months as a research assistant, for his thorough library research and diligent support in preparing many of the figures used in the book.

Susan McEachern, executive editor at Rowman & Littlefield, patiently and skillfully encouraged me throughout the preparation process. I am grateful to Susan for her expert editing and guidance in bringing this project to fruition. I also wish to thank others at Rowman & Littlefield: Matt Hammon, associate editor; Jehanne Schweitzer, production editor; and Patti Waldygo, copyeditor.

Parts of chapter 14 were first published as "Learning in Guizhou," in *Barron's Magazine,* Dow Jones & Co., Inc., August 14, 1999. Parts of chapter 4 and 8 were also printed in my articles "Hey Coolie! Local Migrant Labor" and "Home-Cured Tobacco: A Tale of Three Generations in a Chinese Village," in *China: Adapting the Past, Confronting the Future,* edited by Thomas Buoye, Kirk Denton, Bruce Dickson, Barry Naughton, and Martin King Whyte (Ann Arbor, Mich.: Center for Chinese Studies at the University of Michigan, 2003), 237–43 and 296–302.

Finally, I give thanks for and to my family. My parents encouraged me by example from a young age to step out of my comfort zone toward a concern for and interest in people different than myself. And most of all, I am thankful to my wife, Guowei, and children, Margaret and Jon. Margaret was two years old and Jon was ten months old when we moved to Guizhou. We have grown together. I dedicate this book to them, my fellow travelers on the journey.

Introduction

Not three feet of flat land,
not three days without rain,
not a family with three grams of silver.

—Centuries-old Chinese saying about Guizhou Province

The view from the porch was as stunning as any cathedral: from the wooden dwelling perched on the steep mountainside I saw only endless mountain ranges and vast, open skies. The luxurious natural beauty defied the poverty that had trapped this farming village. Children, some of them school dropouts, some in their bare feet—all with runny noses—gathered around me, wondering who was this stranger who had come into their midst. But they were hesitant to come close.

I suggested we swap songs. People in southwest China's Guizhou Province rarely meet outsiders. I had to search for commonality, ways to connect, to facilitate conversation. With kids, I often used songs—for the really shy, drawing pictures or just throwing rocks.

The children, eager but unsure, huddled together to decide what to sing. After a few minutes' deliberation, the scraggly band turned to face me, short and tall, boy and girl, and started to sing:

Arise, ye who refuse to be slaves;
With our very flesh and blood
Let us build our new Great Wall!
The peoples of China are in the most critical time,
Everybody must roar his defiance.
Arise! Arise! Arise!
Millions of hearts with one mind,
Brave the enemy's gunfire,
March on!
Brave the enemy's gunfire,
March on! March on! March on, on!

1

They mumbled more than they sang, and empty expressions reflected rote memorization rather than patriotic fervor. Still, they sang the song of the revolution: China's national anthem. And all this somewhere deep in the cash-starved mountains of interior China.

A half-century earlier in Beijing's Tiananmen Square, farther away to these children than the sky is tall, a multitude of 300,000 had stood to sing the same song. The crowd had gathered to hear Mao Zedong, standing triumphantly on the rostrum above, declare the founding of the People's Republic of China. Indeed, it was on that day, October 1, 1949, that Mao boldly proclaimed: "We, the 475 million Chinese people, have stood up and our future is infinitely bright."

But, surely, Mao Zedong had not forgotten his years hunkered down in the gritty caves of Yan'an or the perilous months fleeing from Nationalist forces along the serpentine Long March trail in the mountains of China's far west. Mao had seen his peoples' condition. He knew their reality. When Chairman Mao declared that the Chinese people had "stood up," he was fully aware that much of the country could not even sit up, much less stand—most lay in destitute poverty.

Zhu De, commander-in-chief of the Red Army during that period and loyal confidante to Mao, kept a journal during the Long March, occasionally noting what he saw during that searing, year-long struggle to survive. As he passed through Guizhou's countryside in 1935, Zhu recorded:

> Corn with bits of cabbage, chief food of people. Peasants too poor to eat rice. . . . Peasants call themselves "dry men"—sucked dry of everything. . . . Three kinds of salt: white for rich, brown for the middle class; black salt residue for the masses . . . Poor hovels with black rotting thatch roofs everywhere. Small doors of cornstalks and bamboo. . . . Have seen no quilts except in landlord houses in city. . . . People digging rotten rice from ground under landlord's granary. Monks call this "holy rice"—gifts from Heaven to the poor.[1]

For these young singers' grandparents—like those Zhu De observed—Mao Zedong's promises were rhetoric, not reality. The Communist Revolution made promises of liberation from oppression, of serving the people, of justice, of equality, and of disciplined, clean government.

Fifty years ago, revolutionary hope and longing rallied the masses. What about those pledges in the country's poorest regions today? What has become of that "infinitely bright future"? What have Mao's promises, Deng's reforms, and the efforts of Jiang Zemin's third-generation leadership meant to those born under the red flag, deep in China's hinterland?

Beneath the sweeping events of the last five decades—land reform and communes, the Great Leap Forward, the Three-Year Famine, the Cultural Revolution, Deng Xiaoping's ascent to power that ignited both stunning economic growth and tragedy in Tiananmen Square, and the decade-long leadership of Jiang Zemin—lies the reality of individual human drama. The masses, after all, each have a name.

Every individual has a story to tell, an account of how he or she has progressed, struggled, and survived through revolution and reform.

Based on my two years of living among the people of Guizhou Province in southwest China (1997–1999), hundreds of interviews, and five subsequent return visits to the province between 1999 and 2002, *The Promise of the Revolution: Stories of Fulfillment and Struggle in China's Hinterland* provides an on-the-spot account of this broad range of human experience. An ethnographic record of life far from the country's relatively well-known coast, the book reflects everyday voices, people like migrant laborers who identify themselves with the old dockhands—"coolies"—of Shanghai; a twenty-one-year-old illiterate peasant woman; crooked local-government officials; a private-school principal who teaches computer skills to mountain kids who had never seen a PC, much less dreamed of the Internet; a grandfather, father, and son, three generations of change in a mountain village; affluent CEOs, new members of Guiyang's first country club; a vice governor sent from Beijing by Premier Zhu Rongji, charged to awaken economic reform; and unemployed factory workers who strike in frustration at city hall.

These and others process through *The Promise of the Revolution,* together providing glimpses into the lives of millions who populate China's backwater mountain regions. Call them living portraits depicting a vivid landscape dotted with both fulfillment and complaint. How better to assess the promises of the revolution than to observe and listen to Mao's descendants today? In doing so, the volume places a bookmark in time, recording China's grassroots interior fifty years after the Communist takeover.[2]

The extraordinary opportunity I had to live for two years in Guizhou Province was provided through a fellowship with the Institute of Current World Affairs (ICWA). Since ICWA's founding in 1925 by Charles Crane, who served as American ambassador to China under President Woodrow Wilson, the Institute has sent eight fellows to China, most notable among whom was A. Doak Barnett (1947–1949).[3] The fellowship's format, which is quite different from those in traditional research institutes, has been the same for the Institute's seventy-five-plus years: ICWA sends its appointees around the world to immerse themselves in societies with the purpose of gaining an in-depth understanding of life as it is lived by the people. These reflections are recorded monthly and sent back to the Institute, which then circulates them in report form to a limited number of interested people in academia, government, business, and journalism in the United States and abroad. Individuals given an unusual assignment have the opportunity to provide unique insight into undercurrents that are shaping societies worldwide.

Consistent with the fellowship's distinct agenda, the goal of *The Promise of the Revolution* is to seek understanding—as opposed to conveying information alone. As former U.S. Ambassador to China Stapleton Roy says, "knowledge does not equal understanding." Knowledge combines information, theory, and fact. Understanding brings nuance, subtlety, the intangible. Knowledge is bones and flesh; understanding is soul and spirit. We need both, to be sure. But particularly in the information age, when it is so easy to acquire data, we must be very careful not to mistake knowledge alone for *knowing* China. The goal of the ICWA fellowship, and this book, which in many ways is a product of that experience, therefore, is to move along the continuum from information toward understanding. This can best be achieved through on-the-spot observation, people-to-people contact, and the kind of enduring search exhibited by A. Doak Barnett when he wrote:

> Trying to understand China has been a lifelong commitment for me. I was born in Shanghai in 1921, spent my childhood there, and began systematic study of the country when I was in college. Most important, I have been professionally engaged in this task in a variety of jobs in journalism, government service, and academia ever since World War II. Throughout these years, I have written and edited 20-odd books about China and U.S.-China relations, but I am less impressed by what I have learned over the years than about what I still must try to learn to understand China. One thing I certainly have come to know is that because China is so huge and complex, and because it has been undergoing constant and turbulent changes throughout the modern period as the Chinese people have grappled with the enormous problems of development and modernization, one must be extremely wary of generalizations about the country that are not rooted at least partially in study, observation, and experience at the grass-roots level. Unfortunately the images of China prevalent in the West have too often lacked such a basis.[4]

The twenty-four monthly reports I wrote during our stay in Guizhou Province form the core of this book. In all essentials, they are presented as originally written (with the exception of chapter 18, which was subsequently added), though in assembling them for book form, I added academic research to anchor the content, as well as suggested readings at the end of each chapter for the scholar or student who would like to explore further any of the topics I raise.

Consistent with the character of the ICWA fellowship, several qualities distinguish this volume from most other books on China. First, the book is distinctly personal. My writing often has the feel of a journal—a record of my encounters and experiences. However, my intent is not to write about myself; rather, through participant-observation, my goal is to consistently communicate to the reader the voices and perspectives of those I met along the way.

Second, the book is not prepared in the form of a conventional scholarly work. The style is a nontraditional mix of interviews, travelogues, case studies, data analysis, policy prescriptions, and personal reminiscence. Just as Cheng Li describes in the introduction to his post–ICWA fellowship book *Rediscovering China,* "I intend to guide the reader on a journey that shows the transformation of China not only through the eyes of a Western-educated political scientist but also from the vantage point of a local resident who lived through many changes in daily life."[5] While I include analyses of the major issues that face China's interior today—topics like widening disparity, poverty, migrant labor, education, corruption, economic reform, and local-level politics—clearly, the book's intent is to convey these issues within the context of the people, sights, and sounds of China's hinterland.

Finally, the book does not track one topic through its entirety. Instead, I examine a potpourri of issues as I experienced them. One of the beauties of the ICWA fellowship is that Executive Director Peter Bird Martin does not require a preplanned research agenda. Instead, Martin encourages his fellows to "follow their noses" as they encounter people and have experiences that help explain grassroots realities. Melded together, and organized in a thematic sequence, the blend of subjects, stories, and analysis provides a montage of the realities of grassroots hinterland China, fifty years after the Communist Revolution.

The Promise of the Revolution is divided into three phases of time—past, present, and future—general partitions that divide an otherwise cohesive flow of people, stories, and issues.

Part I explores the people's experience of history. Remember, for many the memory of the revolution is fresh, just beneath the surface of the conscious. To probe further, I hiked 150 miles of the Long March trail, winding through the mountain paths and villages of northern Guizhou Province, where Mao Zedong, in Zunyi, was recognized for the first time as the leader of the Communist Party. My walk into history passed through the town of Maotai, known around the world for its fiery liquor, and over the intimidating Daloushan mountain pass, where the Red Army in 1935 engaged Nationalist soldiers in bloody battle. But the richest insights as I hiked along the Long March trail came from dozens of porchside chats with villagers who welcomed this weary traveler with a cup of cool tea and conversation.

Full of nostalgia and pride, older people vividly recalled the day the Red Army had marched through town—one showed me a room where Mao Zedong and Zhu De had slept; another pointed to the sky as he talked, recalling Nationalist bomber raids. Meanwhile, most of their children and grandchildren appeared unimpressed that Mao Zedong had once walked through their neighborhood. They would rather tune in to the latest Taiwanese pop song than listen to the older generation's revolutionary lore. Even so, they are *all* Mao's descendants, children of the revolution.

Yet most are consumed with the present rather than the past. Parts II through IV build on local history by entering the people's current realities—rural and urban. This section begins with human illustrations of the contradictions of Mao's promise of "shared prosperity" and perhaps the longest shadow associated with Deng Xiaoping's economic miracle: growing disparity between coast and interior, and between urban and rural life. In response to this inequality—a growing unevenness that mocks Mao's egalitarian goals—a peasant army of at least fifty million men and women has risen up and voted with its feet. This army is China's migrant laborers, the human response to social and economic disparity.

Just after Chinese New Year, a peak two-week period when migrant laborers return home to celebrate with family and friends, I made the return trip to China's coast with them. My migrant-labor comrades and I stood, squatted, and sat together as the train crawled for thirty-five hours through the mountains of Guizhou Province over its 1,600-kilometer route toward the fertile farmland and wealthy cities of Guangdong Province, just north of Hong Kong. I discovered through the grueling trip that for most who have come out on the short end of Deng's economic miracle, they are more eager to take advantage of the income gap than to despise it.

Their number-one complaint is corruption, better described as issues of social justice and fairness. And they are furious. The more time I spent in rural society, including visits to more than thirty villages and one month living in a poor rural community, widespread frustration over corruption among local-level officials repeatedly struck me as one of the most biting realities of rural life today. Indeed, the very phenomenon that enabled Mao Zedong to whip up and overturn rural society's order fifty years ago has crept back to dangerously unstable levels.

But life is not all negative in rural Guizhou. Many villages I visited, even those hours of hiking on narrow trails from the nearest road, have been wired for electricity just in the last few years. Light bulbs, television, radio, even electric rice cookers—combined with the infusion of ideas and demands of returned migrant laborers—are generating historic change.

Economic "modernization" in the hinterland's rural areas has also had its costs: traditional culture, particularly among the poorest of the poor—ethnic minority peoples of Guizhou's mountains—has come under the powerful influence of Han-dominated urban prosperity. How to keep the finest of traditional culture from getting washed away by the floodtide of modernization? Traditional culture is under attack, soon perhaps to be seen more frequently in museums than in the open forests and villages of southwest China.

Guizhou's urban areas have seen dramatic change as well. I was most shocked by the appearance of private schools. One of more than fifty thousand private schools nationwide, Qiannan Computer Vocational High School teaches data entry and basic computer repair to teenagers from Guizhou's mountain towns, kids who had never seen a PC before the first day of class. Now those same kids "go online" at the local Internet café. Less than ten years ago, the same city, Duyun, had one telephone for its junior college of two thousand students and faculty families. Now, nearly every family home has a phone, and mobiles chirp like crickets in the summer night.

I also investigated a major government push to utilize Guizhou's natural beauty to attract tourists—and investment. A seemingly inevitable byproduct was the arrival of golf: Westernized leisure for Guizhou's tiny but affluent elite.

In the urban areas of China's interior, the economic achievements of the last five decades—more specifically, astonishing advances over the last ten years—are surpassed only by the mounting challenges of reforming state-owned enterprise.

Unemployment, social unrest, and urban poverty all have a human face, stories to tell.

Finally, part V concludes by reflecting upon what farmers and workers in China's hinterland say about their future. Despite striking advances for most, a surprising level of complaint fills many a conversation, feelings rooted in the unfulfilled expectations of the revolution a half-century ago. In so doing, the people—young and old, rural and urban—reveal from their perspective the greatest threat to the future of China's Communist Party: growing disparity, endemic corruption, and a self-described spiritual vacuum.

By concluding with a look to the future, *The Promise of the Revolution* acknowledges the realization that despite all of China's dramatic advances, the fifty-year-old promises of the revolution—and Deng's subsequent promises of reform, characterized by the saying "Our policy is to allow certain groups of people and certain regions to prosper first"—are inadequate. Will the Communist Party evolve in its ability to create and deliver promises to the people? Will those young mountain children—and their children after them—keep singing the songs of the revolution? Or will their tune change? Will the people of China's hinterland pick up and begin to sing the line one elderly, uneducated farmer casually mentioned to me one summer evening after he had returned from working in his mountain fields: "*Chaodai yao bianle*" (It's time for the dynasty to change)?

After five years of listening to the people of Guizhou Province, I have come to the conclusion that the old man is probably wrong: the dynasty, despite its fundamental flaws, is not necessarily on the eve of change. The people are not looking for a revolution. China is not about to collapse.

But the alarm has sounded. Complaint is on the rise. Deteriorating social justice, yawning inequality, and stubborn poverty—three core themes addressed in this book—offset and blur the dramatic material advances most have experienced over the last decade. The paradox of the revolution creates a dynamic that drives both the need for and the opportunity to address change. In fact, with growing challenges to its legitimacy and relevance, the Communist Party's ability to design and effectively implement reform policies, change that moves beyond past promises to respond to and provide for the needs of its people, will be critical to the party's and the country's future. How better to seek to understand these matters than through the stories and perspectives of those who live amidst them: China's hidden but no longer quiescent majority.

I

PRINTS OF THE PAST
Local History

1

The Paradox of Perspective
Colorful Guizhou

"We bandaged their sore feet," this elderly man told me about his experience as a child with the Red Army. Notice his plaited-straw sandals, the same as those worn by soldiers over sixty years ago.

Our journey began in Shanghai. For the multitudes who streamed passed us as we strolled along Shanghai's Bund the evening of October 1, China's National Day, the issues of their country's interior regions must have been far from their minds. My wife and I, however, as we wandered through the sea of celebrants, our two young children strapped in backpacks, could think of nothing else. China's hinterland dominated our thoughts; mountainous Guizhou Province—one of the country's poorest regions, with a per capita GNP twelve times less than Shanghai in 2000—was our destination.[1] The Shanghai celebration was festive. Like a block party along Zhongshan Road, which parallels the river front, Shanghainese had appeared en masse to enjoy the merriment: high school kids raced through the crowds, batting each other with inflatable, oversized hammers and beachballs; young couples led their children around with candy and plastic glow-strips; elderly couples walked contentedly, seemingly oblivious to the entire commotion—all under the glow of flashing neon lights that lit the street like Times Square. The view of Shanghai's nightlights was striking: on one side of the river, the solid gaze of the 1930s downtown New York–style buildings, which front the Bund, appeared serene, if not a bit embarrassed to be dressed in flashing neon lights; on the other side, the ominous 468-meter-high Oriental Pearl TV Tower—the Pudong Area landmark that uneasily combines the look of a giant oil rig with a Star Trek spacecraft—stood erect in the night, colorful lights racing up and down its legs.

Dynamic and historic Shanghai. Glitzy Shanghai, which has been transformed over the last twenty-five years by an outward looking, export-oriented economy.

11

"We built this monument with our own money," said this man who lives along the Long March trail. He was seven years old when the Red Army passed through his town. His neighborhood has special significance because during a Nationalist air raid, a bomb dropped right into the middle of a bedroom sheltering Mao Zedong and Zhu De. The bomb did not explode. Had it, China's modern history would have been quite different.

"Die! Die! Die!" shouted the old man seated in the middle (his mind a bit feeble), as he reenacted the day in 1935 that he and others lined up Red Army soldiers on reconnaissance, decided they were bandits, and executed them. Their township was a warlord stronghold and resisted the Red Army's entrance.

From its legacy as the "Pearl of the Orient," to the days of foreign concessions, to Pudong and now Intel, General Motors, McDonalds, Amway—even Starbucks— Shanghai represents the China Westerners think we know. Yet Shanghai, however familiar, does not represent the broad experience of the majority of Chinese people. For most Western observers, Shanghai offers the point of departure from which we observe and study China; we look "down" and "in" at this vast country. My fellowship with the Institute of Current World Affairs provided me the opportunity to view China from the other extreme: from the bottom looking up and from the country's hinterland looking back to the coast—the perspective from which most Chinese people see their country. We were bound for the small city of Duyun in southeastern Guizhou Province.

"COLORFUL" GUIZHOU

In retrospect, the Shanghai-to-Guizhou flight attendants' lipstick-red outfits and the airplane's powder-blue seats suddenly seemed bright and especially clean. It was as if the "color television" we had been watching in Shanghai had just crack-led, sizzled, and popped to grainy black and white. Drizzly, muddy, drab gray, the portion of Guiyang—Guizhou's capital city—we drove through looked more like slums than "little Hong Kong," as Guiyang is described by those who live in other areas of the province. If this is "little Hong Kong," I thought, what would our final destination—Duyun—be like? (I later found out that those from the city's surrounding counties call Duyun "little Guiyang"!)

Over the initial weeks and months, as we settled into Guizhou, Duyun's drab environs, which seemed so uniform when we first arrived, somehow sharpened into distinctive shades and contrasts. "Gray-zhou," as one American friend called the province, became more than a monochrome—there was the carbon-black-gray of raw coal, the white-gray of the overcast sky, the greasy brown-gray of sludge, the orange-gray of dirty brick, and the ever changing gray hues of moun-tain mist at dawn and dusk. Against this "colorful" backdrop, occasional wild-flowers, tender-green vegetables, or red chili peppers (easily passed by when we first arrived) leaped out to announce their beauty and vitality. Guizhou Province began to come to life—or, better said, we began to come to life in Guizhou.

As I began to encounter and become familiar with the people of Guizhou, a unique social landscape also began to emerge. This panorama was one of subtlety and dimension. Yet how easy it is to overlook the complexity and depth of the past for the seemingly obvious, one-dimensional present. To better understand the contours of Guizhou's present realities, I began my research by digging into the province's history.

EARLY TWENTIETH CENTURY: CHAOS

Like the fog that rests over Duyun at dawn, Guizhou for the first several decades of the twentieth century cowered under the stupefied haze of opium and the arbi-trary reign of warlords.[2] Not that there had ever been a time when Guizhou had flourished; this frontier region had always been known for its harsh mountain ter-rain; scarce, rocky farmland; and lawlessness. But to make matters worse, Guizhou, like the rest of China at the turn of the century, existed in a political vacuum. The Qing dynasty had collapsed in 1911 and competitors vied to fill the vacancy; strug-gle, chaos, and abuse were pervasive. The warlords, who fought constantly, depended on the size of their private armies for their ability to control; the armies' survival depended upon what they could take from the countryside. The poor peasant was forced to foot the bill.

And Guizhou's peasants were already bitterly poor. What very little they had left was sold off, or bartered, to support the widespread and debilitating use of opium. Harrison E. Salisbury, in *The Long March: The Untold Story*, recounts:

> This (Guizhou) was opium country. Here, as Peasant Zeng observed, almost everyone of the age of fifteen and above smoked opium. They sat outside their huts puffing

their pipes with glazed eyes, men, women, and teenagers. The men and teenagers often wore nothing but loincloths, the women not even that. The opium was piled up in brown stacks in the sheds like cow dung put out to dry. . . . Nothing was as bad as the opium. Guizhou was saturated with it. It deadened, drugged, and immobilized the naked poor and it drenched the local armies. The warlord troops of Guizhou were known as "two-gun men"—one was a rifle, the other an opium pipe.[3]

Guizhou's warlords and the power of opium immobilized Guizhou for the first several decades of the twentieth century. The havoc and oppression that resulted were unimaginable.

1930s–1940s: WAR

Through the 1930s and 1940s, warlords and opium commingled with the growing tide of civil war and, simultaneously, Japanese occupation and oppression.[4] Japan's efforts to turn China into a colony, which swept from northeast China down the coast and then inland, functioned intermittently to join the battling Communist and Nationalist parties in a united front. But whatever the alignment—Chinese against Japanese, or Chinese against Chinese—it was, again, the common people who suffered through it all. Peasants became cannon fodder, their crops often confiscated at gunpoint to feed any hungry invader.

In the midst of this turbulent period, a struggling movement of young Communist men and women, under the constant threat of enemy and starvation, straggled into Guizhou Province. Just months before, ninety thousand had survived a Nationalist offensive in Jiangxi Province by breaking through the enemy encirclement and scattering to escape Chiang Kai-shek's war planes. This band set forth on a strategic retreat—the Long March—through China's interior.

When the Red Army entered Guizhou in 1935, however, its eventual success was by no means apparent. In fact, by the time the Red Army arrived in Guizhou, it had narrowly escaped total defeat. In the city of Zunyi, Red Army leaders held a meeting in January 1935 (later referred to as the Zunyi Conference) to debate their next steps. Some participants advocated a turn on the Nationalists to engage in decisive battle. Mao Zedong, however, persuasively articulated guerrilla tactics and a "strategic retreat" away from the Nationalists further into the interior. The decision to follow Mao Zedong proved to be the means of survival for the Red Army. Mao emerged from Zunyi as the leader of the Communist Revolution.

Just as grass began to grow on the trail of the Long March, however, an effort by the Japanese in the late 1930s to complete the colonization of China drove hundreds of thousands of coastal Chinese to seek refuge in China's interior. Precedent had been set by the Nationalist Party, which had relocated its headquarters from Nanjing to Chongqing in Sichuan Province, and by the Communist Party, which had settled in Yan'an. An internal migration, no less extraordinary than the

Long March, ensued. For over a year, a continuous flow of people, carrying goods and children, fled the coast for the interior. Entire classes of coastal university students trudged cross-country to relocate in campuses hoped to be beyond reach of the Japanese. Key factories were disassembled by workers, packed in crates, and dragged cross-country. One account reports that an entire textile mill was loaded onto 380 junks and transported up the Yangtze River. A third of the boats that sank in the Yangtze rapids were raised, repacked, and started on their way again.[5]

In the winter of 1944, after a Japanese surge into Guizhou, the enemy advance came to an end on the province's frozen mountain roads. Overextended across Asia, the Japanese discovered that the war had finally begun to turn against them. They withdrew completely from China one year later.

POST-1949: "LIBERATION"

After Japan's departure, Guizhou became a scene of protracted civil war, a sort of free-for-all in which the greatest menace to Guizhou's people, besides hunger, became bandits. In the absence of order, bands of marauders—some well-organized, others not; some politically motivated, others just out to reap material reward—plundered what little was left throughout war-torn Guizhou.

I met an elderly woman who, when in her early thirties, had fought such bandits in an effort to restore order and justice to her rural home in southeastern Guizhou. Meng Shihua, a stout, tough, but kind woman who stands not a hair over 4 feet 10 inches tall, told me of her adventures in guerrilla warfare against the bandits just after the Communist Party's victory and establishment of the People's Republic of China—after "liberation."

In 1955, Ms. Meng became mayor of her mountain county—Sandu Shui Minority Autonomous County in southeastern Qiannan Prefecture. She served in that position until 1977.[6] Over dinner one evening, Mayor Meng shared a big occasion—perhaps her life's greatest moment—with me.

In 1957, at the invitation of China's State Council, she was selected to represent her Shui people, as one of China's fifty-six ethnic groups, to attend that year's three-day Labor Day celebration in Beijing. This was her first trip to the country's capital. As a gift from her people to the central government leaders, she took with her fifteen bottles of a Sandu County specialty: *Jiuqian tujiu* (home-grown rice wine from Jiuqian Town). A day after her arrival, one of the organizers heard of the young Shui minority woman and the gift she had brought. He arranged for this young woman, dressed in her traditional costume, to offer the toast to Chairman Mao Zedong at the celebration's most important banquet, the final evening at Zhongnanhai (the Communist Party's primary office compound and home of senior Party leaders—China's equivalent of the White House). Ms. Meng described the encounter so vividly that I felt I was with her in the grand hall as she sat in her chair, waiting through the meal to be called to offer the toast. I asked if she was nervous during the wait. She grinned:

No, I was very brave. And plus, the organizer had reviewed the toast with me in advance and had shown me how to respectfully back away from the table after presenting the toast. I felt well prepared, and waited patiently. When the moment came, the attendant came and tapped me on the shoulder. I stood up, and walked toward the front of the crowded ballroom, toward the head table where Chairman Mao Zedong, President Liu Shaoqi, Premier Zhou Enlai, and the other leaders were seated. The waiter poured the wine. Chairs slid back, and the table rose. According to Shui custom, the women sing their toasts to the men. So standing there next to Chairman Mao, who towered above me—he was very tall, even taller than you—I sang a traditional toast in my native tongue: something like, "I've come from far away; I really have nothing good to offer, but this wine is the best we have, and it's made with the sweat of our brow."

As she recalled her experience, she picked up a porcelain shot glass from the dinner table in her weathered hand and continued:

As I completed the song, Chairman Mao suddenly raised his arm, stopping me in motion. Instead of inhaling the drink, he first sipped, then asked me what kind of wine this was. I replied that it was homegrown wine from my county in Guizhou. He paused, said "it tastes so sweet," and, raising the shot glass back to his lips, tilted his head back and drank it down. The ballroom erupted in applause; the entire place seemed to shake. As I was shown back to my seat, I felt so light, as if I was floating.

For Ms. Meng this was a profound event, a moment of incredible affirmation for the bandit-fighting, country-girl-turned-mayor from the mountains of southwest China, suddenly to be toasting the most important person in the entire country.

After "liberation" in 1949 and the establishment of the People's Republic of China, Guizhou Province became more fully integrated into national life. When I asked a former bureaucrat how his county's experience paralleled the rest of the country after 1949, he responded, "We experienced it all . . . land reform, Great Leap Forward, Cultural Revolution, reform." "In fact," he said, "we were probably a lot more enthusiastic than other areas of China in carrying out these policies."

Perhaps he was referring to the radical, cataclysmic policies of the Great Leap Forward (1958–1961) and the subsequent famine during which between twenty and forty million people died nationwide—likely the largest famine in human history.[7] History shows that Guizhou's leaders, though cautious at the beginning of the Great Leap Forward, accelerated their implementation of the policies in 1959, and it became one of the most extreme provinces in the country. This is best demonstrated in the implementation of "mess hall eating," the touchstone of communal living during the Great Leap period. By 1960, over 90 percent of Guizhou's people were eating in mess halls. Guizhou's exemplary pursuit of these all-you-can-eat dining halls was noticed by Mao Zedong in 1959. He called the entire nation to emulate Guizhou Province.[8]

The devastating results of the Great Leap policy also reached national extremes

Meng Shihua at the 1957 Labor Day celebration in Beijing (second from Mao Zedong's left, in dark outfit, clapping and looking toward Mao). Ms. Meng said she had been standing immediately to the left of Mao Zedong and just in front of President Liu Shaoqi (behind Meng in photo), "when suddenly, just before the photographer snapped his camera, a Mongolian girl burst through from the second row, almost knocking the chairman over. I restrained myself and did not push back." The others in the picture are representatives of other ethnic minority groups, dressed in traditional costume. Note Zhu De standing at the far left. Zhu De was Mao Zedong's chief military adviser and commander-in-chief of the People's Liberation Army.

in Guizhou. Guizhou's mortality rate in 1959, 1960, and 1961 was 20.3, 52.3, and 23.3 (per 1,000 population), respectively—among the highest in the country. Compared to Beijing (9.6, 9.2, and 10.8), Shanghai (6.9, 6.8, and 7.7), and coastal Jiangsu Province (14.6, 18.4, and 13.4), the numbers demonstrate the horrific effects of the Great Leap Forward on Guizhou Province.[9]

1960s–1970s: THIRD FRONT AND CULTURAL REVOLUTION

As China hobbled into the 1960s, Mao Zedong became increasingly concerned that China was vulnerable to attack from foreign forces. China's relationship with the Soviet Union had been broken off, and the United States was increasingly involved in Vietnam. Chairman Mao was also concerned that Taiwan might take advantage of the Great Leap Forward crisis to launch an attack on the mainland's coastal cities. In August 1964, just two weeks after the United States escalated its bombing raids on North Vietnam, Mao Zedong convened a special meeting in which he called for the rapid development of a Third Front industrial structure in inland China, including the relocation of key coastal industries and machine-building factories, the development of electric power, and the construction of rail-roads through Sichuan, Guizhou, and Yunnan.[10]

The objective, therefore, of Third Front construction (as distinguished from the first and second lines of defense on China's coast) was to create an entire system within the country's most remote and strategically secure region: China's moun-tainous hinterland. Mao ordered the plan to be implemented with maximum speed. It was. As China seethed in the turmoil of the Cultural Revolution (1966–1976), an average of over 40 percent per annum of China's national investment during those ten years was poured into the accelerated development of this strate-gic industrial network—one of the most aggressive, centrally planned investment programs of all time.[11] For Guizhou Province, in addition to the intellectuals who had been "sent down to the countryside" (many came to Guizhou) during the Cultural Revolution, Third Front construction brought an infusion of new infra-structure, immigrants, skilled engineers, and factories. The significant contribution of this massive influx of skill and capital to Guizhou's development is undeniable. Guizhou has experienced positive growth since the days when the investment pro-gram blew in. Yet economic decisions based on perceived external threat, with little if any consideration given to profitability or sustainability, planted seeds for eventual problems.

When the political atmosphere in China changed, and the rationale for Third Front construction disappeared, the central government modified (mid-1970s) and then abandoned (late 1970s, early 1980s) the inland development strategy. Instead, new precedence, under Deng Xiaoping, was given to a coast-based growth strat-egy—an approach that looked outward, not inward.[12] Though some of the inland industries have creatively found ways to team with coastal factories, most of the enterprises have become unsustainable welfare institutions that, destined to fail without an inexhaustible supply of funds, were left to rust throughout the prov-ince. Today, the legacy of these Third Front factories has left Guizhou with a major reform dilemma.

LATE 1970s TO PRESENT: REFORM

For Guizhou's masses, urban and rural, pragmatic policies of the reform-minded Deng Xiaoping and Jiang Zemin eras have led in absolute terms to a dramatic stan-dard of living increase and relative calm. Without a basic understanding of the chaos, war, and bitterness of Guizhou's twentieth-century history, however, it is impossible to appreciate the relative peace and prosperity now enjoyed by most. The last twenty years of Guizhou's history—and for that matter, of the entire country—have been the most peaceful and prosperous in at least the last two centuries.

This is in no way, however, to minimize the problems that persist in Guizhou— tragedy and misplaced hope have left their damage. Add to that floundering state-owned enterprises, many of which cannot even pay their workers' salaries and benefits; intractable rural poverty; enlarging wealth disparity between urban and rural areas, and the inland and coastal regions of the country; growing corruption and crime; and a gnawing vacuum of belief. Guizhou Province, as does the rest of the country, has its plate full with challenges as it enters a new century. Yet, for all of its struggles, Guizhou Province has come a very long way.

SUGGESTIONS FOR FURTHER READING

Barnett, A. Doak. *China on the Eve of Communist Takeover.* New York: Praeger, 1963.

Baum, Richard. *Burying Mao: Chinese Politics in the Age of Deng Xiaoping.* Princeton, N.J.: Princeton University Press, 1996.

Becker, Jasper. *Hungry Ghosts: Mao's Secret Famine.* New York: Henry Holt, 1998.

Corrigan, Gina. *Guizhou: Southwest China's Mountain Province.* Lincolnwood, Ill.: Passport Books, 1995.

Goldman, Merle, and Roderick MacFarquhar, eds. *The Paradox of Post-Mao Reforms.* Cambridge, Mass.: Harvard University Press, 1999.

Li, Zhishui, and Anne F. Thurston. *The Private Life of Chairman Mao.* New York: Random House, 1994.

Short, Philip. *Mao: A Life.* London: Hodder & Stoughton, 1999.

Yang, Dali L. *Calamity and Reform in China: State, Rural Society, and Institutional Change since the Great Leap Famine.* Stanford, Calif.: Stanford University Press, 1996.

2

A Walk into the Past
Hiking the Long March

Mao Zedong, pictured in 1935, the year in which he became de facto leader of the Communist Party while in Zunyi, Guizhou Province.

Like the Red Army in 1935, my friend and I entered Zunyi City on foot.[1] And like many of its beleaguered company, both of us limped from physical pain and exhaustion—but that's where the similarities end.

When soldiers of the Red Army passed through Guizhou Province on their epic 6,000-mile Long March in 1935, they were constantly beset by Nationalist Army raids, blockades, and bombers. The only opponents we faced on our 150-mile hike were physical and mental. The Red Army numbered in the tens of thousands, as troops wound their way through the mountains of northern Guizhou; we were but two. Theirs was a struggle to survive; ours was a personal challenge to revive the memory and significance of the Long March.

Despite the tremendous gap between our experience and that of the Red Army sixty-three years before, the opportunity to trace its trail—over five mountains, through a cave, a canyon, and numerous towns and villages—provided powerful insights into the enormity of its struggle and the impressions its journey left behind on the people and places the army passed through.

Our feet not only carried us into the past, they enabled us to move slowly enough to experience the people of northern Guizhou Province as they live in the present. How else could I have enjoyed the many families along the way who invited us to sit on their porches and chat? How else could I have, while sitting with these locals, observed township-government officials parading a confiscated television set down the street—the price a neighbor family was forced to pay for giving birth to one child too many? How else could I have been refreshed by believers in a vibrant rural Catholic community? How else would I have stumbled across the terrifying scene of a man beating a woman with a leather whip in their

21

dimly lit, roadside home, as she crouched, begging for mercy? And how else could I have experienced the awesome, devastating beauty of a 6,000-foot mountain peak that, as did the Red Army, we crossed by narrow trails worn into the mountainside by generations of farmers?

Fundamentally, our journey was about discovery: the pursuit of understanding about this segment of the Long March, deep in the country's interior, that provided a crucible for the development of China's Communist movement; a search for knowledge of the people, young and old, who though carrying the distinction of being born in a cradle of the Communist Revolution, live in the middle of all of the issues that face China's interior.

By the time the Red Army troops entered Zunyi in January 1935, they had narrowly escaped total defeat. Just months before in Jiangxi Province, the movement's 160,000 followers had been encircled and assaulted by half a million Nationalist troops and bombed by two hundred warplanes. The offensive was an attempt to annihilate the growing Communist movement. During the night of October 15, 1934, some 90,000 survivors, coordinated by Zhou Enlai, broke through enemy lines to the west and, scattering to escape Chiang Kai-shek's bombers, set forth on a strategic retreat—a 6,000-mile saga that would last 370 days, average 24 miles of foot travel per day, and include a full-dress battle every two weeks.[2]

Edgar Snow, an American journalist, introduced the Long March to the West shortly after its conclusion. Basing his writing on personal interviews with Communist leaders, he described the magnitude of their accomplishment:

> Altogether the Reds crossed 18 mountain ranges, five of which were perennially snow-capped, and they crossed 24 rivers. They passed through 12 difference provinces, occupied 62 cities, and broke through enveloping armies of 10 different provincial warlords, besides defeating, eluding, or outmaneuvering the various forces of Central Government troops sent against them. They entered and successfully crossed six different aboriginal districts, and penetrated areas through which no Chinese army had gone for scores of years. However one may feel about the Reds and what they represent politically . . . , it is impossible to deny recognition of their Long March as one of the great exploits of military history.[3]

As remarkable as was its achievement, the Long March was a trail of death and escape, not a parade of conquering victory. As I interviewed people along the route, this reality impressed me the most. In almost every town we hiked through, locals recounted stories of loss: "Nationalist bombers flew in very low over those mountains," an elderly man recalled as he pointed to the sky; "thirteen soldiers killed over by that bridge"; "hundreds slaughtered in that forest"; "two died of exhaustion at the crest of that hill."

In fact, by the time the Red Army reached its final destination one year after setting out, the movement had lost 90 percent of its strength, shrinking to 7,000–

8,000 men and women (of the several hundred women that began the Long March, no more than 30 survived).[4] Some deserted along the way, intimidated by hardship. The vast majority, however, perished under the merciless onslaught of fatigue, hunger, frost, and enemy fire.

But a remnant is sometimes enough to save a revolution. The survivors—"a hard core of tempered steel, a reliable, and disciplined force"—settled into the desolate, dusty caves of Yan'an for the winter of 1935.[5] And thus began a twelve-year period (the Yan'an Period) during which the Communist movement—saved by coinciding Japanese invasion and a temporary truce with the Nationalists—enjoyed a period of recovery, consolidation, expansion, and eventual total victory.

It is impossible to overstate the importance of the Long March in the development of China's Communist Party. The Long March's significance lies not only in the fact that it preserved the life of the movement, but also in the role it played in determining its leaders, its support-base, and the heroic myths that would come to undergird the Party's legitimacy for decades to come. Central to these areas of importance were the three months the Red Army spent winding through the impoverished mountains of northern Guizhou Province—approximately one-fourth of the yearlong march.

At Zunyi, for example, Mao Zedong achieved primacy within the Communist movement, a position he would not relinquish until his death in 1976. When the Red Army arrived in Zunyi, its leaders were divided; spirits were low; total defeat seemed imminent. An emergency meeting was called, and twenty of the movement's leaders met in a large, two-story home to deliberate their future.[6]

Key to the three-day meeting (January 15–17, 1935) was a heated debate over military strategy. Comintern military adviser Otto Braun and Soviet-trained Chinese Communist leaders advocated conventional, positional warfare to engage the pursuing Nationalist Army. Mao Zedong, however, articulated guerrilla tactics and a "strategic retreat" away from the Nationalists, further into the interior. By the end of the three days Mao's position had prevailed and the leaders agreed to head north from Zunyi toward the Daloushan Mountains on a serpentine escape route deep into the peaks of Guizhou.

Beneath the argument over tactics, however, lay a deeper layer of significance. At the Zunyi Conference the Communist movement took a decisive step toward becoming more fully Chinese. In Zunyi, the Chinese Communist Party, now separated from direct contact with Moscow, had recognized its national leader. Moscow-influenced cadres (those who had up to that point overseen the movement) were relegated to a back seat. With Mao at the helm, the rural-based revolution—a characteristic that would shape its rise to victory through the 1940s and distinguish it from Soviet communism—was set in a new and different direction.

With the movement's leadership and military strategy realigned at Zunyi, enthusiasm was rekindled. The renewed sense of energy and camaraderie among Red Army troops is nowhere better expressed than in the experience of a foreign missionary, who had been captured by Red Army soldiers while working in Gui-

Map 2.1.   The Long March

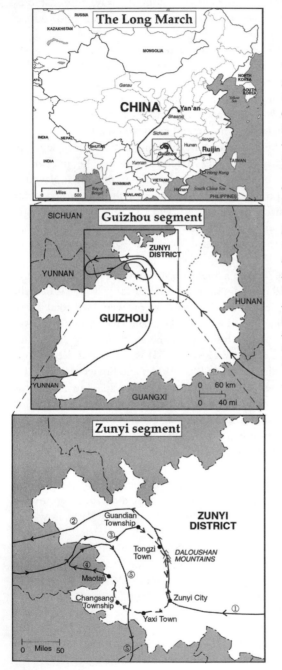

The Red Army spent three months of the twelve-month Long March in Guizhou Province. The troops entered Zunyi District from the east (1); went north through Daloushan Mountains and east into Sichuan (2); then circled back through Guandian Township, Daloushan Mountains, and Zunyi City (3); circled again through Yaxi Town, Changsang Township, and Maotai (4); finally headed south and west through Guizhou and Yunnan (5). The author's journey traced two important sections of the Long March, averaging twenty-five miles a day over six days. As we passed over centuries-old mountain trails, villagers confirmed specific directions based on their memories and local Long March legends.

zhou Province, as he marched toward the Daloushan Mountains just days after the Zunyi Conference:

> The stony track leading north through the Daloushan Mountains toward the border of Sichuan was hard with frost beneath Jakob's callused feet, but as he climbed in the gathering dusk at the end of the line of prisoners, the faint, sweet fragrance of winter plum blossom unexpectedly teased his nostrils. In the gloom he could just see the outline of a grove of trees whose bare branches were speckled with the early blossom, and the perfume of the white flowers lifted his flagging spirits. Ahead of him the troops were lighting torches made from bunches of mountain bracken lashed to staves: they flared brightly in the half-darkness, casting a warm glow over the long, winding column of marching men, and spontaneously the soldiers began to sing as they climbed.
>
> As they marched in the stillness of the approaching night, the rough voices of the peasant troops raised in unison carried clearly along the winding tracks, echoing from the funneled walls of ravines and flowing invisibly up and down the bare hillsides of the Daloushan. The singing, Jakob could sense, was binding the column together, fusing thousands of marchers into one serpentine body, imbuing each man with renewed vigor from a common well of energy. Although he did not join in and the sentiments bellowed into the night were crudely exhortatory, in the deep silence of the mountains the songs in their essence took on the emotional force of hymns and Jakob felt himself strangely stirred by them.
>
> Not for the first time, the cadences of the youthful voices inspired in him an illogical feeling of community with the multitude of troops marching around him. He felt keenly the power of the common loyalty which bound them together; he felt the intense shared excitement of the challenge they faced, fleeing from a superior enemy into an unknown future, every man equal and carrying only the barest essentials for survival on his back—chopsticks, a rice bowl, a quilted blanket, an umbrella of oiled paper, a rifle. Jakob sensed that having survived the fiery slaughter of the Xiang River, each man felt himself chosen to fight on for his fallen comrades as well as himself and faith in their cause seemed to ring from the soul of every man when they sang on the march.[7]

As the Red Army set its face north toward the Daloushan Mountain pass—which would become a bloody battlefield two months later—it began a circuitous route deep into Guizhou's mountains. "Under Mao's new strategy of 'strategic retreat,'" said a guide at the Zunyi Conference museum, "the Red Army ran the enemy in circles until they were totally confused."

According to locals I spoke with, however, including those we spoke to as we hiked over the Daloushan Mountain pass, the enemy was not a bit confused. During this period, even Nationalist leader Chiang Kai-shek flew to Guiyang to personally oversee military operations. The Red Army's refusal to fight a decisive battle, as well as a scrappy ability to persevere, resulted in dwindling numbers—but survival.

And survive it did. Almost all of the nearly ten thousand Communist soldiers who survived the Long March later became the country's political elite. Their experience became the foundation of the People's Republic of China, just as their hardship became the legitimate base for their rule. Indeed, the Long March veterans experienced an unusual camaraderie and a unity that lasted for thirty years, until the Cultural Revolution.

A final and important point of significance of the Long March from a national perspective is the basis it provided for heroic myth, an epic story that bolstered the legitimacy of the Communist Party in the eyes of the people. Every government needs a story to tell. For China's leaders—who until the 1990s were almost all Long March veterans—the march was their ordeal in the wilderness.[8]

This is what the Long March meant to those who would eventually make it all the way to Beijing and into Communist Party history. But what about local folk in the Zunyi area who, though unwitting hosts to the Red Army in 1935, have never even left their villages? What does the Long March mean to them? I was struck by the pride among those I spoke with, particularly the older people. Their attitude was, "We may be poor, but we helped make history." Even some of the young people along the way, who spend most of their days loafing around soda stands and talking about migrant-labor life on the coast, when asked, said that the spirit of the Long March encourages them to persevere.

From another perspective, locals said that the Long March acquainted them with the ideals of the movement. Just as the march has been described as an "involuntary and monumental study tour" for China's future leaders in regions of the country that would have otherwise remained unknown to them, the Long March familiarized those in China's interior with a movement that would have otherwise remained distant and abstract.[9] As the Red Army marched through their towns and villages, its leaders held mass meetings, discussed land reform, and distributed confiscated goods to the poor. The message was attractive for a people who at the time experienced a 50-percent infant mortality rate, thirty years' life expectancy, and near total illiteracy.[10] The Communist message, in its ideal, appealed strongly to the poor of Guizhou's mountains.

There must have been, however, many who resisted the Red Army—powerful family clans, warlords, even remaining loyalties to the Nationalist Party that existed throughout the interior at the time.[11] Nevertheless, the result after Communist victory in 1949 was an interior region more fully integrated with the rest of the country; a degree of cohesion that could not have existed had it not been for the Long March.

The most practical difference the Long March made for many I spoke with, especially among those who live in nonfarming communities (i.e., town [*zhen*] and township [*xiang*] centers) is the economic development that came years after the Long March.

Over a bowl of breakfast noodles in the town of Maotai, famous for its distillery, a man shared with me the fact that Maotai liquor became especially cherished by Zhou Enlai, who, when he and the Red Army passed through the riverside town, had used the fiery spirits (well over 100 proof) as ointment on his sore muscles. In fact, when Zhou Enlai became China's premier and foreign minister, he chose Maotai as the country's official state drink and his personal diplomatic tool. Maotai, most certainly, has prospered because of it. In 1995, the Maotai distillery produced 4,000 tons of the drink and netted a 270-million-yuan profit (approximately U.S. $34 million).[12]

Though Maotai's example is extreme, the entire Zunyi area (Zunyi City, in particular) has received unusually privileged financial assistance from the central government because of its special place in history. This is not to say, however, that the Zunyi area—especially its rural outposts—has shed its poverty. Far from it. Nevertheless, it is significant that many who live along the Long March's route believe that they have benefited economically by sharing in Communist history.

It was also evident from those I spoke with that the difference between history "I have been told about" and history "I experienced personally" is becoming an important distinction in the way people in Zunyi evaluate their past. Among the young people I spoke with, for example, it was obvious that I was more interested than they were in what the Red Army had experienced in their hometowns. They much preferred to talk about working as migrant labor on the coast and about pop music than about something, however important, that happened forty years before they were born.

The older generation could not have been more different. My interest in their local history was surpassed only by their desire to talk about what they had experienced or had heard about from older friends of the same generation. All this made me wonder what the legacy of the Long March will continue to mean as veterans—both those who survived the March and local villagers who, in their own way, participated in the march—pass away. What is true for Beijing will probably be true in Guizhou as well. As the memory of the Long March becomes more and more "their history"—and not "my history"—China's fifty-year experiment with Communism will be increasingly legitimized by practical, life improvements and less by the prestige earned by eight thousand men and women who believed strongly enough in certain principles to persevere through an incredible ordeal.

I expected to experience the feelings of a hero as my friend and I once again set our aching feet on the sidewalks of bustling Zunyi City, the place we had departed from eight days earlier. Not that I expected applause or anything, but just hours before we had sat with a village family, fifteen miles north of the city, enthusiastically discussing the Long March. The elderly husband and wife offered us tea, as their seven-year-old granddaughter, on her own initiative, cooled us by waving a Chinese fan. And just the evening before we had hiked over the famous Daloushan Mountain pass, drank water scooped from an underground spring, and made a meal of wild blackberries in an uninhabited mountain area.

Instead, I felt a bit like a freak. Unshaven, dirty, and limping, I felt more like a homeless person on K Street in Washington, D.C., than a modern-day hero. It made me wonder how Red Army soldiers felt when they first straggled into Zunyi.

SUGGESTIONS FOR FURTHER READING

Bianco, Lucien. *Origins of the Chinese Revolution, 1915–1949*. Translated by Muriel Bell. Stanford, Calif.: Stanford University Press, 1971.

Bosshardt, Alfred and England. *The Guiding Hand*. London: Hodder & Stoughton, 1973.

Grey, Anthony. *In Peking*. London: Pan Books, 1989.

Mende, Tibor. *The Chinese Revolution*. Worcester: Thames & Hudson, 1961.

Salisbury, Harrison E. *The Long March: The Untold Story*. New York: Harper & Row, 1985.

Snow, Edgar. *Red Star over China*. New York: Grove, 1961.

II

PORTRAITS OF
THE PRESENT
Interior China and the Coast

3
One in Fifty Million
On the Rails with China's Migrant Labor

At a train stop somewhere between Guizhou and Guangzhou my companions opened the window just long enough for me to take this picture of people trying to push their way into the train's doorway. As soon as those in the back of this crowd saw our opened window, they rushed toward us. We were able to close it just before the crowd closed in.

If you want to create wealth in the long-term, plant fruit trees;
If profit in the medium-term, raise animals. But if you need money
now, go to the coast and work.

—Heard around Guizhou Province countryside

Li Wanding spoke with emotion about his role in freeing Guizhou's farmers. Director of Guizhou's Labor Bureau during the 1980s, Li used to lie awake at night, distressed because he knew the province's rural residents did not have enough to eat. And he was responsible for them.

When the Communist Party consolidated power in the 1950s, it implemented an elaborate system of migration restrictions—household registration requirements and rationing—that effectively interrupted almost all free movement of people across the rural–urban divide.

This made existence especially difficult in impoverished regions like Guizhou. Along with occasional government handouts, Guizhou's mountain farmers were given a straightjacket. One size fits all. They could no longer react to hard times—as they had "pre-liberation"—by sending members of their community off to the city in search of employment opportunities. Guizhou's destitute farmers were sealed off behind a locked door.

The result was perhaps the supreme irony of the Chinese revolution—that rural

31

revolutionaries who were committed to combating urban bias ended up institu-
tionalizing precisely that, in extreme and deep-rooted forms.[1]

Then the door sprang open. Li remembers, "The day in the mid-1980s I heard
travel restrictions had relaxed, I knew instantly this was the answer. I began to
encourage local governments to send their people out, to leave their villages for
the cities where they could find cash."

The freeing of China's farmers happened simultaneously with perhaps the most
dramatic economic growth in world history. In post-Mao China, Deng Xiaoping's
reforms stimulated growth that doubled the country's per-capita gross domestic
product *two times* between 1978 and 1996. Compare that to the shortest length of
time it took other countries to double their per capita gross domestic product just
one time: Britain, 58 years (between 1780 and 1838); the United States, 47 years
(between 1839 and 1886); and Japan, 34 years (between 1885 and 1919).[2]

Millions were drawn to China's cities by the "pull" of urban income levels,
convenient lifestyles, and strong labor demand for urban construction and factory
production, combined with the "push" of rural poverty, scarcity of cultivable land,
surplus labor (currently estimated at 200 million farmers!), the low social status of
agricultural work, and unfavorable government policy.[3] By 1998, a conservative
figure of 50 million farmers made up the migrant labor force, though estimates
range as high as one hundred million.[4]

Director Li had requested to meet with me because he had read about my travels
with Guizhou's migrant-labor army. As I recalled my experience to Li, I joked that
I had been one of the lucky ones: I had successfully competed with several hundred
migrant laborers for a seat on train No. 488 for its thirty-five-hour journey from
Guizhou to China's coast. It was just a few days after Chinese New Year, the most
important holiday of the year, and my travel companions were returning to work
after two weeks at home with family and friends. My comrades and I stood, squatted, and sat together as the train crawled through the mountains of Guizhou Province, over its 1,600-kilometer route toward the fertile farmland and wealthy cities
of Guangdong Province.

Despite increased mobility, home remains an important part of migrant workers'
emotional makeup and is central to their sense of responsibility. The result is a
fascinating phenomenon before and after Chinese New Year each year: millions
upon millions of people on the move—crowded into buses, trains, and planes to
celebrate the holiday at home and then flowing back to the coast to continue or
search for work.

In order to form my own opinions on the role and prospects of China's migrant
labor, I had decided that the best place to begin was not in books, newspaper articles, or interviews with government officials, but rather as part of this mighty
annual migration on a piece of hard-fought-for bench.

As I stood outside the Duyun train station, enjoying what would probably be the
last breaths of fresh air I would have for two days, I noticed a steady but quiet
stream of people, baggage in hand, filing through the narrow door of the train

station's tearoom. Naturally curious, I walked over to see what was happening. Two yuan (U.S. 25 cents) for a head start on the rest of the masses, a train attendant announced at the door. I dished out the cash and slipped in the entrance with the others. There in the dimly lit, barlike atmosphere stood at least one hundred people crowded toward a door on the other side of the room that would eventually open onto the platform side of the building.

Imagine the starting gates at the Kentucky Derby, with only one difference: all of the horses have to fit through one gate at the jingle of the starting bell. Once the gate opens, anything goes. And though no prize money is at stake, the difference between getting to sit on a bench for thirty-five hours and having to stand or squat is enough incentive to muster every ounce of energy available, and then some.

Trains in China normally have three classes of tickets: soft-sleeper (a closed compartment with two soft bunk beds), hard-sleeper (rows of three-level bunk beds), and hard seat (rows of benches, each pair facing each other). My ticket read "hard, open seating." The number of tickets sold for soft-sleeper and hard-sleeper class is controlled; each ticket has an assigned bed. Hard-seat tickets, however, are often sold without limit, especially when large numbers of people travel. The result is a wild free-for-all. My hard-seat ticket for the thirty-five-hour, 1,600-kilometer journey cost 88 yuan, or about U.S. $10.

After about twenty minutes of waiting in the dark, crowded silence, the door cracked opened and daylight suddenly shone into the room. The bell had sounded. After initial gridlock, the physics of the mass convergence of flesh began to spit people through the doorway. After almost losing my left arm, I, too, popped into the daylight of the train platform. Once through the door, to my surprise and temporary relief, we were immediately forced into a single-file line and led by train security officers toward the final car, an empty one provided for those in Duyun headed to Guangzhou (train No. 488 had originated four hours up-rail in Guiyang). The rest of the cars already overflowed with people.

Though I was about 40th in the single-file line of roughly 250 and knew there were at least 100 seats in the car, I was suspicious of the fragile order (long, single-file lines are rare in China). The officers had difficulty forcing back the occasional traveler who broke from the ranks in an attempt to get ahead. Though I and those in front and in back of me walked slowly and remained in line, internally I, like everyone else, was coiled like a spring, fully prepared to join a rush at the train door.

Order was preserved—that is, until the single-file line was released into the car. As soon as I was up the steps and had turned down the aisle, I confronted a surprise burst of activity: people scrambled back and forth, claiming seats, throwing luggage onto the racks above, blocking others from their space. As I began to run down the aisle, a stout man wearing a black leather jacket and wire-rim glasses waved me over: "Hey! Hey! Hey! You sit here," he yelled above the pandemonium as he stood blocking a two-seat bench. "I'm saving this other one for my little brother.

You sit in this seat; my brother will sit in this one." I threw my bag in the rack above and sat down.

Though the chaos continued around me, every competitive nerve in my body finally relaxed. When the man's little brother arrived and sat down, big brother slipped out through the train's window, lowering himself onto the gravel below. Now I could focus on the next tasks at hand: sitting for thirty-five hours, getting to know those around me, and considering up close migrant labor's role in the unfolding reality of China's hinterland.

Has migrant labor contributed to China's growth, or is it simply a nuisance, an unwelcome result of reform? Does migrant labor threaten or promote social stability? Does migrant labor leave those left behind poorer, or does it transfer wealth to China's backward regions? Is migrant labor divisive, or does it help integrate a country characterized by pockets of prosperity in the cities and special economic zones? What role should the government play in this otherwise spontaneous flow of human resources?[5] Obviously, the answers to these questions, especially the views of government leaders, create very different policy responses to this unusual population group—growing and on the move—which outnumbers the combined populations of Beijing, Shanghai, Nanjing, and Guangzhou. Lots to think about; lots of time to think.

Right on schedule, the train began to roll down the tracks at 1:11 P.M. Our car, now full of at least three times as many people as the number of seats, began to settle in. As in elementary school days when I traded lunch-bag goodies for others' treats, the first several hours of the ride involved an occasional offer of what each of us sitting in our little group had packed for the long journey: hard-boiled tea-eggs, sunflower seeds, dried fruit, cigarettes, candy, and every form of cured pork imaginable. Some fell asleep, decks of cards were shuffled, magazines and newspapers were exchanged, conversations began. The entire car, divided naturally into groups of four to seven people by the position of the benches, began to get acquainted.

A rare gleam of sunshine lit up the blue sky, and fields of yellow rapeseed blossoms provided a delightful foreground to Guizhou's beautiful mountains. Everyone was fresh; conversation was lively. Even those left standing and squatting in the aisles seemed upbeat.

It turned out that many of those sitting around me were "off-post," or laid-off, factory workers headed for the coast to look for a way to support their families. Directly across from me sat a quiet, self-confident man, about thirty years old, who was returning to his job in a Shenzhen electronics factory, a position he had held for a number of years. The annual journey back to Duyun to see his wife and daughter, for him, was no major ordeal. He was used to it. One of the first things he told me, however, was that people on this train won't tell you, and you can't see it on their faces, but they're scared to death. They fear the unknown that lies ahead of them. Most of them don't know where they are going.

Sitting next to him was his twenty-year-old companion, a friendly, diminutive, and hyper chap. The young fellow enjoyed singing along with the pop music that floated through the train's speakers. He also seemed to take pleasure in climbing across the tops of the benches in his stocking feet. The failing state enterprise he worked for in Duyun could not compete with his hopes for wealth on the coast. This was his first trip to Guangdong.

Another young man, twenty-four years old, who shared my bench with me, had recently been laid off from his Duyun factory job. He was going to see his other brother, who worked in Dongguan, a city near Guangzhou filled with export-targeted manufacturing plants. He hoped his brother could help him land a job.

A woman on the bench behind me was interested to know why I as a foreigner would travel hard-seat class. "Why not at least go hard-sleeper?" she asked. "It's only one hundred yuan (U.S. $12) more."

"If I traveled hard-sleeper," I said loud enough for all of my traveling companions to hear, "I would not have the chance to meet nice folks like you all. And you? Why are you traveling hard-seat?"

"I used to work for a state-owned children's clothes factory in Duyun, but left because it could no longer pay my wages. I'm headed for Shenzhen."

"What would be your ideal kind of work?" I asked.

"*Jiating funu* [housewife]," she joked, "but I'd settle to be someone's maid."

I shouldn't have been surprised that among those I was meeting were laid-off urban factory workers, but I was. I had always imagined migrant labor as folks from the agricultural countryside, part of China's army of surplus rural labor.

As the train rumbled down the tracks, I began to realize that, with the slow-motion collapse of much of China's state-owned sector, traditional migrant labor is absorbing a new type of person: urban factory workers from across the country, some skilled and others not, who are joining the search for wealth in Chinese cities and special economic zones. One fellow on the train told me that in Duyun, a city of 460,000 that was developed around state-owned industry, at least 30,000 people have been laid off, 80 percent of whom have left Duyun to look for work on the coast. This is just a drop in the bucket of the officially estimated 30 million laid off across the country who are being forced to find food outside the "iron rice bowl."

After my dinner (a plastic bowl of instant noodles), I showed the folks around me my one-and-only card trick—a real showstopper. While I was in the middle of my performance, a teenage girl and a boy emerged through the crowd. The boy was very shy and did not speak. The girl, giggling between phrases, asked on his behalf if I would be willing to take a picture of the boy and his four friends. They had noticed my camera. I was in the middle of my card trick and it was already late, so I told them I would come find them the next day. They told me they had seats about halfway down the next car.

The night was miserable. By 11 P.M. I had already been sitting for ten hours. Any discomfort to that point had been diverted by snacks, reading, card games, and, most of all, fascinating conversation. But now, no matter how much I shifted around in my seat, I could not get comfortable. My back ached. My neck was stiff. My buddies—some asleep, some staring in a daze—and I leaned on each other. A man I had not even spoken with, who squatted pitifully beside my bench, rested his head against my thigh, sound asleep. But worst of all, the air inside the car was stifling. The sour stench of urine from the bathroom, mixed with an oppressive haze of cigarette smoke, hung like smog. Trash had begun to build up in the aisles and under the seats. If I hadn't had to breathe, I wouldn't have.

Like a computer in suspend mode, my mind slipped into a fog as I sat shifting back and forth, in and out of sleep. All I could think of, beyond my own physical discomfort, was how much I respected these people for what they were going through just to make ends meet.

By morning's light we had entered Hunan Province. The weather had turned cold and rainy. At most stops we couldn't open our window, fearing that people outside, trying to get on the train, would force their way through our window.

By lunchtime, we were nearly twenty-four hours into the trip. I no longer was a researcher seeking to understand what my fellow travelers were experiencing. By this time in the journey, I, like them, was just trying to get through the trip. A monstrous headache descended. I felt like a fish lying on the ground, out of water—gills moving gently up and down, gasping for life. I began to feel sick.

To get my mind off my discomfort, I decided to visit the teenagers who had asked for a picture the night before. I asked the man who had been leaning on me for most of the previous twelve hours to hold my seat. He was glad for the chance to sit down. As I came into view, the boys seemed delighted to see me. They cleared a space on their bench, pulled out some home-cured ham strips, and asked me to do my card trick again. As I shuffled the deck, I asked them why they had decided to leave home.

"We're from the countryside in northeast Guizhou; it's very poor there. We want to come out, earn some money, and see what we can learn. Who knows what will happen? But we can't stay at home."

I have read the literature that evaluates migrant labor—like these teenagers—as a social, economic, and political threat.[6] Since they form a group outside the system, it is argued, there is no way to organize or control these people. Whether for family-planning purposes, concern over rising crime, or just the menace of the unemployed sleeping in the streets, migrant labor lives beyond the reach of the state. Others also cite migrant labor's vulnerability to exploitation and the lack of basic social services available to them, especially health care. Needless to say, it doesn't take much imagination to envision a chaotic drama of fifty million jobless migrant laborers swamping China's cities.

The teenagers' attitudes fascinated me. They certainly did not consider themselves a threat. They were attracted to, not envious of, the relative wealth of the coast—a part of China they had seen only on television. And as a group of five buddies, traveling together for their first time away from home, they did not seem afraid.

From the way they talked about working the stony fields back home, these young men seemed to represent the views of a large number of China's rural laborers who consider agriculture to be an unprofitable, unattractive, and even redundant economic activity. In the rural regions of China's interior where there are few nonagricultural activities, migration is often seen as the only way out. After all, if one family member leaves home—like these young middle-school dropouts—it means one less mouth to feed. And if the migrant is able to land a job, even the dirtiest of manual-labor jobs, he earns on average in *one month* what he would earn in an *entire year* at home. In this way, one family member who has gone to the coast may be able to support an entire family back in China's rural interior.

More and more government officials view migrant labor as a normal conse-quence of economic reform, which, while loosening control of China's country-side through the breakup of the commune system, encourages some areas and some people of China to prosper first (namely, coastal cities and special economic zones).[7] As a de facto component of government policy, therefore, it is only natural that large numbers of people would flow from the less- to the more-developed areas of the country. The challenges of migrant labor are indeed very real. The contributions the laborers make, however, to both the coastal areas and to their home regions outweigh the costs and risks.

And while migrant labor can be viewed as a threat to stability, an equally persua-sive logic argues that migrant workers are the thread that keeps a rapidly transform-ing China from ripping apart. Migrant labor serves both to relieve pressure from the country's impoverished regions and to transfer resources and skills back to those areas. When I put the "stability" question to a Guizhou government official who works in Shenzhen, he responded immediately with an interesting compari-son: the threat of starving North Korea that looms over South Korea. "If North Koreans could travel to South Korea as migrant labor," he said, "the problem of instability on the Korean peninsula would be solved." His analogy is obviously flawed, but I got his point. The general freedom Chinese labor has had to pursue wealth, regardless of where it may be found, has alleviated what would otherwise be unbearable pressure, and certain instability, in China's impoverished interior regions.

In addition, much of China's economic growth has been built by the callused hands and sweat of migrant labor. In urban areas, for instance, migrant labor often does the dirty work that locals would never touch. China's powerful export mar-ket, as well, has been underwritten by the inexpensive and willing labor of those from the interior.

Like the powerful force of Overseas Chinese—ethnic Chinese who live outside China but who contribute billions in gifts and investment to their ancestral home-lands each year—China's *Overland Chinese* (my term for the millions of migrant laborers who work on the coast but who remit significant amounts of cash to their homes in the interior) play an important role in their local economies. A Guizhou official told me that in 1997, migrant laborers from Guizhou remitted five billion yuan (U.S. $600 million) to family members back home. Equivalent to 10 percent of the province's gross domestic product, the figure equals Guizhou's entire annual local-government revenue. In this regard, one of the most important contributions made by migrant labor is the ability to channel resources directly into the hands of individual families in China's poor interior, something government bureaucracies and aid programs seem to have great difficulty doing.

The Guizhou *Economic Daily* reported the story of thirty migrant laborers, all from the same village in Guizhou but who work in different locations on China's coast, who recently formed an "association" to support their home village.[8] Most funds from migrant labor are remitted directly to family members and do not contribute to village services like education and health care. Nevertheless, the example illustrates the Overseas Chinese–like role that migrant labor plays. To become a member of the association, each worker must agree to do three things: First, learn one skill he or she can share with fellow-villagers; second, provide at least one piece of information to the village regarding work conditions on the coast; and, third, provide an annual donation to the village.

The contribution made by migrant laborers to their home villages is, therefore, not just monetary. Several migrant laborers told me, as we traveled down the tracks, that beyond the funds remitted home, they believe their role is to open their family's minds to new ways of doing things and to try to keep their village from being satisfied with simply having enough clothes to wear and food to eat. In fact, many migrant laborers, after a few years of "eating bitterness" on the coast, wake up to realize that they could be their own boss back home, using the skills they have learned.

As our train crossed from Hunan into Guangdong Province, even though we were at least four hours from our destination, everyone seemed renewed by the reality that we were nearing the end of the trip. Groans changed to humming, card playing started back up, life came back to peoples' faces, conversation picked up. Even my headache went away. Four hours late, we finally arrived at the Guangzhou train station at midnight. After thirty-five hours crowded together, we sent each other into the night with sincere wishes for success and safety.

The labor that surges from China's interior to the coast serves as a conduit to transfer resources, skills, and experience from wealthier areas back home. And while the interior-to-coast flow of labor is the most dramatic illustration of the response to the eased travel restrictions of the 1980s, the longer I lived in Guizhou the more I came to realize that significant numbers of the province's farmers opt to forgo the long trip to the coast. More and more, it appears they are choosing the benefits of work in nearby locations a few hours from their home villages in one of the province's nine cities, like Guiyang, Zunyi, Duyun, and Anshun.

SUGGESTIONS FOR FURTHER READING, CHAPTERS 3 AND 4

Chan, Anita. "The Culture of Survival: Lives of Migrant Workers through the Prism of Private Letters." Pp. 163–88, in *Popular China: Unofficial Culture in a Globalizing Society,* edited by Perry Link, Richard P. Madsen, and Paul G. Pickowicz. Lanham, Md.: Rowman & Littlefield, 2002.

Chan, Kam Wing "Recent Migration in China: Patterns, Trends, and Policies." *Asian Perspective* 25, no. 4 (2001): 127–55.

Li, Cheng. "200 Million Mouths Too Many: China's Surplus Rural Labor." Pp. 111–26, in *Rediscovering China.* Lanham, Md.: Rowman & Littlefield, 1997.

Li, Zhang. *Strangers in the City: Reconfigurations of Space, Power, and Social Networks within China's Floating Population.* Stanford, Calif.: Stanford University Press, 2001.

Solinger, Dorothy J. "China's Floating Population." In *The Paradox of China's Post-Mao Reforms,* edited by Merle Goldman and Roderick Macfarquhar. Cambridge, Mass.: Harvard University Press, 1999.

Whyte, Martin King. "City versus Countryside in China's Development." *Problems of Post-Communism* 43, no. 1 (January–February 1996): 9–25.

4
"Hey, Coolie!"
Local Migrant Labor

A farmer-turned laborer pulls a load of scrap metal. Even the slightest gradation required extra strength from behind. Going over a bridge, we backed up traffic until all three pushcarts crawled across.

Life is hard in Guizhou's countryside, as the lives of my friend's three uncles in a remote village vividly communicated. Roadless sheer mountains, shallow soil, no running water, backbreaking labor, stripped forests, too many mouths to feed, and little money make life a constant challenge. Even so, people's ability to live as well as they do—wood-beam houses built into abrupt mountainsides, terraced rice paddies, recently installed electricity, and now even TV sets and rice cookers for some—amazed me every time I made the trek to Splendid Village.

Lack of food and clothes in this community no longer poses a serious threat. Villagers say their biggest need is cash: the means to pay their children's school tuition, prepare daughters' dowries, and purchase fertilizer and other crucial items like cooking utensils.

As a result, 90 percent of the men and many of the women in their twenties and thirties have departed Splendid Village for the cities as migrant laborers. Despite the strong attraction, however, urban areas stir apprehension in the hearts and minds of these rural dwellers.

One of First Uncle's daughters was deceived while looking for a job in coastal Guangdong Province; she ended up getting sold as someone's bride. She later escaped and found her way home, exhausted but free.[1]

Second Uncle's sister-in-law, who stopped by while we were eating breakfast, lost her husband in a mining blast in neighboring Guangxi Province last year—yet another migrant-labor casualty. Second Uncle says he would be working in a city somewhere, regardless of the risk, were it not for his wife's frail health. Because of chronic arthritis in her hips and knees, she is incapable of managing the affairs of their home on her own. Some days she cannot even get out of bed. So Second Uncle remains with his family. That neither of them is able to pursue cash outside

41

the village has led to a painful family decision: Which one of the three children will drop out of school after Spring Festival next month?

Third Uncle works in nearby Duyun, the prefecture capital, pulling a pushcart from dawn to dusk. He happened to drop by while some of us were visiting at his brother's home. Third Uncle speaks to me without raising his eyes. He says he has no other choice but to do this kind of work. He appears ashamed. Yet after expenses he averages 500 yuan a month (U.S. $60), a bit more than the average annual per capita income for the township! Good money, yes, but he earns every *fen* of it through exhausting labor and the disdain of urbanites. I know—I've seen him around town. Life is difficult in the mountains; but for farmers-turned-migrant laborers in the city, it is bitter, degrading, and dangerous.

Many observers view China's labor migration as primarily a flow from the country's backward hinterland to the more prosperous eastern seaboard. Indeed, it looks this way from afar. But disparity in China cuts most deeply between city and countryside, not coast and interior. Labor on the move responds accordingly.

Most of the farmers I spoke with in Guizhou Province say that more of their fellow villagers seek work in southwest China's urban areas than venture toward the better-known coastal destinations of Guangzhou, Shenzhen, and Shanghai. Two-thirds of those who leave Splendid Village, for example, remain in Guizhou's cities.

China is not a country simply tilted east, with all of its labor sliding toward the coast. Rather, urban centers across the land—small, medium, and large—are like raised magnetic points, attracting China's estimated 200 million redundant farmers from fields and mountains as if they were fine metal filings.

Obscure Duyun, a city of 460,000 squeezed along a river valley in the middle of southern Guizhou's mountains, is one of those points. Just ask some of the two thousand pushcart pullers who run its streets each day.

WARMING BY THE FIRE (*KAO HUO*)

From a distance the parked pushcarts look like idle surfboards lined up on Malibu Beach. It had snowed twice in five days, so I wasn't surprised to see a group of porters huddled around a fire, warming themselves as they passed the frigid January day.

Since returning from visiting with the three uncles just days before, I had become absorbed with the realization that the majority of "migrant" laborers in China probably never even travel beyond their provinces' borders.[2] Compared with the stereotypical "Overland Chinese"—those laborers who work on the eastern seaboard and remit significant amounts of cash back to their homes in the hinterland—what distinguishes this lesser-known but equally significant group of migrants? Why stay closer to home? Does one give anything up by not going to

Map 4.1   Labor Migration in China, 1990–1995

The Largest 30 Inter-provincial Migration Streams, 1990–1995

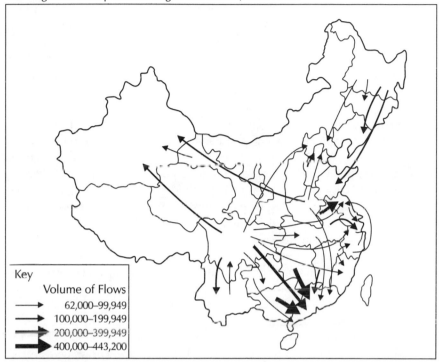

Compiled and Prepared by Kam Wing Chan, "Recent Migration in China: Patterns, Trends, and Policies," *Asian Perspective* 25, no. 4 (2001): 137. Source: National Population Sample Survey Office, *1995 Quanguo 1% Renkou chouyang diaocha ziliao (Data on 1995 National 1 Percent Population Sample Survey)* (Beijing: Tongji Chubanshe, 1997).

Rural Migrant Labor Flows, 1990–1998 (millions)

1990	15.57	1993	34.48	1996	39.84
1991	15.80	1994	39.30	1997	42.13
1992	18.28	1995	30.27	1998	49.15

Kam Wing Chan defines rural migrant labor in several different ways. Here we use his more narrowly defined tally, compiled from State Statistical Bureau surveys, for non-*hukou* migrants (those who do not obtain household registration permits and all of the associated benefits) who work outside their township, excluding those away from home for six months or more and those employed in township and village enterprises (TVEs).

In a 2002 article that demonstrates the rapid rise of China's off-farm labor force, Scott Rozelle and a team of scholars state that by 2000 almost as many of China's 200 million off-farm workers were living away from home as in the village. By including those who remain away from home for longer periods of time, the total shock of migrant labors would be approximately 100 million.

Sources: Kam Wing Chan, "Recent Migration in China: Patterns, Trends, and Policies," *Asian Perspective* 25, no. 4 (2001): 131. Alan de Brauw, Jikuan Huang, Scott Rozelle, Linxiu Zhang, and Yigang Zhang, "China's Rural Labor Markets," *The China Business Review* 29, no. 2 (March–April 2002): 20.

the more prosperous coastal cities? How do urban residents in the interior view this segment of the floating population? What are their pleasures, their hardships?

The next thing I know, I'm in the circle with these guys, chatting about their lives in the city. Surprised, but with typical rural hospitality, they respond warmly to my interest in them. The fire feels good even though they are burning old pieces of board. It turns out they are part of a larger group of thirty that has come from the same home village, about three hours from Duyun. Some are old-timers; one of the young ones has been in the city just three days. Most have been pulling pushcarts for three to five years. They average thirty years in age.

Their huddle occupies a street corner toward the edge of the city. The intersection serves as the terminus for vans and transport trucks that arrive from outlying counties and Guiyang, the provincial capital. The city government has designated their gathering point as an "official" pushcart location—the sign says so. According to the men, it simply means that if their pushcarts are not parked in a row, they may get fined. In addition, porters are required to pay an annual tax of 100 yuan (U.S. $12), the equivalent of about four days' wages. The porters are not aware, however, of any government services they receive in return.

Besides their strategic location, the group has developed a clientele of sorts with a variety of nearby stores, factories, and an auto-repair garage. The porters haul anything and everything: construction materials, furniture, coal, bags of cement, lumber, sheets of glass, scrap metal, sacks of grain, even slaughtered hogs just off the bus from the countryside. If it can be loaded onto an eight- by three-foot flat space, they can deliver it. The porters average 4 or 5 per load (U.S. $0.45). The best haul they can remember is a job that paid 30 yuan; it was a heavy delivery that had to go a long way. After expenses, which are minimal (30 yuan for rent and 100 yuan for food), each porter clears between 300 and 500 yuan (U.S. $37–$45) a month. Compared to the cash available at home, this is a significant sum.

As we speak, an occasional request comes: "*Ban che* [pushcart]!" But they may as well have been calling, "Hey, coolie!" One of the men hops up from around the fire and is off to the job. The circle tightens and expands as porters come and go.

"Why did you all leave home in the first place?"

"We're too poor. There's no money back there."

"Who takes care of your fields and family while you are gone?"

"We all have family members who look after things and do the work. If an emergency comes up, we are not far away."

"How often do you return home?"

"Spring Festival, planting, harvest, . . . about four or five times a year."

"Why didn't you go to the coast to work? Isn't the money better there?"

"The money's better, yes, but the risk is greater. It's much more dangerous there than here, and here is already bad enough. Plus, like we said, we're closer to our village and it's much easier to return home."

"What do you enjoy most about working here in the city?" I ask to see their reaction to something they probably don't think about very often: pleasure.

No response. I don't fill the silence. Finally, one of them says, "Full stomachs."

"And the hardest thing?"

The answer comes more quickly: "City people look down at us. We occupy the bottom of society."

"Why?"

"Because we're from the countryside. The work we do is dirty."

Among the circle, three do most of the speaking; the others just seem to take it all in. One man in particular, an older man about fifty years of age, with a weathered, unshaven face, emerges as the group's spokesman. He's the veteran and has lived in Duyun some thirty years (when he was young, his family moved from the countryside under special circumstances). He points to a shoddy two-story brick structure across the road. "That's my home. My wife, children, and I live there."

But originally, he's from the same village as the others.

At some point in the morning conversation, a cute little girl runs up to him from across the street.

"This is my daughter. Actually, she's adopted."

"What's her name?" I ask, as we squeeze her inside the circle so she can enjoy the warmth.

"Tang Lujuan. *Lu juan* means 'flower by the road.' We found her as a baby, abandoned along the street in front of our house."

Jackpot! He and I have the same last name: Tang.

"We're *jiamen* [relatives]!" Lao Tang declares to all. Family runs deep in China, even with adopted foreigners like me.

"We built the Tang Dynasty," he earnestly says to me, now holding my hand, "but our family name is in decline. There are very few of us left in Duyun. We've got to stick together."

Very pleased, but unable to reciprocate his fervor, I switch the conversation back to the reason I first approached the group: "I'm quite interested in your work, both because it enables you to earn cash for your families back home and because of your contribution to the welfare of this city. How else would the city people transport their things—like furniture, new refrigerators, and television sets—around town?

As I complete my sentence, a young rural woman with a scarf tied around her head strides by, balancing a shoulder pole with a stack of charcoaled sticks fastened to each end. Without telling the guys what I am doing, I stand up and shout, "*Mutan* [charcoal]!" After paying the woman, I instruct her to drop her load over by the circle.[3] When they realize what is happening, the men give a shout of "Hurrah!" We then settle back in around our upgraded fire.

Each day over the better part of a week, I frequented the porters' huddle. I'd sit for a while, chat, warm up, and then head on. I also walked the streets of Duyun, observing pushcarts and pondering this integral segment of the local migrant labor population.

One day, I return, determined to do more than talk. I want to experience a bit of their work firsthand. The fire is already warm by the time I arrive.

"What is the most effective way to find work as a pushcart puller?"

"You can roam or you can park yourself outside a store and hope that someone makes a purchase while you are standing there, but by far the best way to make money is to have a good relationship with a store owner or person at a factory who will direct work to you."

"What's the worse thing that has happened to you all out here?"

"We've had guys killed. Cars drive too fast and don't pay attention."

On this day there are just half a dozen of us gathered around the fire. It's still quite cold. Someone walks up and asks for a porter to haul something down the street.

"How much?" asks Lao Tang.

"Two yuan."

The men laugh off the offer and turn back to the fire.

Fifteen minutes later another call comes—"*Ban che!*" A man, whom they seem quite familiar with, dismounts his bicycle and says something about hauling scrap metal.

"How many of us do you need?"

"Three."

"How much per cart?"

"Twenty yuan for three carts."

"Fifteen per cart."

They settle on ten yuan a cart. Three men hop up; Old Tang is one of them. I follow. We head toward an auto-repair garage that specializes in trucks. Several tons of rusted metal from wrecked trucks need to be hauled away to a man's scrap shop. They load each pushcart, piece by piece, occasionally checking to make sure the stack of strewn metal is balanced by lifting the cart's handles.

After about an hour, all three loads—about a half-ton each—are ready to go. We pull out of the factory compound and onto the main road. Even the slightest gradation requires all four of us to help: one in front pulling, three straining from behind. Fortunately, most of the route is level. We arrive at our destination forty-five minutes later.

Subcultures, whether Washington, D.C.'s homeless population or Beijing's princelings, have their distinct mores, vocabularies, and common experiences.[4] In this way, I was struck by the community experienced by the porters who had left the countryside (and their families) to pursue cash in the city. The relationships were especially strong among those from the same hometown or village.

At the same time, I was equally impressed by the extent to which urban dwellers look down on porters—for that matter, on all laborers who come from the countryside.

EVERY GRAIN OF RICE . . .

"Dirty" is the first word used by a young urban woman when I ask her about migrant laborers in Duyun city. "Of course, though, I don't feel that way," she adds, when she sees the look on my face.

"When we were children," she explains, "our parents often told us that if we didn't study hard, we would end up like them, working on the streets."

At the same time, urban kindergarten children memorize a Tang Dynasty poem called *Min Nong* (Compassion for Peasants):

> Weeding rice paddies,
> while the bright sun shines down from above;
> Sweat off their brow drips to the ground below,
> mixing with soil and seedlings;
> Who knows the toil
> that went into each grain of rice that sits on your plate?

Memorized appreciation? Perhaps. Rural laborers construct their buildings, pedicabs cycle them around town, porters transport their burdens, and women laborers polish their shoes, wash their plates, and care for their children. But prejudice runs deep. In the eyes of most urban residents, rural folk are just, well, filthy.

Though the primary ways in which the urban–rural divide was institutionalized in the 1950s—household registration and migration restriction—have been eased or eliminated, they produced a two-caste mindset that remains until today.[5] The result has produced perhaps China's greatest wall: little understanding or appreciation between its agricultural and nonagricultural populations. Most rural people I have spoken with seem to have internalized this bigotry. A pervasive inferiority complex expresses itself in frequent self-diminishment, like the rookie porter who told me I would lower my status if we had our photograph taken together.

Even so, as long as cash remains difficult to come by in many of China's rural regions and as long as the wage difference remains so unbalanced, millions of rural laborers will continue to migrate to the cities, looking for work. How their urban bosses view them is among the least of their concerns.

In the longer term, practically inexhaustible flows of redundant labor from the countryside to China's cities—coast or interior—must be viewed as a temporary solution to the shortage of cash in the countryside. Both the numbers (approximately 200 million redundant farmers) and the realities of the rural–urban divide are just too dramatic. Market centers must be developed that are more numerous and diverse than simply the urban areas that dot the country.

One obvious need is to promote nonagricultural income-generating alternatives in the countryside. Township and village enterprises (TVEs), for example, brought means of production and capital to the countryside. In this way, TVEs have become an important source for absorbing idle farmers; they have assimilated 27 percent of redundant rural labor nationwide.[6] But that's primarily in eastern, more prosperous China, where rural areas tend to have better infrastructure, access to markets, and traditions of nonagricultural production. As of 1995, TVEs in western China had produced only 4 percent of the total national value, compared to 63 percent in the east and 33 percent in central China.[7] The potential is vast for TVE growth in western China. The need is certainly evident. Still, it takes money to make money. Financial institutions, even of the most basic sort, that extend credit to rural residents must be normalized and made more accessible. For even the better-off poor regions of rural Guizhou, however—like Splendid Village—the likelihood of extending credit in any meaningful way seems light-years away.

Equally vital are infrastructure improvements, which are especially slow to reach desperately poor mountainous regions like Guizhou Province. As policy-makers work to improve conditions in the countryside, the continued development of urban areas must not be overlooked either. Cities and towns will continue to attract rural laborers. As these points across the country become increasingly connected into road, railway, and telecommunication grids, they have the potential of stimulating complementary growth in the countryside. In this way, urban–rural relations need not be seen as a contradiction—rather, as mutually dependent. Generations-deep prejudice, however, is difficult to reverse.

In the meantime, as China faces a declining trend in rural incomes and levels of corruption thwart efforts to institutionalize rural residents' ability to gain access to cash at more local levels (especially in towns and townships), the welfare and stability of the countryside will in large part depend on the ability of migrant laborers to earn money in the country's urban areas.[8]

Despite the unsettling reality of overwhelming numbers of migrant laborers, it is encouraging that significant numbers of rural workers prefer to pursue employment near home rather than simply rush to the coast. Coastal urban residents and policy-makers attempting to address rural stability and the countryside's need for cash-generating activities can take heart that the disparity pie in China first slices vertically along the urban–rural gap, not along the horizontal coast–interior divide.

Still, if migrant laborers have no other way to meet their families' needs for cash, they will continue to be drawn to cities in numbers that could potentially overwhelm all of China's urban areas combined. Irresistibly, one recalls Mao Zedong's theory on peasant revolution: "From the countryside surround the city" (*cong nongcun baowei chengshi*).

During the time I spent with pushcart pullers around Duyun, they would often describe their work as *ku li* (literally translated, "bitter labor"). But it was not until one afternoon that it suddenly struck me: *ku li* sounds like the English word *coolie*. I asked the guys about it. My "distant relative" Lao Tang gave confirmation: "We porters have a long legacy; we are one and the same with the Shanghai dockworkers of old." Indeed, the men huddled around the fire are China's modern-day coolies.

5
Shared Prosperity?

Billboard of Deng Xiaoping in Shenzhen

Our policy is to allow certain groups of people and certain regions to prosper first. The advanced regions are then obligated to bring along and assist the backward regions. We must hold to the course of socialism: the goal is shared prosperity. But an equal pace of development is not possible. In the past we pursued egalitarianism and all ate out of iron rice bowls—this was actually common backwardness, common poverty. We all lost out. First and foremost, reform must do away with egalitarianism; we must smash the iron rice bowl.

. . .

Socialism is not when a small group of people becomes wealthy while most remain poor. Socialism's superiority is found in its pursuit of shared prosperity—this is the embodiment of socialism's most basic value. If, however, the rich and the poor become polarized, this is something very different. Conflict between ethnic minorities, between regions, between social classes, even between the central government and localities could develop, possibly resulting in chaos.

—Deng Xiaoping[1]

The mass movement of tens of millions of men and women flowing away from China's less-than-prosperous regions toward coastal areas of opportunity, as well as those who choose nearby urban destinations, reveals a human drama full of both the attractive lure of pockets of relative wealth and desperation. Together, they have persuaded a population within China—equal in size to the United States population west of the Rocky Mountains—to live and work under difficult conditions often far from home and family.

The spontaneity of this internal migration is striking, especially when one considers that for the first thirty years after the Communist Revolution (1949–1979), almost every aspect of a person's life was organized and controlled. Today, however, market forces are at work.

51

The flip-side of migrant laborers' natural response to their country's unequal prosperity is a series of government policies, developed during the 1990s, that attempts to assuage those who feel passed over by China's economic miracle. One of those central government initiatives—*duikou zhiyuan* (loosely translated as sister-city relationships)—has encouraged wealthy coastal cities to adopt their backward, hinterland cousins. The program illustrates Beijing's growing realization that the disparity gap must be addressed.

COMPLAINT

In early 1992, Deng Xiaoping (eighty-eight years old at the time) made what will be remembered as one of his most skillful political maneuvers: he paid a visit to Shenzhen Special Economic Zone, bordering Hong Kong. One of four "special economic zones" created in 1979 as an experiment in market-oriented reform, Shenzhen—the sleepy fishing village turned high-tech and export dynamo—had become the jewel in Deng's coast-led-development-strategy crown. After inspecting some key factories in Shenzhen, the elderly leader visited some other parts of Guangdong province and Shanghai. At each stop he called for the country to emulate Shenzhen's economic development by pushing ahead with rapid market-oriented reform.

Known as the "southern tour," Deng's trip was strategic because, just months before the Fourteenth Party Congress (convened every five years to evaluate and determine policy and leadership direction), it was an end-run around conservative critics. As a trump card played against retrenchment policies in place since 1989, Deng's outing mandated unequivocal support for continued reform and full-throttle economic growth. His designs were solidified during the 14th Party Congress in late 1992, as evidenced by the creation of the term *socialist market economy*.

Deng Xiaoping's high-profile "southern tour" touched off explosive economic growth and got market-oriented reform back on track. At the same time, however, it disturbed many leaders in China's yet-to-prosper regions. Not only did they feel that Deng Xiaoping's national form of trickle-down economics was not dripping quickly enough, Deng's visit to Shenzhen—symbolic of continued emphasis on coast-led development—indicated no hope for a shift toward, or even equal treatment for, developing the interior. The reform period had brought unprecedented growth to the inland provinces in absolute terms—inland leaders knew that—but compared to the highly favored coast, they were falling further and further behind. Coastal China's high-growth take-off had left most of the less-prosperous interior choking in its fumes.

Leaders from the interior began to express not only frustration with their relatively smaller piece of a growing pie but, perhaps more important, a sense of injustice with biased government policy. Deng Xiaoping's development strategy had created a playing field that leaned hard to the east: special economic zones and other coastal regions received preferential tax policies, foreign investment incentives, as well as lopsided central government investment.[2] To make matters worse, because interior regions had little formal representation in the central government, as coastal economic strength was increasingly parlayed into political capital, impoverished interior regions had less and less voice in central government politics.[3] Hu Angang calls the political-resource bias "the root cause of the sharpened contradictions between the central government and localities and between the developed and less-developed regions."[4]

Complaints continued to percolate during the years following Deng Xiaoping's landmark trip to Shenzhen. In 1994, economist Hu Angang again gave voice to this growing anxiety through two surveys: one with 30 provincial-level inland leaders, the other with 127 county-level government officials from China's Interior.[5] Approximately 90 percent of each group believed that regional disparity had reached extreme proportions, violating socialism's "shared prosperity" principle. Sixty-three percent of the provincial-level leaders and 95 percent of those from the county level believed that a solution to the problem was urgent, that it could not be put off until the next century. Eighty percent of both groups felt that the gap would lead to social instability. Of that group, 16 percent at the provincial level and 12 percent at the county level believed that the development gap could lead to the country's break-up. Hu's survey results were passed along to central government decision-makers.

In February 1995, Chinese Academy of Sciences president Zhou Guangzhao made an unusual appearance on China Central Television's (CCTV) investigative report program *Focal Point (Jiaodian Fangtan)*. In response to the reporter's question on the potential consequences of widening economic disparity, Zhou said, "Chinese history has many examples that demonstrate when society's distribution of wealth becomes terribly disproportionate, social instability can occur, in some cases, leading to a break in social development."[6] Influential academics in China do not speak casually about potential social chaos in public—especially on national television. The situation had obviously become quite serious.

With influential commentators like Zhou Guangzhao and Hu Angang reflecting sentiment that much of China's interior felt passed over by China's economic miracle—while, at the same time, growing numbers of migrant laborers were on the march—it became clear to the central government that regional disparity was no longer simply an economic issue; it had also become a political problem.[7] With that kind of input flowing back to Beijing, central government leaders began to sit up, take notice, and respond.

RESPONSE

As coastal economic growth continued to charge forward—and dazzle the world—central government leaders began to echo back to China's interior their

Figure 5.1.   Rural-Urban Disparity

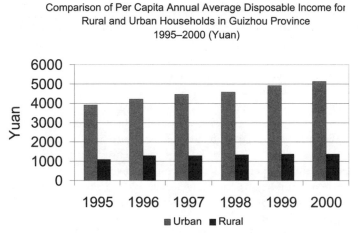

Guizhou's Rural-Urban Divide
Comparison of Per Capita Annual Average Disposable Income for
Rural and Urban Households in Guizhou Province
1995–2000 (Yuan)

Source: 2001 Guizhou Statistical Yearbook (Beijing: China Statistical Press, 2001).

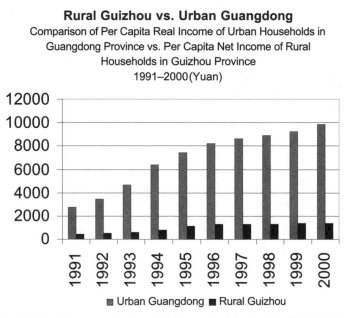

Rural Guizhou vs. Urban Guangdong
Comparison of Per Capita Real Income of Urban Households in
Guangdong Province vs. Per Capita Net Income of Rural
Households in Guizhou Province
1991–2000(Yuan)

*Source: Compiled from the 1992–2001 editions of the annual publication: The China Statistical Yearbook
(Beijing: China Statistical Press).*

concern over the hazardous development gap. In their speeches they began to speak of the disparity problem in a different tone. For example, Jiang Zemin said in a 1993 speech:

> During the development of our nation's socialist market economy, ethnic minority regions of the country—because of a weak economic base—may fall further behind for a period of time. We must pay attention to this problem, we must strengthen our research, and we must develop a policy response.[8]

Li Peng said in a speech the same year:

> We must admit the east–west gap. We must create conditions so that the gap can gradually close. The central government cares very much about this problem and has determined that the west's development is a major issue that must be addressed through policy, funding, and technological support.[9]

And not only did central government leaders respond by speaking to the issue, they responded to a call for "western entry [*xijin*] and not just southern tours [*nanxun*]" by traveling to the interior. China's leaders began to observe firsthand what was actually happening in the backwater regions. In 1996, for example, eleven central government leaders visited Guizhou province.

A significant step was taken in September 1995 at the fifth plenary session of the Fourteenth Party Congress. Whereas China's Seventh Five-Year Plan (1986–1990) explicitly stated that the country would pursue a growth strategy that accelerates the development of coastal regions, at the 1995 meeting the Central Committee put forward the principle of "persisting in the coordinated development among different regions and gradually narrowing regional development gaps." The result was a series of policy initiatives in the Ninth Five-Year Plan (1996–2000). The draft policy package focused on a commitment to increase central government funding for poverty alleviation and infrastructure assistance, improved tax incentives to attract foreign investment to the country's central and western regions, and a policy environment conducive to coordinating the interior's development with the rest of the country. Guizhou province, for example, was designated to receive U.S. $1.2 billion from the central government and various ministries through the year 2000 to support farming and poverty-relief work; preferential treatment in major project approvals involving infrastructure and energy development; and designation as a key province for resource development through the construction of several major industrial bases.[10]

All of this, however, turned out to be a false start. Although the drafting of the Ninth Five-Year Plan included large earmarks designated to the development of China's west, efforts by coastal politicians with interests in preserving the imbalance—in favor of the relatively wealthy east—worked to remove the hard numbers from the draft so that in the end, the plan read nicely, but only discussed the development of the west and a leveling of the playing field in the language of principle.[11]

The Ninth Five-Year Plan (1996–2000) ended up including minimal practical value to the delivery of large-scale central government financial and policy support to China's hinterland.

In fact, it was not until well into the Ninth Five-Year Plan that several top leaders, Zhu Rongji in particular, decided that the matter had become too urgent to continue to discuss in generalities and platitudes. Zhu Rongji set up a leading small group on western development in 1999 and visited Guizhou at Chinese New Year that year.[12] The leading small group was then upgraded into a specific office in the State Council, with coordinating offices in other ministries and commissions like the State Development and Planning Commission and the Ministry of Finance. Large funds were set aside from the central government and large investments began to be made into the development of western China. This initiative became known as the "Develop the West" (*Xibu da kaifa*) campaign.[13]

On a much smaller scale than all of this, but of great interest at the ground level in Guizhou, was a central policy initiative during the late 1990s to create sister-city relationships in which wealthy coastal cities adopt their poor, inland cousins.

SISTER-CITY RELATIONS:
SHENZHEN AND SANDU

As I walked through the school's front entrance into the courtyard, the open area teemed with elementary and middle school–aged children. The impressive four-story, white-tile building belies its location—the remote, impoverished mountains of southern Guizhou province. Shenzhen Hope School was constructed through the donations of seventeen Shenzhen companies that gave 4.35 million yuan (U.S. $526,000) as part of a sister-city relationship between Shenzhen Special Economic Zone and Sandu Shui Ethnic Minority Autonomous County (one of ten counties in Guizhou's Qiannan Miao and Buyi Autonomous Prefecture). The school is located in Sandu's county town, on recently completed Shenzhen Street.

Shenzhen Hope School, with its 1,400 students (800 elementary and 600 middle school), is the largest of 21 Shenzhen-supported schools sprinkled though the mountains of Sandu County. Each of the other smaller, more distant schools, which educate a total of 4,000 students, is sponsored by one Shenzhen company. All began operation the beginning of the 1996 school year, except for Shenzhen Hope School, which opened its doors in September 1997. Because elementary education is so critical to an area's development, Shenzhen chose education as the centerpiece of its support.

Though Shenzhen Hope School has been open for just one semester, it buzzes with excitement. An inscription greets all who pass through the main gate. It begins, "In honor of Deng Xiaoping's words that the first-to-develop regions should help bring along the less-developed regions until, in the end, all reach shared prosperity, the following companies donated funds to the construction of Shenzhen Hope School. . . ."

In the spirit of Deng's intentions, the Shenzhen–Sandu relationship, and others like it across China's interior, is the result of a State Council decision in 1995 to link wealthy coastal cities with backward regions. For Guizhou province, four wealthy coastal cities—Shenzhen, Ningbo, Dalian, and Qingdao—were each selected by the central government to adopt two of the province's eight districts. Qiannan prefecture was paired with Shenzhen. In the first few months after the relationships were established, the four cities signed agreements with Guizhou in over one hundred projects—mainly in education, health care, and tourism development—totaling U.S. $225 million.

During a visit to Shenzhen, I met with the director of Qiannan prefecture's Shenzhen Representative Office. Director Wang has led the office—in fact, the office is a one-man show—since its establishment in 1996. A former journalist from Qiannan prefecture's capital Duyun, Director Wang described his threefold role: to assist in directing Shenzhen donations; to provide information to relevant offices in Qiannan and Shenzhen; and to occasionally help place laborers from Qiannan in positions requested by Shenzhen companies (i.e., organizing migrant labor). Though he says the labor-matching role is the least time consuming, Director Wang told me that a group of thirty young women from Qiannan prefecture had just arrived for training. These would-be Shenzhen maids were staying in his four-room office—one of the rooms had up to a dozen three-level bunkbeds—until they are successfully relocated.

I was surprised to learn from Director Wang that the central government does not require Shenzhen to produce certain funding levels for their contribution to the sister-city relationship. Rather, each city's government is to organize and encourage its companies to give as much as possible to projects in its poor cousin's areas. Director Wang's role, therefore, as information provider is critical both to Shenzhen, as he lets them know of worthy projects, and back home to Qiannan, as he communicates what Shenzhen companies want to and are willing to give.

I assumed that the companies were motivated by tax incentives. I was wrong. Director Wang said there are other incentives at work: Shenzhen's leaders want to do a good job to impress the central government so as to increase their chances of being promoted to a central government position. Shenzhen's leaders also want to look good in comparison to other coastal cities, in the support of their backward interior brethren.

In Sandu County, government officials also told me that the sister-city relationship is not a "give-and-get-out" type of arrangement. After the funds stop flowing, advising, training, and exchange are to continue. The sister-city relationship's objective, beyond providing financial support, is to strengthen understanding between regions.

It is not difficult to see the potential good that can come out of the sister-city relationships. For backward inland areas, the financial support helps alleviate capital shortages and provides education and health-care improvements otherwise not possible. The extent to which this good is maximized on the recipient side, of course, assumes a bucket that does not leak—that is, that those tasked to oversee the handling of the donations get the gifts to their ultimate destination. From what I hear, skimming and resource diversion are severe problems.

Nevertheless, for Sandu County, as an example, twenty-one schools have been vastly improved and are in operation, and four thousand children across the county are receiving a better education than they were two years ago.

From the central government's perspective, the sister-city relationships are an important policy success. Because wealthy coastal companies foot the bill for what would otherwise be government expenditure, the government is able to provide social services without paying for them—a big victory for any politician.

Important as well is that the policy is an excellent mechanism to produce political fruit on the grassroots level, where resentment by the less prosperous may be the strongest. Sister-city relationships communicate that the government cares about the disparity issue. If I'm a poor farmer in the mountains of Guizhou's Sandu County who can now send my child off to Shenzhen Hope School, you bet it seems like the government has done something beyond just saying that it cares about regional disparity; the government got some of those wealthy coastal folks back here to help us out.

The best comment I heard, however, regarding the value of sister-city relationships came from a Qiannan businessman, as we discussed the issue over dinner. He said, "The money is not nearly as important as what sister-city relationships can do for our nation as a people. They have the potential of bringing us together, of helping us understand each other." Well said. Certainly, those in the central government have this in mind as well. National unity has always been a top priority for China's leaders; it is also one of the qualities most threatened by severe regional disparity.

I quizzed a senior Qiannan prefecture government official regarding potential downsides to the sister-city relationships. His greatest concern was the dependence that charity tends to breed. The opportunity-cost of what these gifts take away from self-reliant initiative is to be weighed against their contribution.

As wealthy Shenzhen company and government officials—symbols of Deng Xiaoping's growth strategy, which sacrificed the interior for the coast—blow in and out of the mountain communities for groundbreaking and photo ceremonies, a passive "We deserve it" attitude undermines solid, much-needed self-initiative. Gifts do not always stimulate responsible action.

To guard against the dependence problem, a Sandu government official told me that Sandu County is currently forming a policy that requires all government cadres below age thirty to spend at least one to two years working as "migrant laborers" on the coast. After the required time period, they can return to Sandu to resume their post if they fulfill at least one of three conditions: First, learn a skill they can teach others; second, bring back capital to their home village or town;

and/or, third, bring back an investor and a project. The rationale is that such "training" not only results in more resources flowing back to Sandu, it is hoped that it creates a leader who is less likely to passively accept poverty. Instead, having seen the relative prosperity of the coast, that person will be more enthusiastic about creating change. If the young man or woman chooses not to come back, that individual's remittance of funds back home alone makes it worthwhile for the county to have him or her remain on the coast.

Since I began to investigate the government's response to its economic disparity dilemma, Deng Xiaoping's frequent use of the term *shared prosperity* to justify his coast-led national development strategy has lingered in my mind.

Shenzhen and Sandu represent two extreme Chinese cities, which have been brought together through a government-directed sister-city relationship. Coastal Shenzhen, with its average annual economic growth of 45 percent and per capita GNP 488 percent of the national level, boggles the mind. Sandu County is equally astonishing: locked away in Guizhou's mountains, per capita GNP less than 45 percent of the national level, at least half of whose people cannot read, and thousands of whom do not have enough food to eat and clothes to wear. Several times—somewhere between Shenzhen's Hard Rock Cafe and the bus ride through Sandu's craggy mountains—I thought to myself, "How can China's leaders even speak of a 'shared prosperity'?"

As Shenzhen Hope School's principal and I leaned over the railing outside his third-floor office, delighting in the hundreds of poor school children as they skipped and played below us—made possible by Shenzhen, Inc.—I asked him, "What about Deng Xiaoping's phrase 'shared prosperity' that I read in the school's inscription? Do you actually believe Sandu County will ever catch up to Shenzhen?"

"There will always be distance between us and Shenzhen," the school principal replied. Then he thought for a long awhile, as he looked over the children playing in the courtyard below, and said, "Shared prosperity? We may never reach it, but it is something we can strive toward."

I suppose that as long as those in China's backwater aspire toward shared prosperity with their wealthy, coastal cousins, and do not burn with resentment, government policy is successfully holding off most of the potential dangers of skewed development. That will give the government more time to address the deeper, more fundamental issues associated with the country's economic disparity.

SUGGESTIONS FOR FURTHER READING

China: Overcoming Rural Poverty. Washington, D.C.: World Bank, 2001.
Hamrin, Carol Lee. *China and the Challenge of the Future: Changing Political Patterns.* Boulder, Colo.: Westview, 1990.

Shirk, Susan L. *The Political Logic of Economic Reform in China*. Berkeley: University of California Press, 1993.

Vogel, Ezra. *One Step Ahead in China: Guangdong under Reform*. Cambridge, Mass.: Harvard University Press, 1989.

Wang, Shaoguang, and Hu Angang. *The Political Economy of Uneven Development: The Case of China*. Armonk, N.Y.: M. E. Sharpe, 1999.

Wang, Xiaoqiang, and Bai Nanfeng. *The Poverty of Plenty*. New York: St. Martin's, 1991.

6

Reason to Hope
The China Youth Development Foundation

China has a large population and many talented people. A few million more illiterates, or a few million less, will not make a huge impact on the country. But for an individual, whether or not he or she can read is a factor of powerful consequence; a few hundred yuan has the potential of changing a person's life.

—Xu Yongguang, founder, China Youth
Development Foundation/Project Hope

Day after day, week upon week, little Ming Yuanxue stood peering through the windowless opening into the dirt-floor classroom. With no desk, no stool, no pencil or paper, Ming Yuanxue's determined mind and scrawny legs provided all the hardware she needed to fix full attention on the teacher. As with millions of children across rural China, Ming Yuanxue's family could not afford to send her to school. But that didn't prevent her from standing longingly outside the classroom, absorbing all she could from the teacher as he stood in front of her seated friends. When test time came, the teacher, who had noticed her persistent presence and big brown eyes, allowed Ming Yuanxue to take the exam. At the top of the test paper she turned in were written four words: *Wo yao xuexi*—"I want to study."

In the spring of 1991, national newspapers, radio, and television carried this story as part of an effort by China Youth Development Foundation to raise funds for Project Hope, their social-welfare program designed to promote the educational rights of poor children. Project Hope was founded by Xu Yongguang. His eyes sparkle as he recalls the success of the program. The "advertisement" was the first time since 1949 that a fundraising letter was publicized by China's carefully controlled state media. By the end of 1997, less than ten years after its founding, China Youth Development Foundation had raised $150 million, and Project Hope had provided almost two million children with the opportunity to go to school. In addition, 5,000 Hope Schools have been built (with 500-volume libraries in each); 6,000 high school and college scholarships have been awarded; and teacher-training programs have been established across the country. Project Hope's activities have involved 695 of China's poorest and most remote counties, covering 23 percent of the country. Not bad for a foundation that started with a $10,000 seed grant from the government! General Secretary Xu is quick to point out, however, that he believes the most important contribution Project Hope has made is the heightened attention now given to the right every girl and boy has to receive basic education, including—especially—children in China's forsaken poor areas.

So there is reason to hope. Especially if you ask the hundreds of thousands of children like little Ming Yuanxue who, because of Project Hope, now sit in classrooms instead of peering in from outside the window.

HOPE VANQUISHED

Yet glimmers of optimism abruptly vanish when one meets children like seven-year-old Chen Chunfen, who lives deep in Guizhou's mountains.[1] Although she is bright and eager, her family cannot afford to send her to school. Chen Chunfen and two million children like her drop out of school each year because of poverty.[2]

Such high numbers are particularly worrisome because primary education is a foundation of human and social development. It is clearly associated with openness to new ideas, higher work productivity, lower fertility rates, improved health, the movement of workers from agricultural to nonagricultural activities, and, just as important, self-esteem. Not that basic education has been ignored by the government. In fact, it has been a top priority for policy-makers, especially since the early 1990s. The results, according to official reports, have been dramatic.[3] According to *China 2020*, a World Bank study, the overall illiteracy rate has declined steadily since 1990, when it stood at 22 percent. Gains are especially impressive among the young. Whereas illiteracy among men and women over 55 years old is 62 percent, only 16 percent of those who attended school since 1949 and just 5 percent among those 10–24 years old are reported illiterate.[4] Perhaps the greatest improvements in primary education, however, have had little to do with targeted policies. General economic growth and standard-of-living increases have had the biggest positive impact on literacy and educational opportunities for China's children.

But impressive national-level gains in educational attainment conceal severe regional inequities. In fact, when one takes a closer look at China's poorest areas, it becomes obvious that for millions of the least fortunate, school remains a remote abstraction. Figures from a World Bank project area in southwest China demonstrate the severity of education deficiencies in China's impoverished regions.[5] The project area includes 35 mountainous and remote counties in Guizhou (13 counties), Guangxi (12), and Yunnan Province (10). Only 60 percent of 7- to 15-year-olds in the project area have ever enrolled in primary school; 65 percent of those are boys.[6]

Inferior education levels are not static. The backward state of education in China's most poor areas not only reflects, but actually reinforces, the existing gulf between Chinese rural and urban society. The poorer the area, the more backward the education system; the poorer the education system, the more backward the area. And round and round the cycle goes. At the center of this troubling reality is decentralized education financing. Most schools now have to depend on local governments for funding. For more prosperous areas, even wealthier rural communities, residents are able and willing to invest in quality education. Even entrepreneurs have been known to donate large sums of money to support their local school. For the better off, the shift away from centralized funding has meant increased participation and improvements in the education of their children.

But the reverse is true in impoverished areas and is particularly acute in the resource-constrained upland territories of northwest and southwest China. In these regions, the lack of meaningful levels of agricultural growth and nonagricultural rural enterprise development retard improvements in education.

The current state of China's education bureaucracy has magnified the negative impact of decentralized financing. A 1998 decision at the National People's Congress annual meeting to downsize the Ministry of Education's bureaucracy by 50 percent was part of a nationwide effort to lighten government bureaucracy. "The entire education system is in transition and lacks vision," a former university president and senior Ministry of Education official told me over dinner. The result is a shrinking and hesitant bureaucracy that has left education in a free-fall, with localities forced to fend for themselves—for better or for worse.

In addition, epidemic corruption at grassroots levels—whether diverting appropriated funds or misdirecting education fees collected from farmers—undermines efforts to improve education.

Anecdotes abound. A schoolteacher in one village complained to me that one-third of their school's expenditures last year went toward feeding local education officials visiting on "inspection." "They travel from one village school to the next eating and drinking," the teacher said. "And we dare not feed them poorly; they have power over us." Meanwhile, that same village has children whose parents cannot afford to send them to school.

If you want to feel encouraged about China's success in primary education and literacy, look at national figures or compare most localities with their past. But if you want a strong dose of the reality that much remains undone, watch two million boys and girls file out the classroom door each year because their parents cannot afford to keep them in school.

HOPE REVIVED

But that is not where the story ends. Closely following, in fact, an integral part of the evolution of Chinese society over the last twenty years, has been the increase of people who, when aware of need, have chosen to act—both individually and corporately. Xu Yongguang is one of those people. In 1986, Xu, director of the Communist Youth League's Personnel Department at the time, spent two months in Guangxi Province. He was appalled by the frequency of school dropouts among the youth he observed. Ninety percent of the children did not attend school past third grade. If these areas are ever going to develop, he thought, education will have to lead the way, not limp along behind.[7]

"Three colleagues who had had similar experiences and I decided that we were going to start something on our own," Xu says, "something new, something that was neither traditional 'thought education' [*sixiang jiaoyu*] nor the latest fashion. My instinct was to organize some kind of activity that would raise money to help children who had dropped out of school. At the time, though, I never imagined it would develop into what Project Hope is today."

His motivation? "My father died when I was young; life for our family was difficult. My brother, sister, and I were able to go to school only because others helped us financially. If we had not received assistance from society [*shehui jiuzhu*], it is hard to imagine where my brother, sister, and I would be today."

In January 1989, with a seed grant from the Communist Youth League and approvals from the Central Committee of the Communist Party, Ministry of Civil Affairs, and People's Bank of China, China Youth Development Foundation was established. That year the foundation sent staff members to Hebei, Henan, and Hubei Provinces to investigate potential project sites. During one officer's visit to Hebei Province, he fortuitously met a county-government official who told him of a nearby village school that had thirteen students, twelve of whom had dropped out because of poverty. The government official recounted a brief letter he had received from one of the students: "Director Che, did your family harvest enough rice to eat this year? We've had another bad crop. I've had to leave school. I have no choice but to carry a sack on my back and beg for food." These thirteen students became the first girls and boys to benefit from Project Hope's assistance.

Two million students later, General Secretary Xu admits that they have learned as they've gone along. He laughs, for example, when he talks about how far they've come since an early fundraising letter that tried to attract donations by offering free tour services for donors who came to Beijing. "We underestimated the desire people have to give just for the sake of giving," Xu says.

Or imagine the scene of the entire foundation staff sitting around the office, hand-copying addresses and stuffing envelopes with fundraising letters, compared to the one-swipe breakthrough when a similar letter was printed by a dozen national newspapers.

Probably the most important development for the organization, however, was in 1992, when Project Hope began to offer to match donors (individuals, companies, and schools) with recipients. Rather than just sending their gift to a common fund, as had been the practice, donors could feel as if they were adding a member to their family, city schools could adopt counterparts in the countryside, and companies could choose their preferred site to sponsor the construction of a Hope School. Giving that year increased by over 500 percent.

Equally significant to the increased level of giving was the improved accountability it placed in the organization. Kang Xiaoguang, whose book *Chuangzao xiwang* (Creating Hope) is a study of China Youth Development Foundation, writes: "The one-on-one giving arrangement brought about guarantees in oversight. Supervision of Project Hope was no longer just internal, it began to come from the outside as well: from society, from individual givers, and recipients whose interests directly affected their concern about how each cent of the donation was used."[8]

Throughout the 1990s, the foundation's reputation strengthened, support broadened, and new programs mushroomed to create maximum and lasting impact on education in China's poorest regions. The result, quite frankly, has been amazing. As Project Hope supported growing numbers of children to re-enroll in school, the foundation began to realize that school buildings were important, too. The result: five thousand Hope Schools have been built since 1990.

But then, if students are in school, in decent buildings, yet there are no books, how much can they learn? In 1994, China Youth Development Foundation invited some of the country's best-known writers and publishing houses to form an advisory committee. The committee selected 500 books to form a set library for each school. The foundation had 10,000 of these mini-libraries printed. But after students, school buildings, and books, what about the teachers? One year later, in 1995, teacher-training centers were established across the country. Typically, during summer vacation, teachers and principals are chosen to gather for three weeks of intensive training and encouragement. While most of the foundation's programs have progressed along expanding circles of need, Project Hope has also responded during times of crisis—like the 1998 summer floods, the worst in decades. Project Hope donated 1,500 classroom-sized tents so that students could resume school on time.

Xu Yongguang's most recent initiative is a highly ambitious plan to place multimedia equipment, educational video CDs, and Internet capability in each Hope School, estimated to reach 8,000 schools. Xu has established a company spun off from the foundation that will sell "the world's one thousand best educational programs" on the market for profit. The proceeds will go to support the placement of the equipment and movies in the Hope Schools.

The China Youth Development Foundation has been savvy with public relations as well. Three Project Hope students, sponsored by the Coca-Cola Company, carried the Olympic torch for a stretch in the lead-up to the 1996 games in Atlanta. Significant corporate giving has also come from Philips, AT&T, and Motorola. A professional soccer match is held annually in Shanghai to raise money for China's poor children. And polished television shows with charitable auctions light up phone banks with calls from donors.

Not that China Youth Development Foundation is without challenges. Xu

Yongguang says his organization's greatest limitations are threefold: policies that require too many strings between the foundation and its host-government ministry; burdensome bank regulations; and the persistent perception that philanthropies are run by ineffective people who could not find other work.

Beyond that, I imagine that an organization that has grown so quickly and that operates in an environment so fraught with corruption would face many hazards. But, Xu insists, under his leadership the organization will remain clean. "Our name is out there in society," he says. "If we become corrupt or stumble, it could set back the progress of China's entire philanthropic sector several decades."[9]

Despite the challenges, Project Hope is making headway to redress the country's severe urban–rural and east–west cleavages. Donor and recipient statistics tell the story. Whereas over 70 percent of donations come from middle- and large-size cities and over 60 percent of donors reside in China's developed eastern region, 75 percent of student recipients and 85 percent of Hope Schools are located in central and western China.

Moreover, the value of Project Hope's donor base is not limited to a one-way flow of resources. Giving benefits people on both sides of the gift. A China Central Television employee wrote to Project Hope:

> What Project Hope is doing is of immeasurable value. We want to make a contribution. My thought is that we would guarantee a young girl's tuition until she graduates from elementary school. My daughter is in second grade. Please choose a girl who had to drop out of school but who is a serious student and who made good grades before she had to leave. After she's re-enrolled, please ask her to write to us. My daughter will be the one who is asked to keep in touch with her. These two girls, who live in very different surroundings, can become pen pals for years to come. I think they'll be able to help each other in a lot of ways.[10]

Not that all who have donated to China Youth Development Foundation get as personally involved as this man and his family, but many do. The result has been the creation of bonds that stretch across urban and rural, and developed and underdeveloped, regions of the country. This is a revolutionary change for what had been for decades a society carefully partitioned along the lines of class and region.

China Youth Development Foundation has taken a leading role in creating a new type of organism in China. Unlike nongovernment organizations in most countries, Chinese "nongovernmental organizations" are required to formally associate with a host-government ministry. For better or for worse, there exists a more interdependent relationship between government and nongovernment in China—an arrangement that does not easily transfer to a Western model of state and society relations.

In fact, Xu Yongguang and academic Kang Xiaoguang do not even use the term *nongovernmental organization*. They prefer *third sector* when characterizing China Youth Development Foundation.[11] Though a Western term as well, *third sector* describes a broader arena that is neither totally government (first sector) nor business (second sector).

School dropouts, the unemployed, the newly urban poor, the sick, and the elderly will remain a challenge for the government. As China continues to reform and as the state seeks to govern more efficiently, a policy environment that provides for the healthy growth of the third sector would do much to promote the general welfare of the country's people. Indeed, no country lacks people who need reason to hope.

SUGGESTIONS FOR FURTHER READING

China 2020. Washington, D.C.: World Bank, 1997

Hannum, Emily, and Albert Park. "Educating China's Rural Children in the 21st Century." *Harvard China Review* 3, no. 2 (2002): 8–14.

Lopez, Ramon, Vinod Thomas, and Yan Wang. "Addressing the Education Puzzle: The Distribution of Education and Economic Reforms." Policy Research Working Paper 2031. Washington, D.C.: World Bank, 1998.

Saich, Tony. "The Chinese State and Society." Pp. 194–211, in *Governance and Politics of China.* New York: Palgrave, 2001.

Salamon, Lester M., et al. *Global Civil Society: Dimensions of the Nonprofit Sector.* Baltimore, Md.: Johns Hopkins Center for Civil Society Studies, 1999.

Strategic Goals for Chinese Education in the 21st Century. Report No. 1 8969-CHA. Washington, D.C.: World Bank, 1999.

Xue, Lanrong, and Tianjian Shi. "Inequality in Chinese Education." *Journal of Contemporary China* 10, no. 26 (November 2000): 107–24.

Young, Nick. *An Introduction to the Non-Profit Sector in China.* Kent, England: Charities Aid Foundation, 2000.

III

PORTRAITS OF
THE PRESENT
Rural Life in China's Interior

7

A Day in the Life of Shui Jianhua
Report from Splendid Village

Shui Jianhua, with his mare and foal, returning to Splendid Village from the township store. Shouldering a 110-pound bag of soil nutrient as we climbed the mountain trail, Jianhua told me he often makes the trip three times in a day.

My internal alarm clock sounded at 4:57 A.M. I drew back the mosquito netting, switched on the lightbulb that hung from a wire above the bed, and pulled on my clothes. In a matter of minutes Shui Jianhua, my twenty-six-year-old farmer friend, and I were off to begin his day. We walked up an uneven stony path through the faint predawn light, passing other villagers' sleepy wooden homes, and headed toward a series of terraced rice paddies that cut into the mountainside like a staircase. "I can already feel that it is going to be another hot sunny day," Jianhua said. "If we have many more days like this, those who haven't yet planted their rice seedlings will be in trouble. Look at the village party secretary's paddies over there; he hasn't even plowed yet. It's a good thing I've already gotten all of my seedlings in."[1]

As we continued along the path, a solitary, bent-over figure became visible in the morning darkness, standing knee-deep in a paddy. "That's villager Meng," Jianhua told me after he greeted her. "She's had a difficult life. Her husband was killed by a car in Duyun, while making a delivery with a pushcart. He was just trying to earn some money for the family. Both of her daughters were deceived and sold as wives while working as migrant labor in Guangdong Province. And her two sons are not good for very much. The woman carries tremendous burdens."

We continued along the path. "Here are some of my paddies," Jianhua said proudly, as we stepped onto a narrow mud retainer wall that separated two levels of paddies, each the size of a small putting green. Carefully placed rows of tender-green rice seedlings, each row separated by about four inches, poked above the surface through the water-filled plots.

Surprised by a sudden movement in the dimly lit water, I asked, "What's that in the water over there?"

"Oh, those are just little fish we put in the paddies. By the time harvest comes and we drain the paddies, they'll grow as large as my hand. You should come back then. We have a fish feast. It's a lot of fun."

Jianhua's first task of the day was to divert the flow of a spring-fed rivulet that emerged from a rock-faced cliff above his paddies. During the night the stream had been used to water a neighbor's network of paddies; now it was his turn. Before he introduced the flow of fresh water, Jianhua first inspected each paddy's outlet, a six-inch-wide opening that functions to retain water or to release it into a spillway that leads to the paddy below. At some of the outlets he constructed a small mud wall in order to dam the flow of water. In other paddies that were more full, he patted the mud wall down a bit or adjusted several stones to release a trickle of water. The understanding and skill that enabled Jianhua to maintain appropriate water levels—with the use of gravity only—in this labyrinth of irrigation channels halfway up the side of a mountain was quite impressive.

"Every other day from 6 A.M. to 10 A.M. and from 6 P.M. to 8 P.M. it's my turn to use the stream's water to irrigate my paddies."

"How long has this system been in place?"

"Four years. Before that, there were too many arguments among villagers over who would get to use how much water, and when. So the village leaders put this arrangement into place; things are much better now. A 24-hour-a-day system that gives people several hours access at a time ensures that most get the water they need." (Some paddies and fields are totally dependent on rainwater.)

"This section of the trail is very steep. You continue at your own pace," Jianhua continued. "I'll go up to the top, up where the trees begin, to switch the flow of water into my paddies. I'll meet you up there." As he finished his sentence, Jianhua skipped up the steep path into the darkness.

Thus a day in the life of villager Shui Jianhua began, with the diverting of life-sustaining water into his network of rice paddies.

Shui Jianhua lives in a mountain community called Splendid in southern Guizhou Province. To get to Splendid from Duyun, one has to travel by bus for several hours, hike for sixty minutes along a crystalline mountain stream, and then climb straight up for thirty minutes. The village sits perched among rock ledges, waterfalls, and pine forests. The view from his home is breathtaking.

Typical of the area, Splendid Village's one thousand members work hard just to maintain a subsistence level of living. The village homes are divided into eight subcommunities (zu) that dot the mountainside. Primary crops grown are rice, maize, potatoes, wheat, and cabbage. All work is done manually. A "man's best friend" is the beast that pulls the plow: water buffalo, oxen, or horse.

Agricultural goods for the most part are consumed by the villagers themselves. Other sources of income include raising pigs and capturing wild animals such as snakes. The biggest income-producers for Splendid Village, however, are family members who have left to work as migrant laborers in either nearby urban areas like Duyun or in faraway coastal cities like Guangzhou and Shenzhen.

Almost everything in Splendid Village is handmade. Houses and most furniture are built from local pine; roof tiles are baked in local kilns; every part of the plow except the iron blade is made from tree limbs; and baskets are made from local bamboo.

Items that are not made by the villagers (such as pots and pans, rope, plastic items, rat poison, and fertilizer) are purchased or traded for at the nearest market town, which is a three-hour hike away. Markets are open on calendar days that end with the numbers "3" and "8." On market days over ten thousand residents from the surrounding mountains pour into the town to buy and sell.

Though Splendid Village belongs to one of the poorer townships in the area (average annual per capita income hovers around 450 yuan (U.S. $56)), there have been improvements in recent years. The most exciting was the introduction of electricity in December 1997. The villagers say the most important way electricity has changed their lives is convenience. Instead of having to build a separate fire to cook rice, for example, many of the village homes can now accomplish the same task by flipping the switch on an electric rice-cooker. Jianhua even has a used black-and-white television that receives one channel. The reception is horrible, but it's television—and for the first time in Splendid's history.

While electricity has kindled enthusiasm in Splendid Village, poverty remains a chronic reality. The village's remote location, transport (everything must be carried by men, women, or animals from the nearest road), and other infrastructure limitations are key determinants of the village's poor living standard.

Education levels reflect the hardship. Of the three-hundred-plus Splendid elementary school–age children, less than half attend school. Many families who cannot afford the U.S. $12 tuition choose not to send daughters to school.[2]

Similar to much of the southern half of Guizhou Province, Splendid Village is populated by ethnic-minority people and is composed of a mix of ethnic groups that intermarry. Splendid Village is 60 percent Shui, 30 percent Miao, and 10 percent Buyi ethnic minority. Because the majority is Shui, and the village is located near a county primarily populated by Shui people, most of the villagers have adopted Shui customs and language. Actually, the men dress like Han Chinese (Mao jackets, etc.). The women, however, wear traditional Shui dress. In addition to speaking Shui dialect, most villagers speak a local variety of Mandarin Chinese.

Shui Jianhua's family is typical. His father is Buyi and his mother is Shui. Though Jianhua's wife is also Buyi, neither of them can speak Buyi. And because his wife is from another county, she cannot speak Shui either. As a result, Jianhua and his wife speak a local variety of Mandarin with each other. Jianhua's family and Splendid Village are a fascinating medley of language and culture.

Though Jianhua's family farms six *mu* of land (a bit more than half an acre) spread over twenty-one paddies and has plenty of grain to eat, the family members realize that they must find income outside of Splendid Village to maintain a stable life.[3] In Splendid Village, at least one member of nearly every family has left to find work in urban areas. Three of Jianhua's five immediate family members are part of China's migrant labor force. His parents both work as janitors in Duyun, and his brother has been working in a Guangdong Province factory for three years. Jianhua's sister was married several years ago; she lives in a nearby village. Even Jianhua, who is just twenty-six, has done construction work on the coast of Guangxi Province for five years and drove a pedicab in Duyun for three years. As long as one family member remains in the village to tend the paddies and animals, Jianhua's family believes that it is best that everyone else work in urban areas.

Life, then, for Shui Jianhua and the rest of his fellow villagers, is lived on the margins. And though Splendid Village appears to be a well-integrated and basically self-sufficient community, I realized after joining Jianhua for a typical day of work that life in Guizhou's mountains is a tremendously challenging way to live.

After Jianhua diverted the water's flow into his paddies, we headed back toward the village. Predawn darkness had given way to morning light. It was a few minutes after 6:00 A.M. and the village had come to life: women stood in rows across paddies, bent over as they planted rice seedlings; a man with a plow over his shoulder walked by, leading a water buffalo by a rope connected to the animal's nose; small groups of children gathered to make the thirty-minute descent to the elementary school that sits alongside the stream at the foot of the mountain.

When we reached his home, Jianhua's wife, Meili, had already left to help others plant their paddies. Several days ago Jianhua and Meili had finished their planting with others' help; now it was time to return the favor. Their twenty-month-old baby, Xiao Xia, was still fast asleep. That is, until she heard Daddy's voice.

Jianhua went to the back room and the family bed where Xiao Xia sat crying. He brought her out to the opening in front of the house, crouched, and held her over the edge of the wall. As was the morning ritual, Jianhua whistled to help her urinate. He said proudly that little Xiao Xia almost never wets their bed.

Jianhua began to fix breakfast: potatoes we had dug out of the ground the previous evening, pork fat I had brought from Duyun, and a flavorful chili pepper sauce. He prepared the soupy mixture in a wok that slowly cooked over a charcoal fire.

As I sat outside waiting, a news broadcast began to blare over a loudspeaker installed on a villager's roof. After the thirty-minute program came announcements from the township government. "String must be used when planting your rice seedlings," said a stern voice. "If you are caught planting without string, all of your rice will be pulled up." Using string helps to align the rows of rice and increases productivity, Jianhua said. At the same time, however, it slows the planting process that everyone is so eager to complete.

The loudspeaker is part of a one-way communication system between the township and its villages. The township government uses it to broadcast news and make announcements, and it can even pass messages to individual villagers over the system. But there is no way for the village to communicate back to the township.

After breakfast—Jianhua ate five large bowls of rice, compared to my one—we fed the animals. Jianhua owns a strong mare that had borne a foal just a month earlier. The mare was given raw grain (leftover wheat from last year's harvest); the foal still drank its mother's milk. Two large sows and three younger pigs were fed slop: an assortment of wild greens cut in the mountains, the tops of the potato plants we had pulled out of the ground the day before, and leftovers. Jianhua's two chickens were left to forage for food on their own. Nothing is wasted in Splendid Village. The major event of Jianhua's day was to hike to the township to purchase fertilizer, transport it home, and spread it over the paddies.

Meili, Jianhua's wife, returned for breakfast; the two of them discussed the day's agenda. They depended on each other and seemed like a good team. Today, little Xiao Xia would ride on her mother's back as she worked in the paddies with the other women. The baby was secured to her mother's back with a wraparound cloth backpack.

By the time Jianhua's mare had finished eating, we were ready to set out. Jianhua attached a saddle pack to the mare's back that would be used to carry the fertilizer. He was quick to say, however, that because the mare had worked so hard for the past two weeks plowing and was still nursing the foal, he would lighten her load by carrying a bag of fertilizer himself. Leading the mare, and with an empty, X-shaped wooden rack on his shoulder, Jianhua set off for the ninety-minute hike. This was the foal's first trip beyond the village paddies; she skipped along beside her mother, not wanting to be left behind.

Jianhua was quite proud of his animals, especially the mare. He commented on what a great worker it was, how responsive it was to his verbal commands. He could release the mare from miles away with a load, and it would return directly home. Jianhua said his secret was that he does not strike the animal unless it is disobedient, and he is careful not to overwork it. As we navigated the incline that led down to the village elementary school, the mare slipped occasionally because the decline was so sharp.

When we arrived at a stall that sells cigarettes, drinks, and odds and ends next to the school, Jianhua's cousin, who runs the shop, motioned us over. A few others had already gathered and were peering into a burlap sack that had something alive in it. I looked in—and jumped back. The bag was thick with snakes. "The poisonous ones bring the best money," the cousin explained. He asked Jianhua if he wanted to buy them. Jianhua told his cousin it was not worth his money to make the selling trip to Duyun unless there were more of them.

As we continued on our way Jianhua explained that he knew four snake traders from wealthy Guangdong Province who live in Duyun. "My friends and relatives know I have these contacts, so they like to sell to me. Then I sell to the traders. But I would not dare let them know how to contact the traders directly," he added. "They'd undercut me."

Though not yet noon, the sun shone brightly. An unusual string of about eight sunny days had concerned farmers, especially those with paddies that were not fed by spring water. Our path traced a beautiful stream that wound through towering mountains.

In the distance, heading our direction, I could see four colorful umbrellas. The four men beneath them looked like city folk on a field trip. "Who are those people?" I asked.

"They are township officials who have come out to inspect whether or not we have used string to align our rice seedlings."

We exchanged greetings as we passed each other. They looked surprised to see a foreigner walking with a villager, a horse, and its foal.

"All four of them are wicked," Jianhua said with spite after they passed. "Especially the guy that's walking in front. When we had our baby, I got fined 100 yuan (U.S. $12) because we did not register first. When he came to collect the money and I didn't have the cash, he threatened to take my horse 'til I paid up. I'd like to box his ears!"

"Have you ever considered running for village head?" I asked. "You seem to have a strong interest in the way things are run, and I can tell a lot of the people in the village respect you. You have village elections coming up the end of this year, don't you?"

"You're right, we have elections in December. But in Splendid Village all politics are determined by the township government. So while there are village elections in Splendid Village, they are nothing more than a farce. I'm not interested in village politics."[4]

We hopped across the stream. The mare and her foal stopped to drink.

"You spend a lot of time by yourself working in the paddies and transporting goods back and forth from the township," I said. "What do you think about when you're alone?"

Jianhua thought for a while and replied, "I mainly think about the tasks that have to be done around my home and fields. I also recall the years I worked as a migrant laborer. I've been back in the village for only two years; we returned home after we were married." He paused, then added, "I also think of how I might be able to make a little extra money, ways to support my family, especially as our daughter grows."

"Why did you head to the coast to work in the first place?"

"Just after I graduated from junior high school, I got into an argument with my father. I simply left a note the following morning, saying that I was on my way to the coast to work. It probably wasn't the best way to plan, but that's the way it happened. Though living far from home was difficult and working conditions as a construction worker were bitter, I'm glad I did it. I stayed on the coast for five years. Then after that I drove a pedicab for several years in Duyun. That's when I met my wife. My years working outside were tough, but they were good. I wasn't married at the time and I was able to save some money."

We walked for a while in silence and then asked each other more questions. Jianhua wondered about life in the United States: Do you have farms? Do you grow rice? Do you plow with water buffalo, oxen, or horses? How much is your salary? How do you figure ways to make money in your country? Most of the questions he asked me were about work and money—I suppose they reflect much of his own life's preoccupations.

"Do you have any dreams for the future?" I asked.

"How can you have dreams when you live in a place like Splendid Village?" We walked a bit farther, then he added, "If my brother returns from the coast to take up the family responsibilities in the village, I'd like to head back out for more work in an urban area. I think it's the best hope I have. I'd have to be away from my wife and daughter, and I don't like that, but there's no other way."

By this point we were almost to the township. Jianhua began to see people he knew and greetings were exchanged. "Come to our home and sit for awhile," said people who weren't working in the paddies. Those in the paddies said, "Come down here and give us a hand."

Not wanting to offend anyone, I asked Jianhua, "Are they serious? Do all these people want us to come to their home, and do the others expect us to roll up our pants and get in the paddy with them?"

"That's how we greet each other around here. They're just being polite. Just respond that we'll come on another day."

Shortly thereafter, we arrived at the township store. It was like a scene from a Western movie. We left our horses out in an open area while we looked for the woman who ran the store, which took awhile. We then purchased our goods: two 110-pound bags of soil nutrient (they were out of fertilizer) and a few pieces of candy for Jianhua's little daughter. Jianhua said she always inspected his pockets for goodies when he returned home.

The township center is not impressive. It is a modest collection of a few buildings—some concrete, some dilapidated wood—that house a few dozen township government officials and a junior high school.[5] The township center is more an administrative hub than a community. Splendid Village is just one of twelve villages (more than ten thousand people) under the township's administrative umbrella.

We split one of the bags into two 55-pound sacks and strapped them onto the saddle pack that rested on the mare's back. Jianhua fit the other bag onto the X-shaped wooden rack and groaned as he hoisted it on to his shoulder. We were off.

For the return to Splendid Village, Jianhua decided to take a route that was a bit shorter but much steeper. It was past noon by this time, and the unusually bright day made the sun feel especially hot. We didn't talk as much on the way back. At one point, about twenty minutes into the trek, though, as the four of us (mare, foal, Jianhua, and I) hiked single-file across the face of a steep mountainside, Jianhua said to me, "If you get tired, let me know." I shook my head and grinned to myself—Jianhua was shouldering over one hundred pounds; I was carrying six pieces of candy for his daughter in a plastic bag.

As we zigzagged through rice paddies and rock ledges, we passed hikers and paddy workers who knew Jianhua. The closer we got to home, the more everyone seemed to be related. "That's my sister-in-law's father," or "that's my second-cousin's wife," he would endlessly explain.

"When you're not working hard to keep up your farm and are not with your wife and daughter," I said, "what do you do when you have spare time?"

"I love catching and raising mountain thrush. I'm raising three right now. They sing beautifully, but best of all they like to fight. I take one of my caged thrushes high up into the mountains and let it sing. Its singing often attracts other wild thrush. The wild thrush comes near the cage and begins to sing along, but soon they begin to try to fight. At that point I throw a big net and try to capture the wild bird. Besides enjoying raising them myself, I can sell a good fighter for over 100 yuan (U.S. $12) in Duyun."

We passed a paddy that looked dangerously dry. Jianhua said, "Whoever plants that paddy will be in big trouble if it doesn't rain within the next day or two."

"Has there ever been a famine or a natural disaster in Splendid Village?" I asked. "In the early 1970s there was a famine and many died, but nothing on that scale has happened since then."

The mare, which Jianhua felt sorry for because it had not been fitted with horseshoes, struggled up sections of the mountain, especially where there were smooth rocks and footing was unsure. The little foal appeared exhausted but seemed even more scared of being separated from its mother.

We arrived home at about 2 P.M., more than four hours after leaving. As anticipated, little Xiao Xia searched her Daddy's pockets and was given her candy.

We ate a stew of cabbage for lunch, with rice and chili pepper sauce. After lunch we had originally planned to spread fertilizer in the paddies during the afternoon, but because the township store was sold out, the job would have to wait for another day. As a result, the late afternoon was more relaxed. Jianhua's wife and little Xiao Xia returned to their friend's rice paddies to help plant. Because of the dryness, Jianhua decided to check his fields again—proper water levels are important for a good crop, he said. While crossing from one field to another, Jianhua spotted a mongoose family in the brush—a mother and three offspring. Quite by accident, he found himself standing between them and their den. As the mongooses scurried in desperation, Jianhua ripped off his shirt and lunged at them, capturing one of the little ones in his shirt. Though the mongoose bit him, Jianhua could not have been happier: "This little guy will solve our rat problem. One sniff of the mongoose and the rats will flee our home."

The rest of the afternoon was spent admiring the caged mongoose as it snapped at live frogs that Jianhua dangled from strings. Village kids, arriving home from school, peered admiringly at Jianhua—their hero who had captured the vicious little critter.

By about 8 P.M. it was too dark to work outside. Village fires and rice cookers began to do their work. We began dinner at about 9 P.M., which Jianhua said was normal. Before dinner began, however, all animals were fed and watered. As we ate, I asked Jianhua and Meili if they remembered the first time they spoke to each other. Meili blushed, but Jianhua started right in. "At the time, I drove a pedicab in Duyun and Meili sold shish kabobs with her cousin. We rented rooms on the same street and I would notice her as we often passed each other on the street. I began to try to find a way to say something to her. One day it was raining very hard and as I was walking down the road, she, quite unexpectedly, walked past me very quickly. I yelled out as she passed, 'Hey, you splashed mud on me (even though she hadn't).' She said she was sorry. I teased, 'Well, just be careful next time.' She hurried on. And the rest is history."

Meili, who was quite shy, blushed and squirmed as her husband talked—but you could tell she was enjoying it. Jianhua then asked me to answer the same question about when I first spoke to my wife. We laughed a lot.

As I got to the part in my story where I say, "and the rest is history," Splendid Village's party secretary and the village head (the number one and number two of the village) knocked on the door. They were both Jianhua's relatives.

We spent the next hour talking about the village's history, its struggle with poverty, its successes (such as the recently supplied electricity), and its future. It was an enlightening conversation, but by about 11 P.M. I could barely keep my eyes open. Jianhua was still going strong, but I decided to turn in.

My bed was on the second floor of his two-story home. I pulled off my clothes and lay down. It was 11:01 P.M. During the night it began to rain. And it poured. Spring-fed rivulets gushed white-water mud, and streams turned into flooding torrents. Next morning, word reached the village that three elementary-age children had been swept off a single-log bridge they had tried to cross on their way to school. They were not hurt, but it was a close call.

"For most of the farmers," Jianhua told me over breakfast, "the heavy rain has saved them. But not everyone is happy about it."

Across the valley from Jianhua's front door a rice paddy's earthen wall had collapsed during the night. Three men feverishly shoveled the mini-mudslide with hoes, trying to divert the cascading water.

"I'll have to get out to check my paddies," Jianhua said. "I'll adjust the outlets a bit and I should be fine."

Though there was initially some question—and much debate among the villagers—about whether I would be able to hike out of Splendid Village because of flooded streams, I was able to make it without any problems. As I hiked along the muddy trail that just twenty-four hours earlier Jianhua and I had walked with his mare and foal, I considered the extent to which a day in the life of this twenty-six-year-old farmer speaks of a greater reality of village life in China.

Like his father, Jianhua has to work extremely hard just to subsist, and the lack of cash is a constant problem. Yet whereas his father knew only communes, campaigns, and revolutions as he was growing up, Jianhua has known only reform. In addition, Jianhua has seen and experienced much more as a migrant laborer, something his father could never have done as a young man. As a result, Jianhua has higher expectations and hopes for his life. According to Jianhua, for example, he and other young villagers now complain more about what is unjust; they recently protested against a corrupt township education official. Jianhua also has better access to material goods. Hey, he can even watch his new used television!

SUGGESTIONS FOR FURTHER READING, CHAPTERS 7 THROUGH 10

Friedman, Edward, Paul G. Pickowicz, and Mark Selden. *Chinese Village, Socialist State.* New Haven, Conn.: Yale University Press, 1991.

Gamble, Sidney D. *Ting Hsien: A North China Rural Community.* New York: Institute of Pacific Relations, 1954.

Lewis, Oscar. *The Children of Sanchez: Autobiography of a Mexican Family.* New York: Random House, 1963.

Li, Lianjiang, and Kevin J. O'Brien. "Villagers and Popular Resistance in Contemporary China." *Modern China* 22, no. 1 (January 1996): 28–61.

Parish, William L., ed. *Chinese Rural Development.* Armonk, N.Y.: M. E. Sharpe, 1985.

Scott, James C. *The Moral Economy of the Peasant: Rebellion and Subsistence in Southeast Asia.* New Haven, Conn.: Yale University Press, 1976.

Skinner, William G. *Marketing and Social Structure in Rural China.* Ann Arbor, Mich.: Association for Asian Studies, Inc., 2001 (sixth printing).

Tawney, R. H. *Land and Labor in China.* New York: Brace, 1932.

Unger, Jonathan. *The Transformation of Rural China.* Armonk, N.Y.: M. E. Sharpe, 2002.

Yang, C. K. *Chinese Communist Society: The Family and the Village.* Cambridge, Mass.: M.I.T. Press, 1959.

Zhou, Kate Xiao. *How the Farmers Changed China: Power of the People.* Boulder, Colo.: Westview, 1996.

Zweig, David. *Freeing China's Farmers: Rural Restructuring in the Reform Era.* Armonk, N.Y.: M. E. Sharpe, 1997.

8

Home-Cured Tobacco
A Tale of Three Generations in Big Nest Village

Three generations of change: Chen Dam (grandfather), Chen Meixian (father), and Chen Dongfang sit together at a meal. Seven-year-old Chen Chunfen, Chen Dongfang's youngest sister, sneaked into the picture.

Chen Zhixian, a shy, twenty-one-year-old woman from Big Nest Village, hasn't been the same since returning from Zunyi City four years ago. Her first time away from home as a would-be migrant laborer, Chen Zhixian found out she was different from most in the city: she was illiterate. In fact, when asked by a potential employer to sign a simple contract, she couldn't even write her name—the minimum requirement. Chen Zhixian returned home in defeat, completely humiliated. The sad truth: Chen Zhixian has never attended a day of school in her life.[1]

Within months of his sister's crushing experience, her brother Chen Dongfang, two years older and the eldest of seven children, returned from a distant vocational school to begin teaching at Big Nest Elementary. Chen Dongfang says that his parents, poor farmers and illiterate themselves, could afford to send only one of their children to school. As the oldest son, he received the privilege. After completing his primary education, Chen Dongfang went on to star as the number-one student at the township middle school and then studied elementary education at the vocational school.

Upon returning to Big Nest and a paying job, Chen Dongfang's first thought was his sister. He walked with Chen Zhixian down the hill to the elementary school and inquired if she could enroll. She'd have to start from the beginning—from first grade. School officials laughed. A seventeen-year-old sitting at a wooden desk in a room full of seven-year-olds? No way. The request was rejected; Chen Zhixian's trauma deepened.[2]

Since then, she has suffered from depression, expressed through lethargy and lingering sickness. The evening I arrived at the Chen village home, I caught only a glimpse of Chen Zhixian. I found out later that she had been sick and was taken that evening to a relative's home for "treatment." The distant cousin, I was told, would use "spirits" (*shen*) to attempt to cure her. The following morning Chen Dongfang apologized to me in private: the chicken that the family was going to slaughter for us as a welcome dinner was given to the witch doctor-relative as payment.

Chen Dongfang has one overriding concern in his life: that his younger siblings do not experience their older sister's misery. Besides Chen Zhixian, who stays at home, four siblings attend school and the youngest is expected to begin first grade in September. Since he was nineteen years old when he began teaching, Chen Dongfang has paid each of their tuition. "Tuition" for one semester of elementary school in Big Nest Village is 80 yuan (U.S. $10)—or $20 for the academic year. Middle-school tuition is about $30 per year.[3] For families in Big Nest, whose annual incomes average less than $80, sending their children to elementary school is a costly decision—a luxury item—especially because some adults, never having attended school themselves, are not always convinced of its value.

Second sister, Chen Zhifen, now fifteen years old, is in fourth grade. She's the hardest working of the siblings, says Chen Dongfang. First brother, Chen Zhihua, thirteen years old, is in sixth grade. He's an introvert and has terrible grades. He'd much rather hole up in a room taking things apart and putting them back together. Second brother, Chen Liping, twelve years old, is in fifth grade. He's a peaceful boy, but his heart is not in his studies. Third brother, Chen Xiaobo, eleven years old, is also in fifth grade. He's smart and loves to talk. The youngest, Chen Chunfen, a playful seven-year-old sister, begins first grade this September. She's Chen Dongfang's favorite sibling. Chen Chunfen is courageous, he says. She'll do well.

Apart from their studies, the Chen children are part of a tightly knit household economy. Each child has daily chores: taking the water buffalo to graze along mountain paths (*fang niu*), cutting wild grass for pig fodder (*ge cao*), washing clothes by hand, sweeping the dirt-floor home, and helping with food preparation, such as grinding chili peppers, washing vegetables, and peeling potatoes.

With big brother hovering over his siblings, they will all—with the exception of Chen Zhixian—learn to read and write. But that doesn't mean they enjoy it. Each of the children told me at some point during my visit that they do not like school.

"Why not?" I asked.

"My teacher doesn't care about me," was the common reply.

Little appreciated by villagers, elementary-school teachers in this region's rural areas lack incentive to put their hearts into their work—unless they are exceptional, like Chen Dongfang. During the four years he taught at Big Nest Elementary, Chen Dongfang spent evenings visiting village families to stress the importance of education. He also pled with family heads to enroll their children in school. As a result of his efforts, which were completely of his own initiative, the number of students at Big Nest Elementary increased from 100 to 500 during the four years he taught at the school. The number of students, however, dropped back down to 350 within one year of Chen's departure for vocational school. After the Chinese New Year that followed his departure, only 100 students had enrolled for the second semester. The cause of the volatility: A government corruption–induced tobacco-price debacle—families suddenly did not have enough money to send their children to school. Months later, the number crept back up to 350 students.

I asked Chen Dongfang about his own dreams and plans for the future. "I have only one goal," he replied without hesitation, "to continue to raise the money each of my five younger brothers and sisters needs to complete middle school." The twenty-three-year-old spoke with the seriousness of a parent.

This type of commitment would present a dilemma for most young people. Not for Chen Dongfang. Though his heart's desire is to remain in Big Nest to teach, and he is at the age most in his village marry, he has shelved all personal desires until he secures his brothers' and sisters' education. Because of expected tuition increases, Chen Dongfang is even considering going to China's coast after he completes his teachers program next summer to look for a construction job. If he could find employment, he would make possibly four times what he makes as a teacher. But it's a risk, he admits. Travel to the coast would mean forfeiting his guaranteed monthly teacher's salary. And plus, it's no sure bet he could find a job, especially with the economy as it is.

Chen Dongfang has the sharp, distinct facial features characteristic of someone from the mountains of Zunyi District. Add a Red Army cap to his head and some revolutionary fire in his eyes and he'd look like something off a poster from the 1950s. But this young man is a child of a different age. Education and travel outside his village have opened horizons not previously known in Big Nest. Witness an uncle's sincere question as we sat around one rainy afternoon, chatting with family and village friends: "Is China at the center of the world?"—a fascinating question from someone who has never left his village. In response, Chen Dongfang held up a ball and patiently described to his father's brother that the earth is round.

Big Nest exists somewhere between centuries-old living conditions (wooden plows, cooking over open fires, smoke-cured ham, and paraffin lamps) and urban values of the late 1990s, as the village is pollinated by young people who travel back and forth from China's urban centers as migrant labor. The result is village life in which young and old, though living together, seem at times as if they belong to worlds that are shaped very differently.

During my first of two homestays with Chen Dongfang and his family, I began to sense the intriguing mix of continuity and change that exists in rural-interior China. Most of my insights came as Chen clansmen and I sat on wooden benches in a small, barren room (used also as the eating area), chatting as we dodged drips from a leaking roof, swatted pesky flies, and shooed away scrawny chickens that kept sneaking into the room, convinced they would find grains of spilled rice.

Atmosphere was created by pipe smoking, an important activity in this tobacco country. Each man had a plastic bag stuffed somewhere in his clothes that contained chocolate-brown tobacco leaves. Each also had his own pipe, made with a polished-brass mouthpiece, a thin five-inch-long piece of bamboo, and a small brass bowl just large enough to hold the end of a rolled piece of tobacco leaf. These pipes are their prized possessions. As conversation circled the room, a man, empty pipe in mouth, would pull out a crumpled plastic bag from his pocket, remove a broad leaf of tobacco, carefully tear a strip about one-inch wide and six-inches long, roll it into a tight cylinder, and then stuff one of its ends into the pipe's bowl. The men shared lighters or matches, and when one of them had problems getting his pipe lit, they would all laugh, joking that his lungs were not strong enough or that his tobacco (each grows his own) was inferior.

As we sat around, each man puffing away and enjoying conversation, Chen Dongfang's grandfather, Chen Daru, told some of his life story. Though he is almost deaf, his eighty-year-old mind is lucid. He spoke as if the events of his life sixty years ago had happened just yesterday. No one I met in Big Nest is more thankful than Chen Daru that the past is history.

GRANDFATHER

When Chen Daru was his grandson's age, destitute poverty, opium smuggling, warlords, salt monopolies, and clan warfare strangled northern Guizhou Province. To illustrate how difficult life was in the 1920s and 1930s, Chen Daru told us how a cousin of his hiked two weeks (each direction) to Chongqing in Sichuan Province just to purchase two buckets of salt and then transported them all the way home on a shoulder pole. Farmers in salt-deprived Guizhou had no other choice because of exploitative salt monopolies.[4] Despite the continual struggle to live off his land, Chen Daru enjoyed considerable standing in the Chen clan, some one thousand families spread over five villages.

Chen Daru's social position was strengthened because his best friend, also from Big Nest—a dynamic, eloquent young leader—was recruited by the local warlord as his lead assistant. With his own army and political administration, the warlord controlled a piece of northeastern Guizhou Province, equivalent in size to a present-day county. Like many warlords at the time, he entered an uneasy alliance with the Nationalist government.[5]

Within the warlord's stronghold, however, clan warfare was common. On the eve of the Communist takeover, sporadic hostility between the Chen clan and neighboring Ye clan increased at an alarming rate. Chen Daru claims that the Ye clan was the aggressor and the Chen clan fought strictly out of self-defense. The timing of the skirmishes could not have been worse. At the high point of the Chen–Ye feud in the early 1950s, the People's Liberation Army marched into northern Guizhou to "liberate" the area—that is, to mop up after their victory against the Nationalists and to consolidate power. The new regime investigated the existing power structure and eliminated potential opposition. Chen Daru's best friend was summarily executed; Chen Daru was categorized as a counterrevolutionary, a label he would not shed for thirty years when Deng Xiaoping rose to power in 1978, and far-reaching rehabilitation and other policy changes were ratified at party sessions in late December 1978 at the Third Plenum of the Eleventh Central Committee of the Chinese Communist Party. The meeting marked Deng Xiaoping's rise to power as the country's paramount leader and ushered in a new era in Chinese history.

Even so, Chen remembers, as if it was yesterday. "I never did anything wrong," eighty-year-old Chen says quietly between puffs. "We were just trying to defend ourselves. I am *not* a counterrevolutionary."

FATHER

Regardless of what Chen Daru says about his innocence, among those who paid the heaviest price for his "crimes" were his children. "Growing up was very difficult," says Chen Daru's oldest son, Chen Meixian. A man of few words, he enjoys the circle of conversation but says little. After learning more about his youth as the son of a "counterrevolutionary," I understand why he does not speak much.

Born in the early 1950s, Chen Meixian grew to maturity through years of class struggle, communes, mess hall eating, the famine created by the Great Leap Forward, and the tragic Cultural Revolution. Because of Chen Meixian's father's special status, other children were not allowed to play with him, he was not permitted to move freely around the village, and he was denied the opportunity to attend school. Toward the end of the Cultural Revolution a marriage was arranged for Chen Meixian to a young woman from a village three miles away. They gave birth to their first child, Chen Dongfang, in 1975. Life turned for the better in 1978 when his father was rehabilitated, but for someone—by that time in his midtwenties—who had never known anything other than labels and class struggle, change was not automatic. Children are like wet cement that quickly dries. His personality had been formed; he had learned to mind his own business.

Though China's "one-child policy" was instituted in 1979, Chen Meixian and his wife gave birth to seven children by 1991. Villagers say that birth-control enforcement has not been strict in Big Nest until just the past few years. Now, after a family is discovered to have two children, the woman has no choice but to be sterilized. Township-government officials enforce these efforts.

Prior to that, clan mentality drove considerations of family size: the number of people relative to rival clans measured Chen strength. Village leaders, who are also clan heads, until late, encouraged families to have more children. The leaders, in turn, would falsify reports to township officials on the number of people in their village.

Today, Chen Meixian and his two younger brothers live in adjoining homes. His sister lives in a distant village with her family. According to custom, his father lives with the youngest son. And though their living space is separated, and they cook and farm according to their nuclear-family units, they share much of their lives in common as an extended family.

Chen Meixian is a gentle man. Though he appreciates the fact that his oldest son feels so strongly about education, his preoccupation in life is farming, seeing that his crops (tobacco, corn, rice, and potatoes) succeed. After all, he and his wife have a family to feed.

SON

Chen Dongfang is keenly aware of the profound changes that have occurred within his family in just three generations. He is the first in his family to know how to read. The opportunity to study has clearly provided Chen Dongfang with new prospects and improved thoughts of how to care for his family. How else, he wonders, can his family and Big Nest Village ever break their isolation and cycle of poverty? Higher literacy rates in rural areas, especially among women, are fundamental to improving Big Nest Village's economic situation.

Chen Dongfang is also part of an increasingly mobile generation. Even those in Big Nest who have received little or no education now flow to China's urban and coastal areas. In fact, an entire age group—those in their late teens through early thirties—is conspicuously absent from Big Nest.[6]

One afternoon conversation included two brothers Chen Dongfang's age who work construction in Kunming, the capital of inland Yunnan Province. They had returned for a brief visit with their wives and children. Though they come home only once or twice a year and have not lived at home since they were teenagers, they bring new ideas—and cash—every time they return. The result, as their experience is replicated millions of times throughout Guizhou Province and China's interior, is a pattern of increased interchange between China's urban and rural areas.

These brothers' absence and hundreds of others like them from Big Nest make Chen Dongfang's presence all the more meaningful. Though away at an education college most of the last year, he remains an inspiration for the village children.

Besides the young, Chen Dongfang also has the attention of Big Nest's older generation. To watch those his father's age sit like children as they listen to him tell stories of life in faraway cities and newfound information is quite a role reversal from decades ago when I imagine the young would sit wrapped in their fathers' stories about the production brigade or the latest clan skirmish.

But perhaps most interesting is the way Chen Dongfang and his family relate to each other. The respect he receives from both siblings and parents make it seem as if his siblings have two sets of parents: their mother and father who put food on the table, and Chen Dongfang who keeps pencils and notebooks in their hands. This dual parent–like family structure demonstrates the ways in which education and mobility among young people in Guizhou's villages are influencing family relations.

Dramatic change has occurred in Big Nest since Chen Dongfang's grandfather was a young man, when this community, hidden deep in Guizhou's rugged mountains, was mired in a high infant mortality, low life expectancy, and near-total illiteracy. Even so, Chen Dongfang is painfully aware—he is reminded every day by his sister's suffering—that too much remains the same.

Maybe that's why it bothers me so much to imagine Chen Dongfang crouched on a floor of scaffolding at some construction site in Guangdong Province. Migrant laborers have a contribution to make, certainly; but Big Nest Village needs Chen Dongfang.

9

They Call Me "Brother"

Report from Big Nest Village

Family fun: *Everyone joins in as family members make homemade tofu. Sister pours soybeans and water into the hole in the grindstone, while Father and Brother push and pull the long wooden crank, suspended from a roof beam, that rotates the heavy stone. White, milky soybean liquid oozes out of the press and into the basin below.*

And many strange things there were I had never seen or heard before.

—Mao Zedong, in 1927, after spending thirty-two days in Hunan Province's countryside investigating the beginnings of a peasant movement[1]

Chen Dongfang and I were walking from the township center toward his village home. Just as we stepped off the stony country road onto a shaded side trail, five young boys dashed up to us from behind. "Ge [Big Brother], you've come back," one of them said shyly, nudging me on the arm to make sure I had heard him. During my summer stay with this boy and his family, his grandparents, parents, brothers, and sisters became like family to me.

Back in the 1930s, my "grandfather" participated in local clan warfare. My "father" wears sandals made of straw and smokes a homemade pipe. "Mother" never went to school, but in her no-print world she is the last to care that she cannot read or write. She weighs about eighty-five pounds but can carry loads twice her weight with ease. I have seven "brothers" and "sisters." They are all good kids and hardworking, but their worlds are limited to the poor mountains of northern Guizhou Province. They live somewhere between the secure but narrow predictability of farm life and wildly unpredictable dreams of cement, television, and cash, the attractive-but-risky potential of life outside the village.

For part of a summer, this indeed was my family. We ate together, worked together, and played together. The experience, like no other, provided up–close insight into family life in one of China's poorest counties. It also offered matchless opportunity to enter the rhythms of a village that had never seen a foreigner.

Call it a rustic vacation. The weather most days in northern Guizhou, even in

July, is mild, ranging in the 70s to 80s. The air is fresh, the mountains are tall, shooting stars race across clear night skies. Chickens and finches greet each day with song. Water buffalo graze on lush hillsides, looked after by young cowherds. Tall dark-green corn, tender-green rice paddies, and yellow-green broadleaf tobacco plants demonstrate that nature gives back what is well cared for. The soothing sound of a gurgling stream is never distant. Naked boys play in the creek's big pool. Family members work together. Village adults sit on their porches, chatting after a long day in the fields. That's life with the simple, slow-paced, but hardworking peasants of the good earth.

Idyllic? Hardly. Raging flash floods wash out flimsy bridges and collapse terraced rice paddies. Sisters-in-law screech at each other from across their porches, continuing an ongoing quarrel. Peasants spread rumors behind each other's backs. Smudge-faced children's brown teeth rot from neglect. Fleas crawl on our bodies as we sleep at night. Flies swarm on a chunk of raw pork that dangles from a meat hook. Maggots and mosquitoes, not to mention the stench, make one think twice, and thrice, before visiting the outhouse. Curable sicknesses go untreated. Oppressive local-government corruption keeps resources and opportunity beyond the reach of most. Ignorance cripples. Worse, it kills.

A certain tempo dictates life in Big Nest Village. That, I suppose, is inherent to life lived close to the soil. By about 6:00 each morning, Second Uncle sharpens sickles on a stone slab outside my window, occasionally dipping the heated blades into a basin of cool water. The roosters' crowing competes with barking parents to make sure all the kids are out of bed and into action. From youngest to oldest, each has a role to play in the family-based economy.

By breakfast, the Chen family accomplishes what many would imagine consuming an entire day: the water buffalo is led out to graze; bushels of weeds are cut and chopped up for the two pigs, which are fed three times a day; baskets of potatoes that grow between rows of corn are dug from the earth (some are washed, diced, and mixed with the weeds for the pigs; others are cleaned, peeled, and boiled with rice for the family); the home is swept; tools are readied; the fire is started; and breakfast preparation begins.

Breakfast, which is not served until 10:00 A.M., takes more than an hour to prepare and requires two people: one to continually stuff dried weeds, straw, or cornstalks into an opening in the kiln-like stone hearth, while the chef, standing on the opposite side, prepares the food in one of three large iron woks mounted into the oven. Mother or the oldest daughter usually cooks; a younger child tends the fire.

Rural Chinese have prepared food this way for generations, if not centuries. It's like a scene from a Civil War–era historic-preservation farmhouse in the United States. The kitchen is dark, musty, and damp, but the fire is hot, and with a farmer's appetite the food tastes good.

The family's staple consists of rice mixed with steamed potatoes, but the kids always try to get the bowl with the fewest potatoes possible. "Breakfast, lunch, and dinner, everything is made of potatoes," one brother complains. "It's all we eat."

Slight exaggeration. Yes, there are potato cakes, potato chips, and even thick noodles made from potato powder. But there are also vegetables (mainly cabbage), wheat noodles, homemade tofu, and occasional pork (fried fat, meat cubes, and sausages), as well as the variety of goods bought in the township on market day: soybeans, tofu skin, peanuts, seasonal fruit, and other kinds of green vegetables. And there are lots of chili peppers cooked into everything. Big Nest Village is located in the heart of China's "chili belt."

Until just five years ago, sufficient grain was far from certain in these parts. By July each year, families often were forced to purchase rice at the market. Since a new strain was introduced a half-decade ago, however, there is enough grain even for this large family that lives off of four peoples' worth of land. In the late 1970s, when the government decided to disband communes, arable land was divided into bands of quality, and then parceled out according to the number of people in each family. Because the Chen family had only four members when the land was distributed, the clan, now numbering nine, feels the pinch. Populations expand, arable land does not.

After breakfast, then again after a quick lunch break around 3:30 P.M., the family members divide up and head to their plots of land, spread unevenly around nearby valleys and mountainsides. Routine chores keep everyone busy: hoeing, pruning, digging more potatoes, weeding (weeding and more weeding!), and herding the water buffalo and the just-bought ducklings.

Besides the daily chores, however, occasional tasks often force the family to juggle responsibilities: transporting buckets of human and pig waste out to the corn and tobacco fields, spreading store-bought fertilizer and insecticide in the rice paddies, preparing tofu with the large grindstone, washing clothes in the stream when the sun shines, bathing in the river, drying rice and rapeseed on large mats, sewing, and making and repairing tools.

With the exception of blades, most tools, even plows, are made by hand. Every family has a bamboo grove—what for urbanites may simply be a picture of traditional Chinese art is for them a forest of rake, sickle, and broom handles; flutes; children's toys; basket-weaving materials; even tobacco-pipe shafts.

Recycling is big in the countryside; little goes to waste: human and pig excrement becomes fertilizer; clothes are patched and worn for years, then handed down (one elderly man told me that until just recently, he wore a jacket purchased in 1947!); straw is woven into rope; homework assignments become wallpaper.

By dinner, everyone looks tired from a full day. We sit quietly on hard wooden benches, squeezed around a small table under the dim light emitted by a 25-watt lightbulb that hangs from a wire in the ceiling. Food is gobbled down with little talking.

After dinner, some retire to their rooms (two kids to a bed). Others sit outside on the porch in the dark, sharing local gossip. The buzz one night was about a household that had been caught by county-government family-planning officials hiding a one-too-many child of another family—in fact, the child's father was a township-government official! Big trouble; lots to chat about.

The most constant thing about after-dinner is Father twisting off a strip of sun-dried tobacco leaf, rolling, then stuffing it into his pipe's bowl and enjoying a smoke. He's usually the last one sitting at the table.

That is, unless the kids play a game, like the night I introduced them to "paper football." The activity evolved into the most playful night of the month. The excitement attracted neighbors and relatives, who squeezed into the small dining room to watch competitors, taking turns, slide a thick, triangle-shaped piece of folded paper across the table, trying to score a "touchdown" by getting some part of the three-sided object to hang beyond the table's edge, without falling off. Extra points were made much like a place-kick: by booting the paper object with a flip of the finger through goal posts formed by the opponent's extended fingers.

Most nights, however, the dining room is vacated quickly, leaving Father smoking his pipe in silence and one of the more studious children working on his summer-vacation homework assignment. The rest fall quickly into bed. No one is awake past 10:00 P.M.

Outside the expected activities that occupy the Chen family's time and energy, larger parameters of village life provide cadence as well. Besides the major annual markers—holidays (the highlight of which is Spring Festival) and the twin peaks of busyness, planting and harvest—the strongest beat in life's meter is market day.

On each day of the lunar calendar ending with "1," "4," and "7," the township center swells from its normal population of about 500 to nearly 10,000. On days ending with "2," "6," and "9," the market-day crowd gathers at a different nearby township; on "3" and "8" days at yet another. These three townships (*xiang*) form what was once a district (*qu*), an administrative layer between the township and county that no longer exists. Prior to the revolution, townships were home base for rival clans that fought bloody hand-to-hand, sickle-to-sickle, and gun-to-gun battles.

Nowadays, itinerant vendors follow the market as they alternate among the three townships. Rain or shine, farmers from surrounding villages converge on the township nearest them to join in the festivities.

There are many reasons to go to market day. People gather to socialize, to hear and spread gossip, to tend to business at the township government, to get a tooth pulled or their hair cut, to have their fortunes told, and, of course, to buy and sell goods. Half trade fair, half carnival, market day is more than anything an event, a welcome respite from work in the fields.

By about noon each market day, after completing the necessary chores and finishing breakfast, an expectant atmosphere begins to build in the village. People change their clothes, prepare their goods, and pack for the four-kilometer walk to the township. Unmarried young men and women wear their Sunday best. I made sure each market day to wash my hair in a bucket and shave before setting out with the others.

"*Gan chang?*" ("Are you headed to market?") becomes the rallying cry as people greet each other. "*Zou ba!*" ("Let's go!") friends and neighbors shout, as they strike out on the dirt trail toward the township.

Farmers from a radius of ten kilometers gradually converge on the township center: a concentrated space not more than 100 square meters large. What begins as a rivulet—a few people who set out together from their cluster of mountain homes—becomes a steady flow by the time one reaches the stony country road.

Some strain under shoulder poles, bent with weighty bags of seed, others under a wood-frame rack that supports a butchered hog, split down the middle. Most women carry bamboo-woven baskets on their backs to transport whatever needs to go to or from market. Some, of course, carry nothing—especially young people who want to look just right. Whatever their age, everyone tries not to get their shoes dirty. On rainy days, it's impossible.

The stream becomes a river as we close in on the township. Then, finally, the river dumps into the ocean: a tremendous crowd squeezed onto the township's narrow main street. A strange sensation overcomes me as I step onto the paved township road, boiling with people—as if I'm suddenly floating, carried by the movement of the masses.

Hours later we step off the pavement back onto our stony mountain road to return to our village—like an ebbing tide.

As my brother and I tiptoed across the narrow, muddy embankment that separated the paddies, I could hear the slow, steady pounding of what sounded like the heavy head of an ax striking hollowed wood. The noise echoed through the ravine. Then, as we neared the house, I saw them: two corpses lay side by side on tables in front of the village home. Disheveled hair and ashen faces partially hidden by a piece of cardboard, the bodies lay covered with a quilt—as if the couple was just sleeping. If only it was so.

It had rained the night before. During the storm, the bare wire that carried electricity to their home had somehow fallen from the pole into one of the rice paddies. The fields this time of year are full of water.

That morning, sometime before breakfast, the couple's five-year-old son was playing near the paddy immediately across from their home when he saw what looked like an egg beneath the water. He reached in to retrieve it, but slipped and fell in. The electrified water stung him. He cried out in pain.

Hearing the scream, the child's mother raced over to him. She hopped down into the water, just as she always did when she weeded or spread fertilizer, only this time she received a strong shock as well. The young mother then made a fatal mistake: she reached over and grabbed the live wire.

According to the boy, his mother "got twisted up in the wire."

Father heard the commotion. He, too, sprinted to the paddy. When he saw his wife, writhing in the mix of green rice and now-muddied water, he leaped into the paddy. The father quickly set his little boy up on the bank, then reached for his wife's hand.

Villagers say the young boy ran back to his grandparents, screaming, "Mummy and Daddy are holding hands and they are all tangled up!"

Tragically, the boy was right: His mother and father perished, hands frozen together by a deathly charge of electricity.

Later that same day, we, like others in the village, walked over to the stricken family's home to express our condolences. It was a sight I will remember for a very long time: relatives and friends sitting in disbelief, the two corpses lying next to them in chilled silence.

The hollow rhythmic sound of a hatchet hewing two coffins continued to beat. And it happened on market day.

10

Team Water Buffalo
Report from Big Nest Village

Team Water Buffalo: *Chen Zhibo and Chen Xiaobo, cousins and best friends, take a break halfway up the mountainside.*

During my second homestay in Big Nest Village, two of the children, twelve-year-old cousins Chen Xiaobo and Chen Zhibo, and I became especially close. These boys are cowherds— "Team Water Buffalo," as I came to call them—charged with the daily task of grazing the family water buffalo. During my summer stay in Big Nest, these children became my buddies as they allowed me to join them each day in their work. By doing so, they also introduced me to a fresh angle on village life in China's mountainous hinterland: the children's perspective.

SEND OUT THE COWS

After Xiaobo removes the slats from the pen's opening, the first thing to emerge is the water buffalo's enormous head.

"Come on, you lazy, good-for-nothing!" Xiaobo yells at the buffalo—just as his parents barked at him minutes before. It's not yet 6:00 in the morning. We're all groggy, including the buffalo. The split-hoofed beast knows the drill: it steps out of its weed-bedded pen, turns left, then a quick right and up the trail. Within five minutes the animal has emptied its bowels, creating some of the biggest "mud pies" I've ever seen. With an amazing sense of timing, other cowherds and their buffaloes begin to congregate on the mountain trail.

Bamboo switch in hand, Xiaobo rips into the buffalo's leathery rump, already lined with stripes from lashings on days gone by. When the cowherds really want to sting the animal, they strike it on the back of the calves.

Most of the whipping has little to do with getting the lumbering water buffalo to walk faster. The key, it appears, is to let the animal know who's in charge. After all, what fifty-pound child wants to lose control over an object many times his or her own weight? It's also about twelve-year-old boys becoming men.

The bumbling buffaloes appear to be on autopilot as they walk toward one of two areas where they are led each morning. The most frequented destination is an untilled mountainside about twenty-five minutes from the Chen home. Because of its rocky soil and boulders, little grows there except for grass and weeds. Perfect for pasturing. If the weather is exceptionally hot—something water buffaloes are especially sensitive to—the cowherds send the animals up a wooded mountainside that is a fifteen-minute walk behind their home. Rain, sun, snow, or sleet, "Team Water Buffalo" is responsible for making sure the family cow gets out to graze and safely home by the end of the day. Once the buffaloes are sent to pasture, they usually stay put. This way, the children can go to school, play, or help with chores after they return home for breakfast. Should the animals get into trouble, news usually comes back quickly through a villager who has seen the problem.

One afternoon, for example, I was playing with the boys back at the house when word came from an urgent-sounding uncle: "Your cow's in someone's corn patch, and the field doesn't belong to our village!" Zhibo took off like a rocket. By the time he had arrived at the scene of the crime, his cow had done quite a bit of damage. The angry villager had arrived as well. There was twelve-year-old Zhibo, embarrassed and unsure of what to do, standing by his massive, naughty animal. The following day, after a bit of negotiation, Zhibo's father compensated the farmer with ten pounds of corn seed.

Despite the occasional hassle, cows are an essential part of family life—the equivalent of what would be for many the family tractor. Though plowing is all they do and they are mainly put to work to prepare for planting in the spring, their role is indispensable. Most families have one water buffalo. A few families in the village use "yellow cows" (*huang niu*), which look similar to beef animals. Yellow cows do not plow as deep, but they are less sensitive to heat and easier to care for. Even so, the water buffalo remains the traditional beast of choice.

No one uses horses in Big Nest Village, though other villagers in Guizhou prefer horses because of their dual-use capabilities: plowing (though their furrows are not as deep as those of either yellow cows or water buffalo) and transportation. By their demeanor, water buffaloes seem to care about nothing. "But you should see when two males lock horns in battle," a villager told me. "Once they do, there is no way for a human to separate them." The simple solution: male water buffaloes are kept separate.

Yellow cows' temperaments are a different story. They seem to be naturally aggressive and are always in a bad mood. They are even more prone to bite and fight when they have young with them. One morning a yellow cow, eyes bulging with fury, tried to drive a water buffalo off the side of a cliff. And for no apparent reason. The 50-pound cowherd took off after the 400-pound beast with his switch, whipping it into submission.

A village boy guides his family's water buffalo to the fields.

LIBERATE TAIWAN

One morning, while Zhibo, Xiaobo, and I walked on the wooded mountainside with the cows, I wandered off to look around the forest. When I returned, the boys were playing a game on a nature-made playing board: a large stone slab, large enough to sit on. They had scratched lines into the rock, in a design that looked like a star-shaped checkerboard.

They glanced up at me with smiles then continued their game. *Jie—fang—tai—wan*, each said in turn as he moved one of his three playing pieces the required four positions. Like chess, the object was to maneuver around the board so that by the third jump he had landed on the opposition's piece. The entire game, in fact every four-move turn, includes the repetitious *Jie—fang—tai—wan*. I couldn't believe my ears: *Jiefang Taiwan* means "Liberate Taiwan!" And here we sat on a hilltop, somewhere deep in the mountains of one of China's poorest provinces.

"What does *'Jiefang Taiwan'* mean?" I asked.

"I don't know," they both replied, shrugging their shoulders.

"Do you know what *Taiwan* means?"

Blank stares.

"Jiefang?"

No response.

Later I asked Xiaobo's older brother if he knew about the game. "Yes, as long as I can remember, the kids in this village have played it," he answered.

They've probably been playing it since 1949!

After "Taiwan" had been "liberated" many times and enthusiasm for the game began to wane, I said, "See that tree over there? I bet you can't hit it with a rock." We started pitching rocks at the tree, shouting in glee when our target resounded with a thud.

WHEN I GROW UP . . .

What better place to get to know "Team Water Buffalo" than sitting with them on a big rock overlooking a valley or chatting as we threw stones?

"Do you enjoy taking care of the cow?" I asked Xiaobo one day.

"Yeah."

"Why?"

"It's not bitter [*ku*]. I don't have to work," he says with a big smile.

Indeed, compared to his brothers and sisters who labor in the fields or haul human and animal waste up and down the mountains, Xiaobo's got it easy. He's been in charge of the cow since he was seven years old. He doesn't see it as work. For him and his friends, even though they have to take out the cows regardless of the weather, it's all play.

Based on their grades, it is obvious that they do not enjoy working in the classroom either. Report cards came out while I was staying at the Chen-family home, and the two boys averaged scores of less than 50 (out of 100). At the family meeting big brother and I called to discuss the children's performance, everyone simply laughed when the scores were read aloud: 30s, 40s, and 50s.

But these kids are clearly intelligent. What's the problem? The most common response was that many do not believe studies will get them anywhere. Few—children or parents—see any direct link between school and their welfare. Not in a society where people become government officials through good connections, opportunity flows not from hard work but from favors, and quick cash comes through construction jobs on the coast. For many, school seems like a waste or, at best, a place to socialize with friends.[1]

The quality of their teachers makes things much worse. With poor training and even worse attitudes, most teachers do little to motivate their students. In fact, they spend most of their day gambling—even while at school. The students are often left on their own. The severity of the "teacher problem" has been evidenced by a few cases of how well classes did when the teachers really put their hearts into the job.

On another day, as Xiaobo, Zhibo, and I sat on a boulder, the cows munching on shrubs ten feet away, I put them to a little test: "Who's president of China?"

"Jiang Zemin."

"Right!"

Who's premier?"

"Li Peng."

"Close. Actually, since 1998 Zhu Rongji has been premier." Their answers impressed me.

"What do you want to be when you grow up?" I continued.

"A government official," Xiaobo replied without hesitation.

"Why?"

"So I can relax and play."

"And you? Zhibo, what do you want to be when you grow up."

"I just want to play."

Certainly, many of their answers revolved around the fact that most twelve-year-olds want to play more than anything else. In thinking about it, though, I realized that these kids are also set on playing now (and when they grow up) because they see how hard and relentless life is in the village—especially when compared to the lifestyle of the government officials they observe.

"Guys, I know you probably don't think about this very much," I said, as we continued to pitch stones at the faraway tree, "but how many children do you want to have when you grow up?"

"Two," Xiaobo responded automatically.

"Why?"

"Because that's government policy."

"Any other reasons?"

He thought for awhile, then replied, "Yeah, they could wear better clothes if there are less children."

In their simplicity, these village children were not just cowherds—they were among the best commentators on life in rural Guizhou that I had met.

学习雷锋好榜样
发扬艰苦奋斗的精神

The poster reads: "Learn from Lei Feng's example. Carry forward the spirit of arduous struggle."

11
Leading on Poverty's Front Line
The Spirit of Daguan Village

Fifty-five pairs of eyes stared intently at me across the classroom. Pensive and serious, the fifty-five town mayors and party secretaries listened as I introduced varieties of worldwide poverty and current economic development models. As we exchanged eye contact, I could only imagine the weight of concern that must occupy these men's and women's minds—they are responsible for leading rural, mountain townships in counties that are poor, so poor they have been designated as "impoverished" by Guizhou's provincial government.[1] And this is within China's most backward province.[2] Indeed, the men and women who sat across from me lead China's poorest of the poor.

Provincial and prefecture leaders realize they must get through to the minds of local officials if poverty-alleviation efforts are to take hold. Toward this end, Qiannan Prefecture's Office of Poverty Alleviation began a project in the late 1990s to organize semiannual, week-long training seminars. Over a three-year period, more than three hundred town mayors and party secretaries were to receive training in poverty-alleviation policy, management techniques, and development models, as well as enjoy the camaraderie of sharing a week with others who face similar challenges.

Qiannan Prefecture's governor, Mr. Wu Jiapu, delivered the training seminar's opening address. "Comrades, each of you comes here today from the front lines of poverty's battlefield." The governor spoke without expression. Mentally pacing back and forth, he spoke in slow, measured sentences; thin streams of cigarette smoke rose gently above his head during the periodic silence. "Your task in the fight against poverty is both challenging and glorious. . . . You carry heavy burdens. . . . You must reject blind optimism. . . . You must emulate the hardworking, never-say-never spirit of Daguan Village."

101

The reference to Daguan Village caught my attention. I am familiar with the Dazhai production brigade of the 1960s, a model commune in Shanxi Province that, because of its residents' hard work, reported a dramatic fivefold production increase. Dazhai's work ethic and stunning results were said to prove Mao Zedong's vision of rural self-reliance and revolutionary zeal. To promote Dazhai's spirit to the nation, a front-page article in a December 1964 edition of *People's Daily* featured a photograph of Dazhai brigade leader Chen Yonggui standing next to Chairman Mao. The caption below the photo read: "In agriculture learn from Dazhai." Chen quickly climbed to prominence, all the way to a position in China's Politburo, China's highest decision-making body.[3]

I have also heard and read much about the revolutionary soldier of peasant background, Lei Feng, who was canonized by Mao Zedong as a model proletarian during the 1960s.[4] Though killed in 1963 by a falling telephone pole, the twenty-three-year-old soldier conveniently left behind a beautifully written diary that displayed an unusual selflessness and passion to serve the people. As one of his many quotables, Lei Feng wrote, "I will be a screw that never rusts and will glitter anywhere I am placed." After Mao Zedong eulogized Lei Feng, he instantly became a model for all to emulate. "Learn from Lei Feng" campaigns—in which his "spirit of the rustless screw" and other admirable qualities were exalted for all to follow—sprang up nationwide in the 1960s; they were resurrected in the early 1980s and then again immediately after the events of 1989.

But I had not heard of Daguan Village. A Dazhai for the 1990s? The spirit of Daguan Village was something I would have to look into after the training seminar ended. Meanwhile, the afternoon session with the town mayors and party secretaries turned out to be quite enjoyable. Many of the serious dispositions lightened a bit as we had time to get to know each other during breaks and after the session concluded. In fact, to my delight, a casual reference I made during the presentation to my love for fishing resulted in invitations from several mayors. "We're poor, but we have lots of fish in our rivers!" one mayor said proudly. "Prefecture leaders from the capital Duyun come to my town to fish; I stand right next to them when we fish, we use the same bait, but they catch all the fish. Could you come to my place and show me some tips?" another mayor remarked. Typical fisherman humility, I thought to myself. "Of course. I'd love to," I accepted. "We can chat as we fish." Others, however, remained quite serious, even in their private comments. "Foreigners underestimate the seriousness of our poverty," one mayor told me. Another official lamented, "Our town faces tremendous difficulties."

I wanted to follow up on these invitations immediately, but I decided it would be best to look first into the ideal each was supposed to emulate in their leadership of local poverty reduction—the spirit of Daguan Village.

EMULATE THE SPIRIT OF DAGUAN

Though Daguan Village sits high in the remote karst mountains of Luodian County in southern Guizhou Province, it has become a nationwide phenomenon.[5]

All major Chinese newspapers and television documentary programs have told Daguan's story. A photographic exhibition has even taken the spirit of Daguan on the road. Daguan Village's leader, Party Secretary He Yuanliang, has risen to national fame as well—he is a "national model worker" and was a delegate to the Fifteenth Party Congress in Beijing in 1997. The Guizhou Province delegation hosted a booth and a press conference at the Congress to promote the spirit of Daguan Village. In the first year after the campaign to emulate Daguan began, some eighty thousand visitors—mainly busloads of government officials—had made the journey to "learn from the spirit of Daguan." That's an average of over two hundred a day! Apart from my disappointment with not being able to interact with Daguan's villagers, my trek to Daguan Village, just a seven-hour bus ride from Duyun, was well worth the trip.

Mr. Chen, assistant party secretary of Luodian County, met me outside the Luodian Guest House at 8:00 A.M. We climbed into the jeep and began our day trip to Daguan Village. After a steep ascent, which seemed to take us into the clouds, the driver pulled off to the side of the road, a dizzying height above the craggy valley below. We climbed out of the vehicle at the first point of interest: a bend in the road that provided a panoramic view of layers upon layers of mountain tops that disappear into the fog—it seemed as though I was looking out of an airplane window. A roadside sign introduced karst geology, including: "Karst geology is not suitable to support human life. In most areas of the world where karst formations exist, emigration is the only solution." We got back in the jeep and Party Secretary Chen began the Daguan story.

Nine times during the 1970s, Daguan's Village party secretary, He Yuanliang, tried and tried again to arrange emigration for his people. In order to raise needed travel funds, Party Secretary He even sold the tile roofing off his home for 60 yuan.[6]

The breakthrough came in 1983 when several Daguan residents, working on a road-construction crew, took note of the way roads are cut into mountainsides: rock is exploded and crushed into gravel, the area is leveled and then packed with ground stone and dirt. They had an idea. Perhaps the same method could be used to turn their rocky landscape into plots of cultivable land. Two village brothers returned home to experiment with a small stony section of hill outside their doorstep. The first harvest from that patch of reclaimed land yielded 25 kilograms of grain. There was hope.

The following winter, Party Secretary He convened the annual village meeting for "three days and three nights." The village emerged united around a plan: "Clear plots of land in the valley rock crevices, plant trees on the slopes to each side; plant enough grain for each family, diversify the rest of the village resources." Equipped with a strategy and under the dogged servant-leadership of Party Secretary He, Daguan's residents began the remarkable journey of transforming—mostly with primitive tools like hoes, sledge hammers, and homemade explosives—rock slopes into step-like terraced plots of cultivable land.

Daguan Village

Who cannot be moved by the astounding achievements of those people [Daguan Village] who, under the most severe natural conditions, persisted for twelve years? Who can resist the tears that well up in your eyes? This hard-working, fighting spirit is the soul of the Chinese people. It is the pillar of China's survival and development. This spirit is not only required during periods of war, it is just as necessary during times of peace. Not only do backward areas of the country need this spirit, prosperous areas of our country need it as well. And not only rural areas, but also every sector of work in the city can learn from the spirit of Daguan. With this kind of spirit, we can find the needed strength to overcome every obstacle. We can continue to advance the formidable task of building socialism with Chinese characteristics.

—Editor's note on the front page of the *People's Daily*, February 16, 1997

Official 1996 statistics show that twelve years of effort resulted in 1,038 *mu* of arable-land plots and an annual per capita income of 1,008 yuan (U.S. $120). Daguan Village's current per capita income surpasses Luodian County's absolute poverty line by almost 500 yuan.

A decade of struggle has given rise to legends as well; these heroic stories are communicated to the visitor on stone tablets placed near where the event occurred. Our jeep pulled over at each of these scenic spots. On the roadside over-looking one series of fields, the sign's heading read "Blood Field." It continued:

> From 1987 to 1988, land reclamation efforts in Daguan Village reached a high level of intensity. Because Mr. Wang Mingguang, a village resident, worked day and night on his field, he became overly fatigued. He was so exhausted that, after igniting a homemade explosive, he did not move to a sufficiently safe distance from the explosion. He was severely injured, including the loss of one eye and three fingers on his left hand. After recovering from his injury, however, Mr. Wang continued to reclaim land. His current total is 7 *mu*—an average of 1.8 *mu* per family member. To commemorate the spirit of Daguan Village, which in order to create a livable home does not fear sweat and blood, this plot of land is named "Blood Field."

Before we climbed back into the jeep Party Secretary Chen reminded me, "This, again, demonstrates the hard-working, never-say-never spirit of Daguan." I nodded my head—the mantra was beginning to sink in: the hard-working, never-say-never spirit of Daguan.

As the tour neared its end, thirty-seven-year-old Chen spun around in the passenger seat and said, "I'm getting my MBA through a correspondence course at Nankai University, Zhou Enlai's alma mater in coastal Tianjin. I'll complete the degree this year. By the way, is Lee Iacocca still a big deal in the U.S.?"

I about swallowed my tongue. "Actually, if I recall correctly," I recovered, "he was more a phenomenon of the 1980s and early 1990s."

"Oh yes, of course, now it's Microsoft's Bill Gates. Gates, he's the man!!" Party Secretary Chen followed this with an exuberant thumbs-up. The irony of it all was just too wonderful. Yet it's exactly the MBA/Bill Gates mix in the life—and aspirations—of a Communist Party secretary in a remote Guizhou county that describes contemporary China so well. And Party Secretary Chen is the norm, not the exception.

Feeling that we had finally connected, I asked Party Secretary Chen several questions: "What do you believe is the usefulness of Daguan as a model village?"

"There are really two answers to that question," Chen responded. "The primary usefulness is the spirit of Daguan. We can all learn from Daguan, regardless of our position in society. The hard-working, never-say-never spirit of Daguan is very much the national spirit of the Chinese people. This needs to be encouraged. The second aspect of Daguan's usefulness as a model village is the 'scientific approach' Party Secretary He used to solve his problem—he used a rational, well-thought-out method to create a living for his people in an otherwise uninhabitable land."

"And what is the main difference between the Dazhai and Daguan models?"

His answer veered from the script, "Dazhai was a model commune in a planned economy; Daguan Village is a success story in a private economy [*siren jingji*—his words]." His response should have read "socialist market economy." Perhaps he was still entertaining thoughts of Bill Gates.

I then asked, thinking out loud, "Do you ever think Party Secretary He wakes up in the morning wishing he had never been discovered? That he and his village could have enjoyed quiet success without all the fanfare and nuisance of two hundred tourists a day treading through his vegetable garden?"

"No. Mr. He is a Communist Party member, a servant of the people. The more he is able to reach with his message, the happier I think he would be. It's his duty."

At what point Daguan Village's success was "discovered" is not entirely clear. The literature says that until 1990, Daguan had not asked for "one penny" from the government. After 1990, Daguan's chronology reports a steady stream of attention and high-level visits, though Daguan did not become a nationwide phenomenon until the end of 1996. My personal impression is that Party Secretary He and his village are legitimate and demonstrate a truly remarkable work ethic. After the higher-ups selected the village as a model, however, I also believe that life became much easier. Party Secretary Chen told me that to date, the government has contributed 520,000 yuan ($65,000) to Daguan Village, mainly in low-interest loans and infrastructure improvements such as road improvements and promotional activities. Perhaps quality dynamite, truckloads of soil, the best fertilizers, and visiting botanists to ensure that crops remain green, as well, I thought. One thing's for sure now: Daguan will not fail. It can't. It's a model village.

The extent to which Daguan Village is self-made, in my opinion, is not nearly as significant as what the hard-working, never-say-never spirit of Daguan communicates about those who promote it. The basic fact that fifty years after the revolution model villages are still in the government's motivational toolbox is interesting. Several years ago a central-government official in Beijing explained to me his understanding of this "model psychology." Deep in the Chinese psyche, he said, is the fear of being different. Like the Chinese sayings, "a man dreads fame as a pig dreads becoming fat" and "shoot the bird that takes the lead," there is a worry over standing out. The government capitalizes on the correlate to this mind-set by elevating model villages and workers, along with the drumbeat to emulate. Like positive peer pressure, once a momentum is created, no one dares to be left behind—at least in appearance.

The Daguan spirit also reflects what the government believes it will take to continue to make progress in the struggle against poverty. In 1978, 260 million people (33 percent of the rural population) lived in absolute poverty. Reform-driven economic growth reduced that number to 42 million (8 percent of the rural population) by 1998. Based on the World Bank's international poverty standard of $1.00 per day, about 106 million people remain in poverty.[7] The majority of rural poor are now concentrated in resource-deficient areas and comprise entire communities located mostly in upland sections of China's interior provinces. Through Daguan, as an example of success amid this form of poverty, the government communicates to the remaining millions (local officials in particular) the qualities it desires to see promoted: self-reliance, creativity, selfless leadership, and the refusal to give up.

Amid ongoing poverty reduction efforts, Daguan Village also serves as a showcase—a government laboratory used to demonstrate poverty-alleviation methods such as land reclamation, Party Secretary He–style: "clear plots of land in the valley rock crevices, plant trees on the slopes to each side." With two hundred visitors a day, Daguan also provides an opportunity to show off new ideas: cement water-storage receptacles (5-feet deep, 10-feet in diameter) used to capture rainwater appear to be the recent push. Daguan Village now has more than 255 of them; one tank built alongside each series of fields demonstrates a solution to mountain-related irrigation problems. The county government provides the materials in the form of a loan; the farmer pays back the loan in increments. The extent to which Daguan marriage and childbirth policy is being promoted as exemplary is unclear, but it's worth mentioning. Before a Daguan couple can get permission to marry, the man and woman must first clear one *mu* of land—six months' to a year's work. A great way to test the relationship, I suppose. Before a couple can receive the required approval to have a child, the man and woman must clear another *mu* of land. According to Party Secretary Chen, this ensures that there will be enough food to go around (the annual production of one *mu* of land supports one adult).

From a broader perspective, the government believes the spirit of Daguan is a message for all—not just for the country's impoverished mountain communities. The tremendous challenges that face China during the post-Deng era, particularly in the areas of economic reform, will leave many needing to take good notes from Party Secretary He and his village. The government realizes that now is the time to remind the country that life-after-Deng is not a piece of cake; painful, necessary reform must be pushed forward. The Chinese people must recall the spirit that enabled them to survive the turmoil common throughout this century.

Enough of the government's perspective. What does the common person think about the spirit of Daguan? What difference does the spirit of Daguan make to those appointed to lead China's poor—the town and village leaders who live each day on the front line, staring desperate need in the face? Is Daguan Village truly an encouragement or have people grown weary of government models? Is Daguan derided as Dazhai theater; scoffed at as a naive, out-of-date Lei Feng? Or is Daguan's model spirit an effective public-relations tool that will motivate people to improve their lives and overcome their challenging surroundings? I sought the perspectives of four of the mayors and party secretaries I had met at the training seminar through follow-up visits to their home areas.

During one of those calls, the township mayor's lack of interest in the spirit of Daguan Village puzzled me. I decided to test his reaction to one final statement: "It seems like the spirit of Daguan doesn't mean very much to you." "Don't get me wrong," Vice Mayor Ni of Boyao Town replied politely, as we hiked along the red-clay mountain road, overlooking a river that snaked through the valley below. "The spirit of Daguan Village is raised at almost every meeting we hold. The spirit of Daguan encourages us; after all, we know they used to be much worse off than we are." Even so, the mayor's flat tone implied that the Daguan Village message had neither captured his imagination nor influenced his efforts to lead his town.

The responses of the other local leaders I visited were remarkably consistent with Vice Mayor Ni's: they could recall (more or less) the story of Daguan Village and, when pressed, appeared to believe and appreciate Daguan's accomplishments. But the message hadn't penetrated their motivations; there was simply no interest. Instead, the mayors seemed consumed with the challenging realities of their own impoverished towns and villages. Voices of local despair and apathy, the appeal of the county seat's relative wealth (*xian cheng;* the next higher layer of government administration), and distant treasures of China's coast—as seen on television—spoke much more loudly than a village success story they had been instructed to emulate.

But neither did these leaders appear cynical of Daguan's success or of the government's use of Daguan Village as a model. The spirit of Daguan Village just didn't stick. Any political reality beyond the county seat seemed quite distant. Whether this was due to political culture or because of lack of funding from above—or both—these town (*zhen*) and township (*xiang*) leaders appeared to be basically left on their own to govern the villages under their jurisdiction.

As the most basic level of governance above villages, towns and townships play a central role in leading China's 800 million–strong rural population. Apart from national and provincial policies and periodic meetings at the county level, a major share of the burden to govern rural China falls on the shoulders of small groups of

Figure 11.1. Basic Levels of Rural Chinese Government Administration

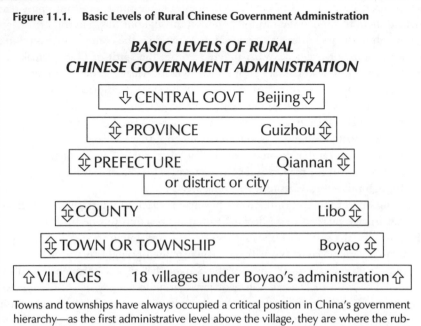

BASIC LEVELS OF RURAL
CHINESE GOVERNMENT ADMINISTRATION

⇩ CENTRAL GOVT   Beijing ⇩

⇕ PROVINCE   Guizhou ⇕

⇕ PREFECTURE   Qiannan ⇕
or district or city

⇕ COUNTY   Libo ⇕

⇕ TOWN OR TOWNSHIP   Boyao ⇕

⇧ VILLAGES   18 villages under Boyao's administration ⇧

Towns and townships have always occupied a critical position in China's government hierarchy—as the first administrative level above the village, they are where the rubber has (or has not) met the road in efforts to govern rural China. Continuity and change at the town and township level throughout the twentieth century have provided a significant weather vane to observe political winds of change in rural China. Following the Communist Revolution in 1949, towns and townships (as well as districts, or *qu* at the time) were the loci of shattering changes as the Communist government sought to totally restructure power relationships at the local level. The tumultuous process included class warfare and the destruction of the power of village leadership groups (for example, struggle sessions against local landlords). As China's Communist government reorganized rural society—from land reform (early 1950s) to agricultural producer cooperatives (mid-1950s) to communes (late 1950s through 1970s)—towns and townships provided center stage for rural change. Again reflecting the times, communes were changed back to townships in the 1980s. Since then, as the ideals of communism gave way to reform and the possibilities of a market economy, a dampening of ideology has been reflected in an increasingly diverse political-economic rural landscape. This is especially visible in the difference between wealthier (coastal) and poorer (interior) areas of rural China.

town and township leaders. For better or for worse, they are in charge. Indeed, "the heavens are high and the emperor is far away."

In impoverished, interior regions like Guizhou Province that face extremely scarce resources and challenging physical constraints, local officials fall somewhere in the spectrum of selfless agents of creative change and heavy-handed officials who abuse their power and siphon limited resources for personal gain. In a political system with little accountability, then, the personal quality of the leader becomes all the more important. Either way, the common person—the villager, the farmer—pays the price, or reaps the benefits, for the quality of town and township leaders.

SUGGESTIONS FOR FURTHER READING

Barnett, A. Doak. *Cadres, Bureaucracy, and Political Power in Communist China*. New York: Columbia University Press, 1967.

Einwalter, Dawn. "Selflessness and Self-Interest: Public Morality and the Xu Hongfang Campaign." *Journal of Contemporary China* 7, no. 18 (July 1998): 257–70.

Friedman, Edward. "The Politics of Local Models, Social Transformation and State Power Struggles in the People's Republic of China: Tachai and Teng Hsiao-ping." *China Quarterly* 76 (1978): 873–90.

Goodman, David S. G. "The Localism of Local Leadership Cadres in Reform Shanxi." *Journal of Contemporary China* 9, no. 24 (July 2000): 159–83.

Kelliher, Daniel. "Chinese Communist Political Theory and the Rediscovery of the Peasantry." *Modern China* 20, no. 4 (October 1994): 387–406.

Lieberthal, Kenneth G. "The Organization of Political Power and Its Consequences: The View from the Outside." Pp. 157–82, in *Governing China: From Revolution through Reform*. New York: W. W. Norton, 1995.

Lu, Xiaobo. *Cadres and Corruption*. Stanford, Calif.: Stanford University Press, 2000.

"Return to Dazhai." *Asia Week* 25, no. 2 (January 15, 1999): 32–33.

Saich, Tony. "Governance beyond the Center." Pp. 141–63, in *Governance and Politics of China*. New York: Palgrave, 2001.

Zweig, David. "Urbanizing Rural China: Bureaucratic Authority and Local Autonomy." Pp. 334–63, in *Bureaucracy, Politics, and Decision Making in Post-Mao China*, edited by Kenneth G. Lieberthal and David M. Lampton. Berkeley: University of California Press, 1992.

12
Still a Song to Sing?
Modernization versus Traditional National Minority Culture

A singing people, the Dong people tell stories, communicate their emotions, and preserve their history through song.

Since a fire roared through mountainous Xiao Huang Village several months ago, torching one-third of the community's wooden homes, none of the people have been in the mood to sing. At least, that is what two teenage girls from the village, both surnamed Wu, say. Singing is the lifeblood of this Dong ethnic village, located in southeastern Guizhou Province's Qiandongnan Miao and Dong Autonomous Prefecture—the heartland of Dong traditional culture. Before the young ladies can remember, their parents and grandparents sang Dong melodies to them. As toddlers, they heard tunes that imitate the sparrow's twitter, the brook's gurgle, and the cicada's whir. As youngsters, the village song master led groups of them after dinner each night, memorizing the richness of Dong culture through song. Safe under the covering of the village drum tower, as children they were taught to sing their people's history, customs, and emotions. What they learned in the dark, they perfected during the day as they skipped along mountainsides, herded water buffaloes, or cut weeds for the family animals.

Adults sing as well. They sing in community groups; they sing by themselves. You name the occasion, there's a song for it: songs to congratulate, for working in the fields, to use when matchmaking, for sacrificing ritual offerings, when receiving guests and seeing them off. And, of course, for funerals. "The dead," according to a Dong saying, "cannot hear any language unless it is sung."

The Dong also have tunes for times of calamity, traditionally sung when driven from their homes by drought or violence in search of food. Even so, the teenage cousins who described their village's sadness in the wake of the devastating fire said they were not in the mood to sing the "rice-begging songs."

These days there's another force sweeping through China's ethnic-minority communities—Dong and otherwise—as destructive as fire and ravaging the traditional cultures of village after village.[1] Call it the power of prosperity, the attraction of Han-led urban modernization.

RONGJIANG ABUZZ

After six long hours on the public bus, traveling over packed-gravel mountain roads and past stunningly steep terraced fields and poor hovels, we finally begin our descent. The bus winds through forests into a gentle valley. A river flows through it.

We step off the bus in Rongjiang County's county seat, population ten thousand. Though separated from prefecture capital Kaili by 200 kilometers and by desperately poor Leishan County, Rongjiang is bright and active: food stalls sizzle, people walk with purpose, bright banners stretch across the road, street-side boutiques overflow with basic but colorful consumer goods, karaoke bars howl, and three-wheeled taxis and pedicabs shuttle up and down the main street.

The town moves with an activity that defies its surroundings. Though no industry besides a small timber trade and some basic processing is evident, it is clear that, like many of the county seats throughout China's hinterland, Rongjiang has become an engine of modest economic growth for its surrounding towns, townships, and villages—at least for those linked to it by roads. As a market center, the county seat draws in resources from surrounding rural areas and gives back through commodities and services. Small-town development is a key component of a strategy to spur growth in China's backward hinterland.[2] Rongjiang appears to be getting it right.

But we were in search of Dong tradition, so we walk along a paved road that traces the gentle contours of the river toward smaller Dong villages five kilometers to the east. Entrepreneurship continues to fill the air. On the outskirts of town, a man has built a footbridge, spanning the shallow river. Sitting in a lawn chair at one end of the flimsy bridge, he collects five *mao* (six cents) from each person who prefers to pay rather than walk the additional fifteen minutes to and over the regular, cement overpass.

Alongside the road, men hammer out quarter-sized plugs from fir tree trunks, then fill the pits with packed fungus spores. Even grandmother joins in the chore of stuffing the holes. The young men stack the pockmarked logs, hose them down with water, and cover them with plastic sheets. Humidity and a few months' time will produce mushrooms. They plan to sell their delicacy to folk in the county seat.

A few hundred meters down the same road, swarms of bees cloud around their boxes, busily coming and going from surrounding fields. It's rapeseed season; there's much nectar to be found in the nearby canary-yellow blossoms. Four years ago, this Dong family purchased 90 bee boxes (10,000 bees in each box) from a Han couple who had traveled all the way from coastal Zhejiang Province with their bees.[3] The Zhejiang beekeepers lived with and trained the Dong family for six months. Now this middle-aged couple, parents of two, spends more than half of the year on the road, chasing blossoming flowers around the country. Meanwhile, elderly grandparents look after the primary school–aged children. It is tiring work, they all admit, but smiles and a sense of drive communicate handsome profit.

The visible activity is just part of the surprising story of Rongjiang. Like bees gone to other fields, large groups of young people from the area, including Dong and other ethnic minority youth, have left Rongjiang for China's coast and nearby cities—such as prefecture capital Kaili and Guiyang—in search of nectar of another kind: cash. And like honeybees, they'll return home. Indeed, the human pollination factor has meant more than just cash for Rongjiang; it has led to more openness to and acceptance of new ideas, in turn generating further development and progress.

Progress? I suppose it depends on whom you speak with. Certainly, from many perspectives, it was not that long ago when Rongjiang County was slow, gray, and somber. The area was closed off, and poverty immobilized the destitute economy. But then again, Dong songs and customs have existed for centuries. And they are anything but dull, drab, and gloomy.

TRADITION!

We hit it big at the Dong villages. Without realizing it, we arrive the day before one of their biggest holidays of the year, *Cai Ge Tang,* a festival that commemorates the Dong's ancestral heroine, *Xing Ni,* or *Sasui* (grandmother), as everyone calls her. We hear distant lusheng pipes and popping firecrackers before we actually see the procession. Then, far off, they appear: led by minstrel-like pipe players and village elders, a long, single-file line of women, all wearing the same traditional costume, parades behind an older woman carrying an opened umbrella. We stand there in awe as the line passes, . . . 10, 20, 50, . . . at least 1,500 women filed by in silence. The only sound is the organ-like lusheng and occasional sputter of firecrackers.

The morning-long procession, which threads in, out, and around the three participating villages, memorializes a long, arduous march Xing Ni made over one thousand years ago, during which she led her people to settle along the banks of southeast Guizhou's rivers. Xing Ni eventually died in her struggle for her people's freedom. When she was killed, legend states, each village sent people to collect rocks from the battleground. These memorial stones were piled in their own villages. Their heroine now deified, these rock collections became the center of each village's Sasui temple. Each pile is topped off with an open umbrella, symbolizing grandmother's protection.

The half-day, single-file procession reaches its climax when the line parades into a large open area—the middle-school courtyard—coiling into ever-tighter circles, eventually four rows deep. Now, all one-thousand-plus women circle around the village elders and lusheng players, walking slowly, hand in hand, round and round. Sections of the women (singing teams) spontaneously break out in song. Then it's over. Everyone goes home for lunch.

CULTURE CLASH

It fascinated me to see how even the entrepreneurial Dong outside Rongjiang's county seat resurrected their traditions during the holiday. The riverside village was transformed from one emphasis to another: from economic activity to rich tradition. Even so, symbols of collision between tradition and modernization kept appearing, demonstrating that though tradition is still alive, customs and beliefs of the past are under siege.

During a quiet moment in the village, I strolled through the narrow lanes that separate densely placed wooden homes, peering into people's living spaces as I walked along (most of the doors are left open). What I saw in one villager's living room stopped me in my tracks. There, pasted to the wall just next to the ancestral family altar, was a poster of Los Angeles Laker seven-foot-plus superstar Shaquille O'Neal. If Shaq only knew he had become a god in Dongland![4]

More telling, however, was the state of one of the village drum towers (*gulou*). These large wooden structures form the traditional center of Dong villages. If singing is the lifeblood of the Dong, the drum tower forms their corporate heart. Each community has one.

For centuries, villagers had met under the drum tower's protection to settle disputes. Elders deliberated, stories were told, and children gathered with their song master to sing. The tower's drum was beaten when the village came under danger of attack. Rallied by the sound, villagers would gather around the clan leader at the tower. Unified strength helped to repel the invader. But not lately, not at the drum tower in the village we visited. Some young fellow had to ride off on his bike to find the key for the padlock on the iron gate that kept the drum tower off-limits to most. The fifteen-meter-tall tower looked more like a dusty museum than the village's pulsating heart.

The drum tower is still used, they say, but only for meetings of the village government and karaoke parties—and from what I could gather, there's a cover charge for the latter. Though it was evident that traditions in the Dong villages we visited are under siege, for a magical half day—in honor of grandmother—all of tradition came to life.

Two years of living and observation in Duyun, the capital city of one of the three autonomous prefectures in Guizhou Province (meaning that the combined minority population surpasses 50 percent of the total), provided frequent opportunity to meet and get to know people other than Han.[5] Farmers and urbanites, uneducated and well-schooled, migrant laborer and government elite, from a variety of backgrounds such as Miao, Buyi, and Shui, revealed with few exceptions that in the face of rapid, Han-led modernization, the more the people are exposed to a "modern" urban lifestyle, the less they reflect the traditions of their respective group. In poorer regions of China like Guizhou, it often comes down to how far these people live from the nearest road. The more remote, the more destitute— and the more traditional—in that order. However, as ethnic tradition meets the modern urban Han population, it all changes. As they say, the person becomes Han-ized (*Han huale*). They begin to dress Han, talk Han, and value things Han.

But what is Han? Confucius was a Han, but he would roll over in his grave if he got a peek at pop-Han culture today. I tried to pin down a definition of current Han culture in a long conversation with a Han television executive in Guizhou's capital, Guiyang. Having been pulled and hauled first by Soviet-style Communism and now by the frantic pursuit of individual prosperity, Han culture today is focused on the pursuit of an urban and materially advanced lifestyle, undergirded by the undefined but gene-deep values of Confucianism, Buddhism, and Taoism.[6] However one tries to describe current Han culture, one thing is sure: it is the most materially advanced of all contemporary Chinese cultures. It is also the greatest numerically (92 percent of China's population is Han). So it attracts and dominates.[7]

Even so, the blind chase of things Han is certainly not because ethnic-minority cultures lack sophistication. The artwork and life philosophies of all the ethnic traditions I have encountered are stunning. But exquisite antiphonies and fine batik do not produce concrete houses, running water, gas stoves, hot baths, refrigeration, color television—and karaoke bars. So they are easily rejected.

Since I am a distant observer who can float in and out of Guizhou's mountain communities without truly experiencing poverty's grind—destitution that most of us cannot even dream about—it is hard for me to relate to the disparity between the realities of mountainous minorities and the attraction of the convenient Han. Passing-through visitors tend to see only the delicate embroidery and hear only the pleasant mountain melodies; we cannot relate to the sweat and hunger of many of the ethnic minority peoples of China's interior.

From deep in the mountains, concrete-and-file Han urban areas look quite different. Subsistence living changes the way people view the role and value of their traditions. The result for most minorities in the mountains is a psychology of inferiority, in which the baby of ethnic identity is readily cast aside with the bathwater of rural backwardness, even if that bathwater holds the essence of what it means to be Dong, Shui, or Miao.

There are refreshing exceptions; there always are. There is the thirty-year-old Song & Dance Ensemble leader in Qiandongnan Prefecture, whose father is Miao and mother is Shui, and who is a standout lusheng player. He's proud of his tradition. The young man designed a lusheng that can play half-notes—the first of its kind, he says. He designed it, his father crafted it. The expert musician complained to me how most ethnic minorities he knows "blindly chase things Han." But even he keeps an electric guitar in his closet.

After listening to Dong choruses at the "grandmother's day" celebration in Rongjiang and observing the relative dynamism of the county seat's economy, as well as considering the identities of other ethnic minority peoples I know in Guizhou, I cannot but wonder—or wish—that there must be some way to combine the substance of tradition with the advances of modernism. But that's the age-old question, isn't it? How to keep the finest of the past from being washed away by the flood-tide of the present. It would be a shame if the best of Dong culture ended up in a museum. Certainly, there still must be a song to sing.

SUGGESTIONS FOR FURTHER READING

Blum, Susan D. *Portraits of "Primitives": Ordering Human Kinds in the Chinese Nation.* Lanham, Md.: Rowman & Littlefield, 2000.

Diamond, Norma. "The Miao and Poison: Interactions on China's Southwest Frontier." *Ethnology* 27, no. 1 (1988): 1–25.

Eberhard, Wolfram. *China's Minorities: Yesterday and Today.* Belmont, Calif.: Wadsworth, 1982.

Harrell, Stevan, ed. *Cultural Encounters on China's Ethnic Frontiers.* Seattle: University of Washington Press, 1995.

Oakes, Tim. "Selling Guizhou: Cultural Development in an Era of Marketisation." Pp. 31–67, in *The Political Economy of China's Provinces,* edited by Hans Hendrischke and Feng Chongyi. New York: Routledge, 1999.

Rossi, Gail. *The Dong People of China.* Singapore: Hagley & Hoyle, 1990.

IV

PORTRAITS OF
THE PRESENT
Urban Issues in China's Interior

13
Coping with Reform in Guizhou's Industrial Rustbelt

Little-heard-of Duyum City, with its 460,000 population, owes much of its past growth to Third Front industrialization. Today, however, some of the city's most important reform challenges trace directly to its Third Front legacy.

> If war breaks out we have nothing to fear.
>
> —Mao Zedong (1965)

Even if you happened to ride right by, you probably wouldn't notice that this factory exists. Tucked down a twisting road fifteen kilometers from Duyun City, "321," as it is commonly called by its central-government designation, is camouflaged by several mountains that press tightly around it. Only a series of three-story buildings peeking out of a grove of trees hint that there is anything in the area besides farmers and paddies. Just outside the factory gate, a series of cement-block apartment buildings, one-room restaurants, a clinic, and a schoolhouse offers further proof. Indeed, the people who stroll back and forth in this self-contained compound belong to a three-thousand-member factory community called "Chuzhou Wireless Communications"—at least, that's the name inscribed on the factory's gate. Actually, even the factory's name disguises the exact identity of the plant: "321" manufactures radar systems.

"The factory sits behind that mountain," an engineer explains as he points beyond the gate—the factory itself still invisible. "It was built at the base of several sheer cliffs to provide 360-degree protection. There is even a large cave the factory can be disassembled and hidden in, if it were to come under attack. But the cave was never used; it's been sealed up for years." A legacy of Mao Zedong, "321" and nearly two thousand other factories like it are sprinkled strategically throughout the mountains of China's hinterland. Though built just thirty-some years ago as part of Mao's Third Front industrialization program, "321" seems like something from a totally different era altogether—those were the years of the Cultural Revolution, Red Guards, and Mao's "Little Red Book." As relics of the time, these industrial dinosaurs that now litter the mountains of inland China are reminders that much of China's current economic-reform agenda is focused on dismantling the industrial policies of the Mao era.[1]

Mao's Third Front industrialization program was a massive, top-secret invest-ment strategy motivated by perceived threats from the Soviet Union, the United States, and Taiwan.[2] The goal of the national plan was twofold: to relocate key factories from the country's "first front" (coast) and "second front" (central China) to the west (the "third front"), so as to minimize the loss of industrial assets in the event of a war and to develop strategic industries in the protected environs of the country's remote interior.

From 1964 to 1971—the high tide of the Third Front—while most of the coun-try reeled in the throes of the Cultural Revolution, the central government sank an astounding 40 percent of its total annual budget into the construction of steel, armaments, machinery, chemicals, petroleum, and railroad base areas in China's remote inland regions. The objective was that, as Mao said himself, "If war breaks out we have nothing to fear."[3]

Map 13.1.   The Three Fronts

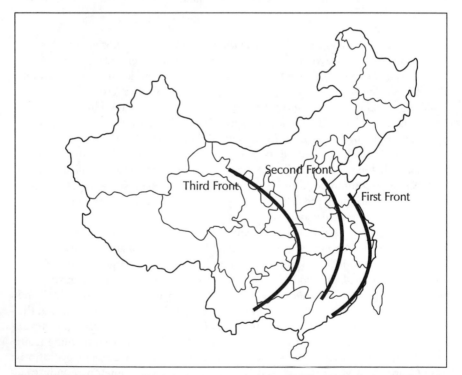

The term "third front" refers to China's remote interior regions, thought in the 1960s to be most impenetrable in the event of foreign aggression. The third front included all of Guizhou, Sichuan, Yunnan, Gansu, Ningxia, Qinghai; the southern part of Shaanxi; and western areas of Henan, Hubei, and Hunan provinces. Much of the economic reform in China today is focused on undoing industrial policies of the 1950s–1970s. In areas like Guizhou Province that means, in part, dealing with the legacy of the third front.

Such a defensive approach is understandable for a country preparing for war, and most of his life, Mao had known only fighting and "strategic retreats"—lessons learned during protracted civil war with the Nationalists, the Long March, and Japanese occupation. Though the international environment during the 1960s was indeed tense, the perceived enemies never attacked. By the late 1970s, the rationale and political support for an interior-looking industrialization ceased to exist. And with the rise of Deng Xiaoping at the end of the decade, national investment priorities shifted completely to a coast-led, outward-focused development strategy.[4] The result was an abandoned Third Front strategy and recognition that, while most of the factories were not viable, they could not be moved, either. For the time being they would have to be supported.

The 1,500 workers and technicians at "321" reflect this history. They, however, face a very different reality today than in 1966, when they and their factory—as national priorities—were relocated from coastal Jiangsu Province. Though they were guaranteed jobs, housing, medical care, and education for their children, the move involved tremendous sacrifice. These young engineers and factory workers were required to give up their lives on the coast and to reconstruct them in a self-contained community hidden amid a grove of trees somewhere in the remote mountains of southern Guizhou Province. Today, though many still speak with a Jiangsu accent, few have ever returned to their coastal homes. A factory worker joked with me that they had felt exiled, as if they had done something wrong.

But until lately, "321" has had it better than many other Third Front factories because it manufactures a technical, defense-related product. Even after central-government attention turned to the development of China's coast, government funding continued for "321." As part of a planned economy, the radar factory produced according to quotas and regardless of cost or efficiency. All this, however, began to change in 1995 when the factory's leaders were told that it was time to face the market. More recently, managers have even been told that they will receive no more government funding. Thus "321" will survive on its own or will become a memory. Though "321" continues to sell a few radar systems a year and is hurriedly trying to develop more marketable products, the people I spoke with believe that the factory's days are numbered. Four hundred laborers have been placed "off-post," and more layoffs are expected.[5]

The magnitude of the challenges "321" faces is by no means unique. Cities like Duyun and provinces like Guizhou throughout China's interior, which at one time benefited from the expensive and urgent push to develop their areas, now face the quandary of how to reform enterprises that have become colossal burdens. Everyone I have spoken with recognizes that positive change will come only at tremendous economic, social, and human cost.

Third Front industrialization came at a huge price for the nation as well. Although the Third Front served to better integrate the country through infrastructure improvements (railway grids, in particular) and sent trained professionals to areas of the country that would not have received such expertise otherwise, the concern for national security and strategic choice behind the Third Front—as opposed to development considerations—created what Barry Naughton calls "a negative impact on China's economic development that was certainly more far-reaching than the disruption of the Cultural Revolution."[6] Naughton believes that China's current annual industrial output is currently 10 to 15 percent below what it would have been if the Third Front had never been undertaken and the funds had been invested in other inland locations.

UNDOING THE PAST

At the Fifteenth Party Congress (September 1997) the central government promised decisive action to address the state sector's massive debts and chronic inefficiencies. This included the Third Front industries. The commitment to reform was furthered by Zhu Rongji's selection as premier in March 1998. At that year's National People's Congress meeting, Zhu pledged to reverse the cycle of state-owned enterprise losses within three years. Complementing the determination to reform from within, China's accession to the World Trade Organization opens the country to external competitive forces that will further drive domestic economic reform.[7]

However, forty-plus years of sediment has accumulated under a planned economy, which requires extensive dredging. As a result, the measures being taken are drastic—massive layoffs and widespread factory shutdowns indicate that there is no other choice. Between 1998 and 2001, more than 36 million state workers, one-third of the total, lost their jobs.[8] According to a 2002 National People's Congress session, 52 million more workers will lose their jobs in the next five years.[9] Add the 12–13 million people that enter the labor market each year, and one begins to get a sense of the burden that weighs down on the state-owned sectors of China's economy. The issues become specific and personal in small cities like Duyun.

Obscure Duyun, a city of 460,000 in southern Guizhou Province that owes much of its past growth to Third Front industrialization, provides a fascinating microstudy of efforts to undo the past. Like the rest of the country, debt, inefficiency, bloated payrolls, and poor management plague Duyun's state-owned enterprises. Listen to what factory workers in Duyun say when asked why their factories are failing:

"There are way too many workers in our factory; at least five people do the job of one person."

"The factory's management doesn't have a clue about how to operate according to principles of a market economy."

"Our biggest problem is that workers don't trust the factory's leaders. The leaders siphon money from factory coffers, enriching themselves, while the factory can barely keep its doors open."

"No one is motivated; there are no incentives."

"The quality of our factory's workers is too low. We are terribly inefficient."

Though these comments come from workers in Duyun, they could just as well be heard in any city around China. And while there are commonalities across regions, there are also important differences that distinguish Duyun's predicament (and those of other cities in China's hinterland) from state-owned enterprise reform in other areas of the country. According to several government officials here in Duyun, these distinctions create a more difficult task of reform.

For one, coastal SOEs were not buried in the mountains, strategically hidden from the enemy, far from major cities, and far from the country's seaboard. What this means for Third Front enterprises in the interior is that while well protected, they exist far from the markets they now need to depend on. Less access to markets and higher transportation costs cripple their ability to reform. Compare this to SOEs on the coast, which, though in difficult straits as well, can at least reach their markets. Mr. Song Min, director of Qiannan Prefecture's Economy and Trade Bureau, told me that lack of access is this region's biggest obstacle to reform.

The challenge of SOE reform in the interior is exacerbated by the unusually large share of the economy occupied by its state-owned sector. In 1995, for example, 67 percent of Guizhou Province's industrial output was produced by state-owned enterprises. Compare this with coastal provinces like Guangdong (18 percent) and Zhejiang (14 percent). Even Liaoning Province, northeast China's heavy-industry center, whose state-owned enterprises produced 44 percent of the province's industrial output, occupies a smaller share than Guizhou Province.[10] For Guizhou Province this reveals not only the weakness of its non-state-owned sector, it also indicates that reforming its lopsided public sector will be all the more difficult.

What is true for Guizhou Province specifically also applies to the region generally. In eastern China, SOEs produce an average 28 percent of all industrial output; in the central regions, 44 percent; and in western China, 55 percent.[11] As a corollary, non-state-owned options of production in provinces like Guizhou are far less than in the country's central and coastal regions. Such alternatives would include collectively owned enterprises, township and village enterprises, private businesses, and foreign-owned companies.

In interior cities like Duyun, there are two extremes: decaying state-owned enterprises and traditional agriculture, with few layers of economic strata in between. All this means that reform of Guizhou's state-owned sector will be more stubborn, as laid-off workers from state-owned enterprises have far fewer options to pursue after losing their jobs.

And finally, officials and factory workers in Duyun tell me that the city's SOE workers are less entrepreneurial and less likely to want to take risks than are workers on the coast, who, though having always worked in a state-owned enterprise, adapt more easily when tossed into a sink-or-swim, market-oriented economy. Less familiarity with and, among some, fear and resentment of life outside the "iron rice bowl" may create a drag on reforming the public sector in Duyun and cities like it throughout the interior.

HUMAN COSTS

Living in China's interior for a period of time allowed me to see the human dimension of policies and statistics that for most can be read about only from a distance. Neighbors filled labor redundancy numbers; local government policy was made and implemented by people we knew. The successes and failures of Duyun's efforts to deal with necessary but difficult reform of its state-owned sector played out before our eyes.

Take thirty-year-old Li Fangfang—our "milk lady"—for example. Since her teens Ms. Li made shoe-heels at a state-owned factory in Duyun. She and her husband both worked at the factory until they were laid off two years ago. But since then, neither has received a penny, even though the factory is supposed to provide 180 yuan (about U.S. $22) monthly compensation to each of its laid-off staff members.[12] Hardly enough to live on, she says, but it would be better than nothing.

With responsibilities to care for a young child and with her spouse laid off as well, Ms. Li is among those for whom transitioning out of cradle-to-grave employment is most difficult. She admits, however, that there is a slightly older age group that is having an even harder time coping with reform.[13] Now in their forties and fifties, the "Red Guard" generation—who as young people in the 1960s during the Cultural Revolution served as Mao Zedong's revolution-makers—is now often considered the least desirable by potential employers. Yet they are also too young to enjoy a relatively more relaxed retirement-age lifestyle, dependent on grown children. Perhaps most difficult for this age group, however, is the sense of victimization they feel. Self-described as China's lost generation because of the opportunities, particularly educational, they missed as youths during the Cultural Revolution, they now face unemployment.

"But feeling sorry for oneself doesn't put rice on the table," says Ms. Li in a husky voice. And though she is not happy about her predicament, Ms. Li is certainly not sitting around waiting for the government to come help her.

Every morning at 7:00 A.M., Li Fangfang and her husband ride their three-wheel, flatbed bicycles to a wholesale milk distributor, package and load 2,000 six-ounce bags of fresh milk onto their bicycles, and prepare the delivery list. Ms. Li then rushes home to prepare lunch for her child. Just after lunch, she and her husband begin their deliveries. From 1:00 to 8:30 P.M., the two of them on separate routes, Li Fangfang and her husband deliver fresh milk to over 400 families. Their reward for this back-breaking work, which Ms. Li and her husband now do seven days a week, is only 20 yuan (U.S. $2.40) between them, per day.

Listening to Ms. Li speak is heart-wrenching. Six hundred yuan per month, she says, is barely enough to make it, and that's if they are very careful with their money and no one gets sick. If a family member were to fall ill, they have no medical insurance; the shoe-heel factory stopped providing coverage long ago. Though she speaks with long sighs between her sentences, I could hear a healthy sense of fight in her voice: "No matter how difficult it is, I'd rather work for myself than for some factory boss who becomes wealthy off my hard work. Though not much, at least the money we make from delivering milk is our own," she said. Although she is beaten down by life's burdens, dignity and self-respect are written on her face. Our neighborhood's "milk lady," in her effort to adjust to the blows government reform has dealt her, is not about to give up.

The ability of Li Fangfang, the "Red Guard" generation, and the rest of the country's laid-off workers to cope with the challenges of being shrugged off by government cradle-to-grave paternalism will play an important role in shaping China's evolving future. Indeed, by virtue of a retreating public sector, the contracting role of the state in peoples' lives has important and far-reaching implications for Chinese society.

COPING WITH REFORM

Li Fangfang is one of 11,000 (if you count officially), or 40,000 (if you listen to local scuttlebutt), former state-owned enterprise laborers in Duyun. The official unemployment figure in Duyun, a mild 4 percent, does not include laid-off workers or hidden unemployment, small comfort to those who have fallen through the cracks of structural reform. Like Li Fangfang, they have to find their own way to put food on the table, regardless of how they are categorized by government statistics.

People across the country are getting quite creative at coping. The old adage "necessity is the mother of invention" certainly applies here. In Duyun, particularly because of the lack of alternatives to state-owned enterprises, the most common way to make money is through service-related activities. Women become nannies, others help with grocery shopping and cooking; beauty salons are springing up like mushrooms after a rain; one family pooled its resources and bought a taxi that family members take turns driving; many have opened little convenience stores and eateries around Duyun.

Family networks—as an informal social safety net—also play an important role in helping laid-off workers weather the storm. One man I know has two sisters, one of whom is laid-off. Because he makes a salary, he and his wife and child provide money each month to help support the sister and her family. The other sister, who is working, and her family care for their elderly parents. "Don't underestimate the strength of the Chinese family," this friend told me.

Family assistance aside, increasing numbers are turning to quicker, more tragic ways of making money: prostitution and drug dealing (heroin is most common). Only fifteen years ago, drugs and prostitution in China were virtually unheard of.

Figure 13.1.   China's Unemployment Enigma

Reminiscent of the early 1980s when official China used the term "waiting for work" (*daiye*) to justify its claim that the country had no unemployed, the present official nationwide unemployment (*shiye*) rate—a rosy 3.6 percent—does not include two important categories: "hidden" unemployment and those who have been "laid-off" (*xiagang*) from their state-owned jobs. The term unemployed is officially defined as permanent urban residents who are of working age, capable and willing to work, and have applied at a local employment center for a job. "Hidden" unemployed are those who are no longer gainfully employed but have yet to be formally let go by their work units.[a] According to scholars at the Beijing-based Development Research Center, a government think tank, a more accurate national average may be 8–9 percent urban unemployment, with the figure spiking to above 20 percent in industrial rustbelts.[b]

The situation in the agricultural sector is different, but even more severe. Zhang Suping of the State Planning Commission's Macroeconomic Research Institute states that current "hidden" unemployment (redundant labor in the case of farming) in rural areas totals 183 million people, or 31 percent of the rural workforce. A Guizhou *Economic Daily* article notes that, when including "hidden" unemployment and combining urban and rural China figures, between 180 and 260 million Chinese people are unemployed—that's about 20 percent of the population. As the article's author is quick to add: "that's about the size of the entire population of the United States."[c]

a. Qian Zhihong and Wong Tai-Chee, "The Rising Urban Poverty: A Dilemna of Market Reforms in China," *Journal of Contemporary China* 9, no. 23 (2000): 116.

b. Matthew Forney, "Workers' Wasteland," *Timeasia.com* at www.time.com/time/asia/covers/1101020617/cover.html (07 September 2002). For an excellent review of the various interpretations and estimates of unemployment in China, see Dorothy Solinger, "Why We Cannot Count the 'Unemployed,'" *The China Quarterly*, no. 167 (September 2001): 671–88.

c. *Guizhou jingji ribao* (Guizhou Economic Daily), 26 February 1998.

Now, though, in even small cities like Duyun prostitutes and drugs are readily available.[14]

For laid-off workers who can't make it in Duyun or who believe that chances for employment are greater on China's coast, growing numbers are heading to the coast to look for employment.[15] There are, however, those who can't cope—legally or illegally. Until the mid-1990s, poverty was a distant reality in China's urban centers. Severe economic hardship was known only by those in the countryside. As the guarantees of socialism, however, weaken under government preferences for competition and an incomplete social-welfare system, urban poverty has soared. According to China's State Statistical Bureau, 5 percent of China's urban population, totaling 12.5 million people, live in poverty.[16] In 1995, the per capita yearly income of poor urban incomes was 1,360 yuan (U.S. $170). Eighty-seven percent of the urban poor are either laid-off workers or retirees.[17] Guizhou Province's 68,000 urban poor constitute 14.5 percent of the local urban population.[18]

Whether out of desperation, anger over corrupt factory officials, or frustration over having lifetime employment and all its benefits suddenly pulled out from under workers, protests have become common.[19] Though there have been no large-scale protests in Duyun yet, organized groups of laid-off factory workers frequent the prefecture government building, demanding compensation payments. But as Li Fangfang says, "These protests don't get you anywhere, and besides, the government doesn't pay any attention to you as you sit at the government headquarters' front gate. After awhile you get hungry and go home. And you're certainly not going to make any money just sitting there."

Though perhaps ignoring less-than-threatening protests, both central and local governments are concerned about laid-off workers. They realize that rough-and-tumble factory workers—what Americans may imagine as West Virginia coal miners or Pittsburgh steelworkers—are as great a threat, if not greater, than any form of student protest.

Stated more positively, the government realizes that effective state-owned enterprise reform and solutions for laid-off workers are at the heart of future economic health for the country. As the overweight government attempts to off-load fiscal burdens, efforts to steer the economy—really, the entire country—in a healthy and constructive direction are critical. But the task is monumental and, quite frankly, beyond the complete control of the government. Besides, is not one of the goals of state-owned enterprise reform to encourage the economy to operate at a safe distance from the government?

A core dimension in the government's effort to facilitate the transition of millions of laid-off workers, and to minimize social unrest, is psychological. Official Chinese newspapers and television programs address, almost on a daily basis, the necessity of reform. Two themes are most prevalent. First, that layoffs are not peculiar to China. "Being laid-off and finding a new job is common for any society; it is certainly not an issue unique to China," reads the front-page story of a Guizhou newspaper.[20] And as if to comfort the readers, the full-page story adds, "In the United States, the average worker is 'laid-off' and transitions to new work twelve times during his life."

Second, the media emphasizes the need for self-reliance. In other words, get off your bum and find a job—find something to do, find anything to do—the government is not going to do it for you, as you've been used to all your life. "There's nothing scary about being laid-off," reads another article, "the road to reemployment is just under your foot; with each step, the road will get wider and more secure."[21] But you have to take that step yourself, the article emphasizes. The same story holds up as a model a former factory worker in Wuhan, who, in looking for a money-making activity, invented a machine to spread polyurethane on wooden floors. "If I hadn't been laid-off, I never would have become an inventor," he's quoted, as if grateful. "I would have operated a lathe all my life."

Beyond government exhortations expressed by the media, national and local governments are making practical initiatives as well. Though Duyun is behind the curve and actions the city has taken thus far are more fluff than substance, efforts to help laid-off workers find employment have begun.

"Laid-Off Workers' Tax-Free Alley," established in 1997, is a highly publicized side street in Duyun that has been closed off to house over one hundred six-by-six-foot stalls, in which laid-off workers are given tax-exempt treatment to sell their wares. Like an athletic locker-room, banners over the alley's entrance, such as "Renew oneself for a new life," aim to motivate those attempting to start over.

Though the stalls are full of goods—nail-clippers, hair clips, kitchen utensils, toiletries, bras, underwear, children's clothing—business is slow. Laid-off workers-turned-salespeople lament that this idea is not working very well. Even an official in the prefecture's Peoples' Congress told me recently that "Laid-Off Workers' Tax-Free Alley" is more of a show than a solution.

In addition to the tax-exempt business opportunity, eight outdoor locations around the city provide information on job opportunities. Handwritten posters glued to a wall provide a colorful backdrop to the Labor Department official who sits at his street-side desk, interviewing laid-off workers looking for jobs. The official I spoke with said that he speaks with an average of 400 people a day, 200 of whom make serious inquiry, and, among those, 12 of whom find a job.

All in all, however, Duyun's efforts lag behind initiatives already underway in major cities across the country. Almost every city has a service center to help laid-off workers connect with new work and training centers to teach new skills—hairdressing, massage, and cooking seem to be the most popular.

Though uncertain about specific measures to take, government leaders at all levels are quite clear about one thing and repeat it often: economic growth is most important to secure the momentum and success of state-owned enterprise reform. And that's where the rub comes in. As if conjuring a magical number, the central government says that 8 percent growth is necessary to absorb laid-off workers and the thirteen million people who enter the labor force each year as a result of population growth.[22]

Regardless of how quickly the economy does or does not grow, everyone I have spoken with—from the engineer at "321," to Li Fangfang the "milk lady," to laid-off workers and government officials in Duyun—even in Shanghai, Nanjing, and Beijing—believes that state-owned enterprise restructuring, as part of the "creative destruction" process of economic reform, places China at a critical stage in its development. There is one other thing that everyone I spoke with agrees on: the situation is going to get worse before it gets better.

SUGGESTIONS FOR FURTHER READING

Khan, Azizur Rahman, and Carl Riskin. *Inequality and Poverty in China in the Age of Globalization.* Oxford, UK: Oxford University Press, 2001.

Lardy, Nicholas R. "China Enters the World Trade Organization." Pp. 1–28, in *Integrating China into the Global Economy*. Washington, D.C.: Brookings Institution, 2002.

Ma, Jun. *The Chinese Economy in the 1990s*. New York: St. Martin's, 2000.

Naughton, Barry. "The Third Front: Defence Industrialization in the Chinese Interior," *China Quarterly* 115 (September 1988): 351–86.

———. *Growing Out of the Plan: Chinese Economic Reform 1978–1993*. Cambridge, U.K.: Cambridge University Press, 1995.

Qian, Zhihong, and Tai-Chee Wong. "The Rising Urban Poverty: A Dilemma of Market Reforms in China." *Journal of Contemporary China* 9, no. 23 (2000): 113–25.

Shambaugh, David, ed. *Is China Stable? Assessing the Factors*. Armonk, N.Y.: M. E. Sharpe, 2000.

Solinger, Dorothy. "Why We Cannot Count the 'Unemployed.'" *The China Quarterly*, no. 167 (September 2001): 671–88.

Steinfeld, Edward S. *Forging Reform in China: The Fate of State-Owned Industry*. Cambridge: Cambridge University Press, 1998.

Whyte, Martin King. "The Changing Role of Workers." Pp. 220–40, in *The Paradox of Post-Mao Reforms*, edited by Merle Goldman and Roderick MacFarquhar. Cambridge, Mass.: Harvard University Press, 1999.

14

Sprouts in a Hard Place
Principal Bi and the "P"-Word

The clatter of students tapping on computer keyboards fills the room, as Qiannan Computer Vo-Tech's students practice their typing skills. Many of these students had never seen a computer before arriving at the school.

Through conversations with school principals in Guizhou, I caught a surprising glimpse of a noteworthy and, quite frankly, surprising development: the emergence of private education. But don't say the "P"-word too loudly; the politically correct expression is "schools established by social forces" (*shehui liliang banxue*).[1] Either way, the significance remains the same. China's education system, which for more than forty years was directed, funded, and managed solely by the government, has begun to make room for others—even in Guizhou, one of the country's poorest provinces.

QIANNAN COMPUTER VO-TECH SCHOOL

One evening, while I was sitting at home watching a World Cup soccer match, a superimposed string of text crawled slowly across the bottom of the television screen: "Qiannan Computer Vocational-Technical School announces openings for new students in both its two-year degree program and short-term training courses. For more information contact Principal Bi Jiangang at . . ."

I usually do not pay attention to such distractions; but this one caught my eye. The next day I was scheduled to meet Bi Jiangang, principal of one of Qiannan Prefecture's first private schools.

"How much does it cost to place your advertisement on television like that?" I asked Principal Bi when I saw him.

"Three hundred yuan [U.S. $35] a pop."

"That's a lot of money."

"Yes, but I have to use every means available to attract students. Whether or not my family and I, and our staff, eat depends on the number of students enrolled at our school. Student tuition is our only source of revenue. We, after all, are a private school."

This year, Principal Bi convinced fifty more young people to invest in Qiannan Computer Vo-Tech's two-year program.[2]

The school's one hundred students, who are fifteen and sixteen years old and have come from all corners of this mountainous prefecture, represent each of the area's ethnic-minority groups. They have enrolled with the hope that computer skills learned through one of two majors (data processing and computer repair) will help them find a job. The program serves the function of a vocational-technical junior college in the United States, only at the high-school level. For most of the students the school is the last stop of their formal education process.[3]

One afternoon I sat with eight of Principal Bi's students in an empty classroom and talked with them about their experiences. I was struck to discover that five of the eight students had never even seen a computer before arriving at Qiannan Computer Vo-Tech!

"I like computers," sixteen-year-old Xiao Qin beams, her smile as wide as she is tall. The first-semester student is from a village in one of the prefecture's poorest counties. There is not even one computer in her hometown of ten thousand people.

In addition to the two-year degree program, there are about eighty adults enrolled in short-term training courses, ranging from several weeks to six months in length.

But computers? In one of the poorest regions of the country? In the vast rural regions of Guizhou, computers—even telephones and, for some, electricity—remain a distant reality, if even heard of. At the same time, however, the province's twelve cities continue to experience the transformation of nationwide economic growth. That includes the recent appearance of computers.

In 1994, for example, phones in our prefecture-capital city of Duyun were unusual; computers were almost nonexistent. Only four years later, phones—even cellular phones and beepers—became common throughout the city. During the summer of 1998, even the Internet became available through a local provider. Business and government documents used to be handwritten; now it has become common practice to have them typed at local word-processing shops.

Though currently an urban-only phenomenon in Guizhou, it is inevitable that the need for computer-literate people will only increase. Even so, three-fourths of Qiannan Computer Vo-Tech's students will travel to China's more prosperous coast to look for work when they graduate.

The school operates at full capacity. But Principal Bi's goal is to double the number of students. "We're flexible," says Bi. "It's one of our strengths as a private school. We could simply hire more teachers and rent more space from our landlords. They certainly have plenty of room to spare." Indeed, when one enters the compound of the Zhenhua Group (formerly known as "083"), the large courtyard and surrounding office buildings are strangely quiet. Not long ago, however, the company was among the largest five hundred state-owned enterprises in China. The Zhenhua Group, which belongs to the Ministry of Electronics, oversaw more than two dozen strategic factories that were relocated to China's interior during the Third Front industrialization period (*sanxian jianshe*) of the 1960s and 1970s.[4]

From its regional headquarters in Duyun, "083" oversaw the colossal operation. Now the company is greatly weakened. Less than five factories continue to operate at more than half-capacity; the rest are simply a memory.

PRINCIPAL BI

Principal Bi's personal history is tied closely to Zhenhua's past. He is a child of the Third Front era. In the 1960s, as a boy, Bi was brought from Beijing to Guizhou by his parents when they were relocated to one of Zhenhua's secluded factories. In fact, Bi's father, as one of the Beijing factory's lead engineers, was called in one day by his superior and shown a topographical map of Duyun's surrounding mountains. His boss then drew a circle on the map and tasked Bi's father to relocate the factory—the entire complex, workers, and families—from the suburbs of Beijing to the craggy mountains of Guizhou.

Thirty-four-year-old Bi has happy childhood memories. "I grew up playing in the mountains that surrounded our factory. There's not a hill I didn't climb."

Because of their remote locations, each factory had self-contained living quarters (*shenghuo qu*) where thousands of families attempted to recreate their lives. Such communities included clinics, theaters, cafeterias—and schools. All were organized by departments within the factory.

After graduating from the factory's vo-tech school (he studied computer design), Bi remained for a few years, first working and then teaching at the factory-school. That's when he learned his first lesson in school management. Call it a model of how not to do things. He observed the rigid, top-down control and poor quality of the factory-school's administration, and remembered it.

His second lesson came several years later as a young adult, when during the economic-boom years of the early 1990s, he headed to Guangdong Province to join in the "gold rush." After a few years, Bi decided to return to Duyun. He had learned much and made good money, but a sense of responsibility called him back. The lesson in Guangdong: Guizhou is backward; education is critical if the province is to progress. "Plus," Bi says, "I like Qiannan Prefecture. It's my home."

So Bi moved back to Duyun in 1993 and established a private computer company with some friends. They believed there was a market that had potential to grow. Along with their business, the group of entrepreneurs developed computer-training courses. In May 1996, the classes were registered as a fully accredited "school established by social forces," the only one of its kind listed with Qiannan Prefecture's Labor Bureau. Earlier this year, Principal Bi separated from the company and now operates on his own.

Principal Bi seems to be at the right place at the right time. In Duyun, even in the midst of an economy slowed by domestic difficulties and the effects of regional financial crisis, the growth of computers does not appear to be lagging. Still, Principal Bi knows he'll need to make full use of his advantages as a private school if he's going to continue to compete.

Principal Bi believes the school's greatest strength is that it must survive on its merits. The school's reputation, its success in helping steer students toward jobs, and teachers who put their heart into their work are its best hopes for survival. The students I spoke with sense this quality. When asked what they like best about the school, they said they appreciated how hard the teachers worked and truly cared for them. As a result, the students say they are motivated to study harder.

Quality also radiated from several teachers I met with one day when Principal Bi was out of town. Their enthusiasm was especially striking because they had all had careers in state-owned enterprises before switching to Qiannan Computer Vo-Tech. "Principal Bi's management style gives us flexibility and responsibility," one teacher told me. "He gives much, but he expects much as well."

Bi rewards his teachers based on performance, not according to seniority, as was true in all the teachers' former jobs. They receive a salary, but their compensation is based on a semiannual review. At first, Principal Bi said it was difficult for a couple of the older teachers who were used to being paid according to seniority. Now they realize that his is the best approach, despite the lack of guarantees.

"Do you ever wish you were back in the security of the iron rice bowl, enjoying the cradle-to-grave benefits of the state-owned enterprise system?" I asked the teachers. "What we give up in security," one teacher replied, "we gain in the enjoyment of our work. Plus, the factories we used to work in are either sinking or have already sunk."

In order to demonstrate that Bi is not a distant leader, his desk sits as one of eight in the main office. The result is a cohesive staff whose members agree that their destinies are tied together in the school's success.

Like private schools in general, Qiannan Computer Vo-Tech's strengths make an important contribution to society around it.[5] Think about it. People used to bureaucratic grip hear how the school's autonomous management provides freedom to innovate and exercise personal responsibility. Those used to low productivity listen to stories of a school that is sustained by hard work and lean budgets. The school's teachers speak with former factory colleagues about the fulfilling risks of making it without government assistance.

Even the students are sold. Before they enrolled, some of those I spoke with were hesitant about the newness of "schools established by social forces." Not now. That's one hundred seeds, which upon graduation will scatter into society's soil. And these types of seeds (the Guizhou variety) are particularly uncommon and valuable.

While it is clear from the students and teaching staff that Qiannan Computer Vo-Tech has a good thing going, Principal Bi confides that at times they struggle just to keep their heads above water. Other than their advantages as a private school, the odds, in fact, do seem to be stacked against them.

For example, there is growing competition from state-owned schools that, now facing their own challenges brought on by decentralized funding, see value in buying a few computers and advertising that they have a "computer studies" program. There's also the endless financial strain of trying to keep up with the latest computer software and hardware upgrades. And Bi himself says that he sometimes feels isolated, as if he were the only one pursuing innovative education. He believes he is doing the right thing with his homegrown management style, but he is not certain. Until recently, he was not connected with others who are pursuing similar goals in Guizhou and other parts of the country.[6]

Though he is not fully aware of it, Principal Bi is not alone in his struggles. Over the last few months I have spoken with a handful of private educators in Duyun and Guiyang. When asked their greatest challenges, they gave a consistent reply: the effort to keep up financially and cope with unequal treatment from local government. With the exception of Principal Bi, who says his number-one challenge is financial, the others' primary complaint is discrimination. Their difficulties point to the realities of a country in the midst of change, existing somewhere between state-planned and market-driven, between controlled and encouraged, between big government and big society.

Amid this passage from then to now, formerly unchallenged interest groups (*liyi jituan*) watch authority slip through their hands as their departments are reduced and "social forces" emerge and gain strength. The common result, especially when those with threatened interests exist within government ministries charged with regulating these "social forces," is uneven treatment.

SOURCES OF GROWTH AND FRAGILITY

Blame it all on growth and reform. Private education in China did not leap forward until 1992, when Deng Xiaoping made his landmark visit to southern China. The public nod of approval he gave to market-based economics reinvigorated growth and policy reform, both of which had been slack since the summer of 1989. Since Deng's "southern tour," the number of private schools has exploded nationwide, totaling more than fifty thousand by 2001.[7]

Take Wenzhou County in coastal Zhejiang Province, for example. The wealthy county represents the antithesis of state-command economics. Only 14 percent of Zhejiang's economy is state-run; in Wenzhou County the number would be even lower. Following suit, 84 percent of kindergarten children and 10 percent of senior high school students attend private schools.[8] Compare Guizhou Province at the other end of the spectrum, where the state-owned sector, though weak, continues to produce 67 percent of industrial output. Private education is rare, with the exception of provincial capital Guiyang, which as an island of relative wealth has

Figure 14.1. The Composition of Private Education in China

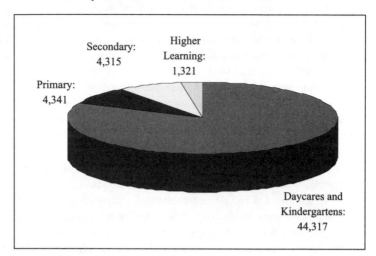

Secondary: 4,315

Higher Learning: 1,321

Primary: 4,341

Daycares and Kindergartens: 44,317

Note: Total Number of Private Educational Institutions: 54,294.
Source: Jing Lin, "Private Education in China: Its Development and Dynamics," *Harvard China Review* 3, no. 2 (Spring 2002): 21.

six private middle schools, more than twenty private primary schools, and several dozen private kindergartens.[9] The rest of Guizhou's cities each have a handful of private schools.

Still, the appearance of the sprouts of private education in the hard ground of interior provinces like Guizhou is remarkable.[10] This is particularly true when one considers that Guizhou, if measured by per capita gross domestic product (an indication of productivity), is the most backward province in China.

The growth of private education, though fueled by market-oriented sectors of the economy, has been facilitated by an evolution in government policy. In less than ten years Beijing has come a very long way. A 1993 State Council report announcing China's educational plans for the 1990s passed over "schools established by social forces."[11] Among the document's fifty articles, only one mentioned private schools, a reference tucked away in a paragraph discussing education for the disabled. That is a far cry from government support headlined in "Regulations for Schools Established by Social Forces," which went into effect October 1, 1997. The central government's position was expressed in sixteen Chinese characters: "actively encourage, firmly support, correctly lead, strongly supervise."

A September 1998 article in the government-mouthpiece *People's Daily* went even further: "Schools established by social forces . . . are an inevitable result of economic construction and social reform. It demonstrates that forty years of government-run education, as a single-system model, is not appropriate for the realities of our country's educational needs."[12] Coming from the *People's Daily,* that is a strong statement indeed.

All this should mean that private educators across the country are "actively encouraged and firmly supported." Right? Local-level officials can parrot the sixteen-character statement of support, but foot-dragging and interference reveal their hearts.

In addition, laws remain incomplete and unclear. This leaves private schools vulnerable. One private school I know was recently taxed twice—once as a private school, again as a private business. Another is having a terrible time with a building permit. The general conclusion I have reached after meetings with government officials and private-school educators is that despite growing support from Beijing, "schools established by social forces" in China's interior remain frail, because of both subtle policy discrimination and now-slowing economic growth.

An article in the *People's Daily* discusses a vision for the future relationship of China's government and society: "Experts believe 'small government' and 'big society' are interdependent. If government is not reduced, its functions not transformed, it will be hard for society to develop, difficult for social organization to be complete; society's life as an organism will lack vitality. At the same time, only as society becomes more autonomous can it take on greater responsibility for its own management and development, and not rely on 'unlimited' government. This can happen only if government is reduced and its functions transformed. The purpose of government cutbacks is not just to lessen expenditures or simply to increase efficiency; the primary concern of government downsizing is to breathe life into society."[13]

Private education, though of mustard-seed proportions at present, holds promise as a contributor to that "big society" vision. Actually, maybe the appellation "schools established by social forces" makes better sense than the "P"-word, after all. "Social force," even if as subtle and vulnerable as a sprout, points to far-reaching change that could not only reshape China but strengthen it in the process.

SUGGESTIONS FOR FURTHER READING

Cheng, Bi. "Exploring the Practice and Theory of Chinese Private Schools." *Chinese Education and Society* 30, no. 1 (1997): 23–38.

Dahlman, Carl, and Jean-Eric Aubert. *China and the Knowledge Economy: Seizing the 21st Century.* Washington, D.C.: World Bank, 1999.

Deng, Peng. *Private Education in Modern China.* Westport, Conn.: Praeger, 1999.

Hou, Wenzhou. "Migrant Children's Education in China: Migrant Private Schools." *Harvard China Review* 3, no. 2 (2002): 27–33.

Lin, Jing. *Social Transformation and Private Education in China.* Westport, Conn.: Praeger, 1999.

———. "Private Education in China: Its Development and Dynamics." *Harvard China Review* 3, no. 2 (2002): 21–26.

Wu, Degang. "An Overview of China's Education Reform over the Past 20 Years." *Harvard China Review* 3, no. 2 (2002): 5–7.

15
"Field of Dreams"
Tourism in Guizhou Province

A postcard promoting Guizhou tourism. Mountains and rivers are trademarks of Guizhou's abundant endowment in natural resources. Several rivers in Guizhou Province now offer white-water rafting.

> Tourism is one of your advantages; you have the conditions to develop this sector. Just focus on making good use of your abundant natural resources. That would be enough. There is no need to invest in all kinds of crazy stuff (*luanqi bazao*), like fancy hotels. You don't need that. Just make sure you build decent bathrooms, and keep them clean. That and a good shower are sufficient. Your food tastes good down here, like what I ate today: not much meat but your vegetable dishes were quite nice, and not expensive. This is attractive. There's no need to thoughtlessly spend money. Focus on efficiency. As tourism develops and transportation conditions improve, that, one day, will be true prosperity.
>
> —Premier Zhu Rongji, during a 1996 inspection tour of Guizhou Province[1]

Imagine, for a moment, that you are a resident of Guiyang, Guizhou's bustling capital city. You have worked hard at your desk job through the 1980s and 1990s to cocoon yourself from life outside the provincial center. Yet while enjoying the conveniences of the city, you have become weary of the traffic, the constant noise, the worsening pollution, and the monotony of your life's routine. You have disposable income like never before and since 1993 you have had two-day weekends.[2] Still, you feel pent up.

You pick up the newspaper sitting on your desk and notice a full-page spread about a newly opened tourist site: highland grasslands just 48 kilometers southeast of Guiyang.[3] The article describes a "Spanish-style" mountain cabin with a stone-hearth fireplace. Outside the lodge and under the expansive canopy of a clear night sky, friends sit around an open fire as the staff cooks a whole mutton on a spit.

There are ethnic dancing and singing performances, horseback riding, and plenty of fresh air. And all this in a place called "Magenuojie"—the local Miao minority language for "where the beautiful women live."

"WHERE THE BEAUTIFUL WOMEN LIVE"

"Only 48 kilometers from Guiyang, huh?" I grumble to myself as my wife, my two kids, two friends who had flown in from Beijing and Shanghai, and I toss back and forth while our van labors through steep hairpin turns up the rugged mountain road.[4] One hour passes, two hours . . . the jaunt just outside the city takes over three hours. The promotional literature doesn't mention that between Guiyang and the grasslands, one's vehicle must climb almost 6,000 feet.

"It's a grassland, all right," we mumble to each other as we pile out of the van, surveying the desolate landscape—the kind of wild beauty you'd find on the moors of northern Scotland. A stiff wind and frigid drizzle chill our bones. It wasn't nearly this cold down in Guiyang. We are all underdressed. "Here we are," I think. "My friends have come from the comforts of the coast to freeze in the distant mountains of the interior."

As we step into the cabin, however, my complaint melts. A crackling fire, prepared well in advance of our arrival, blazes in the stone hearth. The wooden cabin, simple but thoughtfully designed, has a nice feel to it.

"This is well done. It reminds me of a hunting cabin in the pine forests of south Georgia," I say to Director Liu Shijie, head of Qiannan Prefecture's Tourism Bureau, as I move my family closer to the fire. Director Liu beams with delight that a foreigner has said the cabin reminds him of something Western. He designed it himself. He tells me of his "struggle with the elements" in developing the site to the point where tourists could actually visit. "Even bringing in such basics as water and electricity were a tremendous challenge. And there are other issues like how to dispose of the garbage and how to keep away the rats, especially in the summer months," Liu explains. "And if we could just get the road up from Guiyang paved." We nod in agreement.[5]

In the face of all these difficulties, Director Liu is especially proud of what he has accomplished. He should be. "Our focus is to provide Guiyang's two million residents (his target market) with experiences they cannot have at home in the city, memories that will bring them and new friends back. There are plenty of mountains and rivers in Guizhou, but only one grasslands. What I have, no one else does. And where in Guiyang can you warm yourself next to a cozy fireplace?"

"And the 'beautiful women'?"

"That's just what this place is called by the locals. Rather than calling it the Longli County Grasslands, we thought the traditional name given by the Miao villagers added a nice touch."

As a former journalist, Director Liu knows how to package his message. Over the last year, his project has been written up in over a half-dozen newspapers and tourism publications.

Liu is succeeding. In its first full year of operation seven thousand tourists, who pay about U.S. $10 a head per night, have visited the grasslands. At that rate, Liu says, investors—a consortium of three Chinese companies—should be able to recoup their 2 million yuan investment (U.S. $180,000) in just three years.

Liu proudly says, "The government has not spent one *fen* [cent] on this project."

For us, the two days at the Magenuojie grasslands, despite the chill, were full of memorable activities: gathering around the fireplace, eating roasted lamb with our fingers by candlelight (it was raining, so we skipped the outdoor campfire), watching a colorful song-and-dance performance by local villagers, and riding "Japanese thoroughbreds" across the spacious landscape.[6] All this, I imagine, would be very attractive to Chinese urbanites cooped up in Guiyang.

CHANGING TIMES

What fascinated me most as I observed the two dozen Chinese tourists was how this group of people, who only a few years ago insulated themselves from anything outside the city, are now beginning to return to the countryside—at least, when the visit is comfortable and brief.

It is difficult to fully appreciate the depth of emotion some Chinese have toward their personal histories, which led many to escape the hardships of the countryside for the conveniences and securities of city life. Their feelings parallel historical events, as well as government policy, favoring the development of the city while the countryside footed much of the bill. That many urban dwellers have begun to return "to play" reflects a sea change in attitude.

The fact that one of the most popular dishes at the grasslands lodge is *zhiqing chaofan* ("sent-down-youth fried rice") indicates that some who were sent to the countryside as students have actually begun to pursue the memories of their Cultural Revolution experiences. Now parents, these former sent-down youth have much to pass on to their children through stories of "when I was a child."

The chili pepper–eating, horseback-riding general manager of the grasslands project—he's the one who put *zhiqing chaofan* on the menu—was himself "sent down" to Guizhou from Shanghai as a youth. He never returned. This forty-something manager is quite a contrast to the stereotypical Shanghainese.

Some younger urbanites—those in their twenties and thirties, who didn't directly experience the Cultural Revolution—appear to be in search of a feeling when they head for the mountains. The Guizhou *All-City* newspaper article quotes a woman after she returned from the grasslands, where she rode a horse for the first time: "I came back and told a friend that I had found the sensation of being perched out over the bow of the Titanic as it sliced through the vast ocean ahead, just like the movie."

The connection seems tenuous, but what cannot be denied is the significance of how twenty years of economic reform and industrialization are leading to a shift in the way China's urban residents, young and old alike, view the countryside.

On the other side of the equation, what goes on in the minds of the colorfully dressed but poor Miao villagers as they entertain groups of privileged city dwellers? In one activity, for example, Han tourists and Miao hosts compete to see which group can outlast the other in remembering choruses to sing back and forth at each other from across the lodge. A head-on clash of culture? Hardly. The well-rehearsed tunes Miao villagers shoot back are Hong Kong and Taiwanese pop songs. And you can bet the Chinese tourists are not singing traditional Miao folk songs, either. Still, both sides appear to have great fun.

Do the Miao people benefit from this invasion from the city? Tourism brings significantly more cash to the local villagers than they would have otherwise.[7] And if I were a Miao, I would feel proud of my heritage as I compare myself to the sometimes obnoxious tourists. Even so, one has to wonder what they are really thinking as they dance a local version of the two-step with their Han guests. For better or for worse, the city and the countryside, Han and Miao, now meet each day on the Magenuojie grasslands.

The grasslands are but a microcosm of a rapidly growing tourism sector in Qiannan Prefecture, Guizhou Province, and across China. Separate from the millions of dollars foreign tourists inject into China's economy each year, Chinese tourists themselves are swelling in numbers and spreading around significant amounts of cash. In 1996, for example, of the 256 million urban citizens who traveled, 125 million were on vacation.[8]

In poor but scenic Qiannan Prefecture alone, Chinese tourists spent 85 million yuan in 1995, corresponding to a tenfold increase in tourist visits since 1992: 85,000 guests in 1992, 500,000 in 1995, and one million in 1997.[9]

FRESH VISION

Guizhou residents often say to me, "The mountains are our greatest difficulty; they are also our greatest hope" (kunnan zai shan; xiwang ye zai shan).[10]

The optimistic side of this saying refers to more than just the abundance of minerals yet to be mined. People have begun to realize that Guizhou's tourism potential ought to be able to capture more than just the 1-percent share the province currently holds of nationwide tourist-generated revenue. Tourism's multiplier effects within the local economy are also becoming better understood and appreciated. Qiannan Prefecture's government reports that for every person employed in its tourist sector, five jobs are created. Similarly, for every yuan in profit to the industry, nine additional yuan are earned throughout the local economy. "For an impoverished, backward area like Qiannan Prefecture," a Guizhou Daily article

Figure 15.1. Domestic and International Tourism in Guizhou Province

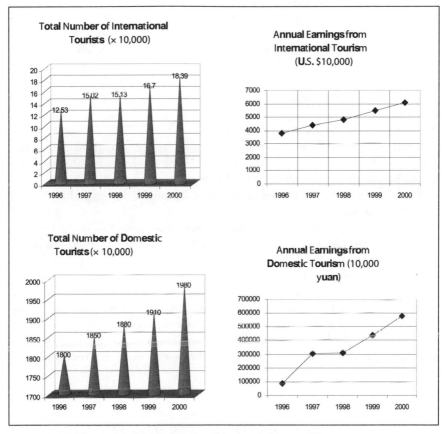

Source: *2001 Guizhou Statistical Yearbook* (Beijing: China Statistical Press, 2001).

says, "the effectiveness of tourism-related development in poverty relief is extraordinary."[11]

But for Guizhou Province, a poor region long used to development along the lines of comparative disadvantage, a relatively recent focus on developing advantages is challenging government official and entrepreneur alike to use fresh eyes and new skills to make use of their "tourism resources": natural beauty, colorful local cultures, and history.[12]

The development of Guizhou Province's tourist industry was given a boost in August 1998, when a young central-government official arrived from Beijing for a tour in Guizhou as vice governor. An economist by training, forty-four-year-old Guo Shuqing is as certain as anyone of the importance of encouraging Guizhou's development utilizing its comparative advantages. Tourism is one of the items in the vice governor's portfolio.[13]

In an October 1998 speech to provincial tourism officials, Guo said, "In Guizhou, there are beautiful landscape scenes wherever you look. We are a 'province of parks' well worthy of the name. . . . There is no other industry like tourism that both affects and is influenced by so many sectors of the economy, including business, transportation, energy, culture, sanitation, public security, even roads and schools. While tourism brings benefits to these areas, if any of these sectors is lacking, tourism's development will suffer as well. . . . Tourism is a service-intensive industry under all the demands of modern society."[14]

In considering priorities to further develop tourism, Guo reminded the officials, "The most important thing we have to do is make the needs and desires of the tourist the number-one priority. We must eliminate placing our own wishes, our methods, and ourselves at the center. We must thoroughly survey and understand the interests of the tourists."

Because he comes from outside the province, Guo brings vision to both the potential and the challenges of Guizhou tourism. Along with a fresh perspective, he brings new momentum.

While able to articulate the big picture, Guo also shows talent in bringing specific ideas to the table. For example, while exhorting the officials to think and prepare toward the future, he suggested constructing a series of "rest stops" along highways yet to be built (with bathroom, telephone, and convenience store). As transportation infrastructure in Guizhou continues to improve and road traffic grows (tourist and otherwise), demand for the convenience of "rest stops" will strengthen.

"IF YOU BUILD IT, . . . THEY WILL COME"

With fresh input from a new vice governor, the entrepreneurial minds of people like Liu Shijie, and increasing demand from urban residents around the country, Guizhou's tourism sector will continue to grow as an important engine of development in the province's economy. But it will not be as easy or as automatic as some may think.

Whether developing grasslands, rest stops along an expressway, or hiking tours along the Long March trail, the obstacles to building tourism in Guizhou are, in fact, as great as the potential. For all the abundance of natural beauty, culture, and history, lasting development is not simply a matter of hanging a sign that reads: "Open for Business."

That is, unless it's Hollywood. In the movie *Field of Dreams,* a miles-long line of cars is magically drawn to a cornfield-turned-baseball diamond in the middle of America's hinterland. For reasons they cannot explain, thousands of baseball fans are attracted to witness what turns out to be a reappearance of "Shoeless Joe" Jackson, legendary slugger of the 1919 Black Sox.[15]

But that's the movies. A Guizhou tourist official, who is not so easily optimistic about the future of tourism in Guizhou, told me that she is concerned because, still, too many people believe that tourism is simple. Just build it; they will come. A mentality that oversimplifies tourism, especially when it's in one of China's most backward provinces, easily leads to careless upkeep, poor service, and nasty toilets. Perhaps this is what Premier Zhu Rongji meant when he toured Guizhou in 1996 and urged local officials to "build decent bathrooms, and keep them clean" as a focus in developing the province's tourism industry.

Zhu's point, though at first blush almost comic, is actually profound. Sure, there are complex, big-ticket items that must be considered—investment and infrastructure are among the largest issues. But in the final analysis, it is not far off the mark to suggest that a significant determinant of the future success of tourism in Guizhou is the quality of the service provided—and how clean the bathrooms are kept.

SUGGESTIONS FOR FURTHER READING

Cheng, Allen. "Cashing in on Wanderlust." *Asiaweek* 27, no. 23 (June 2001): 48.
Oakes, Tim. *Tourism and Modernity in China.* New York: Routledge, 1998.

16
Golfing in Guiyang
Playing with Guizhou's Affluent

Author prepares to sink a putt at the eighteenth hole of the Guiyang Golf Club. A restful clubhouse in the background welcomes weary golfers after a full day of play.

My partners, some of Guizhou's most wealthy businesspeople, and I strode down the fairway of Guiyang Golf Club toward the eighteenth green as if it was Sunday afternoon at the Masters Golf Tournament in Augusta. The manicured lawn's refreshing scent filled the air. The course, thoughtfully designed along the contours of the mountain terrain, delighted the eye. The weather was overcast and cool—great for golf in August. A restful clubhouse beckoned in the distance.

"Hand me the seven-iron," I said to the caddie.

"Sir, you're still one hundred and sixty yards out and the green is set up a bit. I suggest you use your six-iron."

Xiao Ye may have been just a middle-school graduate from Guizhou's country-side, but she spoke with confidence, so I took her advice. The next thing I knew, my ball was on the green. Luck? Absolutely. But as Xiao Ye and I approached the green, I teased her that I should listen to her more often. She dipped her head in embarrassment, her hand covering a smile.

Local farmers-turned-groundskeepers wore faded-blue "Mao jackets" as they trimmed the grounds with imported weed-whackers. Other "peasants" hauled baskets of sand on their backs, spreading it over grass seedlings. It was all part of an effort to grow a golf course on what previously had been barren mountainside.

Five years ago, when the Guangdong Province real estate company began to search for a suitable location in Guizhou Province, the team of developers drew a circle on the map around the capital city, Guiyang, thirty kilometers in radius. Then they began to look.

The golf course's president, Mr. Lin, himself a Guangdong native, says that at the time, a four-wheel-drive vehicle was the only way to get to the resort's present location.

What was then a thirty-kilometer overland adventure is now a thirty-minute zip down the Guiyang-to-Zunyi expressway. Five years ago the mountain was rural refuse. Now—200 million yuan (more than U.S. $20 million) later—the Guiyang Golf Club is a hotspot for Guiyang's wealthy to play and to be seen.

Guizhou's affluent have indeed come out to play. The club is much more than just a place to drive a golf ball; it is an entire complex of sports and relaxation. The facility has tennis courts, a swimming pool, an elaborate fitness center, fishing in the lake that sets the 120-room luxury hotel off from the course, and Chinese and Western restaurants. In addition, the first of more than a dozen lakeside villas has recently been completed. They start at the equivalent of U.S. $100,000 and are selling fast.

All at a 4,000-foot elevation in rural Guizhou! In fact, the rejuvenating mountain air is part of the club's appeal.

But it's expensive air: club memberships cost 200,000 yuan (U.S. $24,000), plus a 250 yuan (U.S. $30) monthly fee. And this in a province of China whose 36 million residents make on average just $200 each year.

There is no need to sign up for tee times yet at the two-year-old resort, but on weekends the course sees a steady stream of visitors. How many members? Company secret, says a course vice president. But it is not hard to find people who will talk about why they joined the Guiyang Golf Club.

I decided that the best place to make my initial encounter with Guizhou's affluent was at the club's double-deck driving range. So, on that pleasant Saturday afternoon, I hit baskets of golf balls and looked for the right people to meet.

I enjoy all sports, but it had been years since I had played golf. Still, I thought, my look as an American—unusual in these parts—would appeal to some, particularly those fashion-conscious golfers, as keen to pursue the right look as they are the low score.

Enthusiasts exhibited their prized Ping and Titleist golf bags for all to see as they reclined in chairs behind the practice tees, sipping green tea. One displayed a different status symbol—a chic, admiring companion in sunglasses and all-black outfit—as he powered balls over the pond with his driver. Ten feet away, a newcomer swung and missed in her high heels and skirt.

Farther down the row I noticed two men, probably in their early fifties, apparently serious about their golf. After I exhausted my basket, I walked over and commented to one of the men, now sitting in a chair and watching his partner swing away, "He's got nice form. Where you all from?"

"We're locals," the gentleman responded as I pulled up a chair.

"You all are from the county here?" I asked with a twinge of surprise.

"Yeah, he's the . . . this," the man said as he showed me a thumbs-up. "He's the county party secretary. I'm the tax-bureau chief."

"You guys are good," I said, realizing that although these two did not fit the exact profile I was looking for, they certainly were among the most powerful at the course.

If practice makes perfect, these two should be close to flawless—the day I saw them, they had played forty-eight holes. They come out most weekends.[1]

The following morning, the three of us, with the required caddies, played the course together.

"Golf is a great way to meet people," the party secretary said to me between holes. "Those who come to play have money. They're usually the company's owner or general manager. We play golf with them. We promote our county. We invite them to invest here. Didn't I meet you this way? If it wasn't for golf, we wouldn't have met."

Xiuyang County is one of the richest in Guizhou, largely due to its proximity to Guiyang. The big-time investment from the golf course certainly didn't hurt.

"But how has the course affected local people who previously farmed the land?" I asked the party secretary.

"Most of it was barren mountain scrabble. And the course agreed to employ the local villagers. The resort has put about three hundred people to work. On balance, it has definitely helped the locals, enabling them to break the cashless, subsistence-level cycle most farmers experience in Guizhou."

I don't doubt him. Though there must be complaints among some about the resort's disturbing the village's sleepy way of life, for many of the locals who would have normally needed to leave for distant cities as migrant laborers, the cash has come to them. My caddie, for example, has worked at the course since it opened two years ago. Xiao Ye comes from a typical smalltown family. Unconcerned about what one does after life as a caddie, she's thrilled just to have a job.

Though interesting, the two officials do not represent the majority who have joined the Guiyang Golf Club. Most of those who pay dues are wealthy thirty- and forty-year-olds from Guiyang, young company heads, many of whom undoubtedly hail from privileged backgrounds. How else could the young businessman I played with on another day thrive as head of a private company that installs electrical hardware systems for entire townships?

On that day, I hooked up with three young men, members of Guizhou's business elite. Each was the president of a company: a real estate firm, a fertilizer company, and the power company. Each had played most of China's best golf courses: Shenzhen, Hainan, Kunming, and Dalian.

"How many are there like you all in Guiyang?" I asked the others in my foursome.

"There are probably one hundred people in Guiyang like us, who have the money to fly anywhere in the country on any given weekend and play golf."

"Why golf?"

"It's a healthy alternative, a great way to relax. A lot of Guizhou's wealthy hang out in nightclubs, and, recently, bowling has caught on. But golf is different. At the end of a day of golf, you're physically tired but mentally rejuvenated. Golf is a game of you against yourself."

The fertilizer executive replied, "I've been playing for just one year. A friend

These lakeside villas at Guiyang Country Club start at the equivalent of U.S. $100,000.

brought me out one day and I've been hooked ever since. Golf is also a great way to spend time with a few good friends."

"And a great place to talk business," another company head jumped in.

"What else do Guizhou's wealthy do for fun?"

"We fish, we bowl, we play mahjong."

"Do your spouses ever join you on the links?"

"No, they prefer shopping."

A few hours at the driving range offer ample evidence that golf is also providing a new way to pursue that stylish, ever-elusive look of wealth and leisure: the right golf shirt, the matching hat, cool saddle shoes, baggy khakis, and for the very sophisticated . . . the golf glove dangling out of the back left pocket. And who better to model that look than Australian golf professional Greg "The Shark" Norman, in a life-size cardboard cutout at the club's pro shop.

"Golf will be the new fashion sport of Guiyang," one of my foursome told me. "In fact, I'm building a three-deck golf range right in Guiyang, with a restaurant, pro shop, and everything. People in Guiyang with a little money want to look stylish, like us. Golf will be the new fad. The driving range opens after the country's fiftieth anniversary, and it should really take off. We're right behind the province's military headquarters; come visit us sometime."

Weeks later, while sitting around a steamy hotpot dinner with a less-monied but well-educated group of friends in Guiyang, I asked their opinion of Guizhou's richest.

"How much money does one have to have in Guiyang to be considered really wealthy?" I asked.

"We have a saying, 'One million yuan is just getting started.'"

"How many in Guiyang are past 'just getting started?' Of those, how many earned their money through hard work, through legal means?"

"There are a lot of very wealthy people in Guiyang, but few outside the provincial capital. The guys you met at the golf club would have been among Guizhou's most wealthy," one quickly answered.

"Wealth in Guiyang really took off in the mid-1990s. Any not corrupt?"

He thought for a second, puzzled. "None."

Whether or not his statement is true, this urban dweller's perception is as important. The automatic association of wealth with corruption illustrates the reality that in many places of the country, political power (*quan*) and special favors are preconditions for making big money (*qian*).

Certainly, there are many talented people in Guiyang, and one must remember that the provincial capital ranks among China's thirty most wealthy cities. Still, it is the endless shades of gray and black between business and government dealings that upset people the most.

Remember as well, one senior government official told me, that with a city as well-off as Guiyang, it takes some pretty drastic poverty to drag the province's overall average down to the nation's cellar. This certainly simplifies and intensifies views about Guizhou's affluent.

While at the Guiyang Golf Club, I happened across a former provincial tourism bureau chief. The cheery Mr. Zhang was a guest of golf club president Lin, part of a review team Lin had invited to observe the resort and share their input. Mr. Zhang spoke glowingly of the tourist value of golf in Guizhou, the pleasing combination of a sophisticated sport and the natural beauty of the surrounding mountains and lakes. "A golf course adds to the attractiveness of Guizhou as a 'province of parks,'" he said, "not to mention its strengthening of Guizhou's investment environment."

The former government official got more serious, however, when he talked about the review team's recommendation that the club find ways to become more accessible to those who cannot afford membership. Their suggestion? Varieties of pro bono services for groups who could come out to the course—say, on a weekday—for a day of rest and relaxation. Companies have already brought their staffs out for half-day retreats. I ran into a group of them. Also, the day before I arrived, on Teacher's Day, several hundred teachers were invited from Guiyang for a day of fun and all-you-can-hit golf balls at the driving range.

But would the exclusivity sought and paid for by those with the bucks get lost in all the public do-gooding? That's part of the balance the course's management must strike between its appeal to those with the deepest pockets in Guiyang and the image the club projects.

Indeed, it harkens back to Mao's revolutionary promise of equality, to the current disparity question, and to Deng Xiaoping's ever-pragmatic, ever-clever logic: "Let certain groups of people and certain regions prosper first."

Sounds nice. But when one realizes that one golfer who chose to give up his club membership could finance the tuition of literally thousands of students for all of their years in school, it makes one wonder if it is even appropriate to allow such a course to set up in a province like Guizhou, where such privilege is astronomically out of reach for 99.9 percent of Guizhou's populace.

Reason, however, suggests that if a market-driven real estate investment company from coastal Guangdong is willing to put up the money, there is no rationale why the course should not be here. And if the course makes Guizhou a more attractive location for business executives, more power to them and to the province. Shared prosperity is not guaranteed by simply maintaining the lowest common denominator.

SUGGESTIONS FOR FURTHER READING

Friedman, Thomas L. "Fine China." *Golf Digest* 52, no. 6 (June 2001): 182–86.
Harris, Dick. "Once Scorned Elitist, Golf Now Enjoys a Mini-Boom in China." *China Today* 43, no. 7 (July 1994): 49.
Watson, Paul. "For All the Tees in China." *BRW* 18, no. 39 (October 1996): 13–17.

V

PROMISES, PROMISES
China's Inadequate Revolution

17
Matters of the Heart . . .
The Rebirth of Religion

Ironies of the revolution. A young boy, with grandmother instructing from behind, bows before a statue of a legendary Long March nurse at Zunyi's Red Army Park. Incense and scarves, placed by visitors, have turned this revolutionary site into a shrine.

> Everywhere in China you hear talk of a spiritual vacuum, an echoing nihilism that quiets this hyperkinetic nation. This week, as China celebrates the 50th anniversary of Mao's October revolution, high-tech military jets will scream over Beijing, foreigners will arrive in search of new investment opportunities, and the government will celebrate a nation transformed. But what will be missing is faith. Fifty years ago, on an overcast day, Mao and his cadres gathered in Tiananmen and stared at a nothing future—no food, no remnants of a healthy economy, no allies. All they had was faith. And it will be the only thing missing from this week's party.[1]

On Sunday morning, April 25, 1999, more than 10,000 adherents of Falun Gong slipped unassumingly past all of the early-warning systems that protected an already-tense Tiananmen Square and quietly surrounded Zhongnanhai, China's White House, where the country's leaders live and work.[2] This, China's largest public demonstration since 1989, consisted of no shouting students. Most of those who sat silently in protest around the government headquarters were middle-aged and elderly men and women—retired factory workers, bespectacled professors, and even some Communist Party members.

After that spring day, when the thunder of silent protest echoed through the halls of Zhongnanhai, the government decided to crack down on Falun Gong. And it has with a fury. Sustained now for more than three years, the political campaign has reached stunning proportions. For several months after Falun Gong was outlawed on July 22, 1999, China Central Television's thirty-minute evening news program aired practically nothing but anti-Falun Gong rhetoric in which academics, former followers, and ordinary citizens spoke about how the cult cheats its followers, separates families, damages health, and hurts social stability. The government operation has been a study in all-out demonization.

In the first seven days after the campaign began, Chinese authorities rounded up at least 5,000 Falun Gong members, ransacking homes and confiscating printed material. Another 1,200 government officials were detained and required to study Communist Party documents and to renounce any allegiance to the movement.[3] Since those early months, the Communist Party has kept up steady pressure in its battle against the movement. But Falun Gong adherents have fought back. In January 2001, five alleged Falun Gong members set fire to themselves in Beijing's Tiananmen Square. A year later, the authorities responded by displaying on national media three of the severely scarred former practitioners, who expressed their regret for setting themselves on fire in Tiananmen Square. "I went to burn myself to demonstrate that Falun Gong is good and true, but I never imagined this outcome," one of the members said on nationwide media through a disfigured face and body. "But now I think it is a cult, and people should understand that and no longer follow it."[4] Months later, members of the Falun Gong took the next step by hijacking a cable television network in the industrial northern province of Jilin, and for fifty minutes broadcast their version of the self-immolations. The battle rages on.

But behind the scathing, high-priced, and wide-ranging campaign, there looms a simple but important question: Why would millions of people, reportedly more in number than the Communist Party membership itself, flock to a belief system that teaches self-cultivation, group exercise, and the end of the world? The answer can be found in the inadequate promises of the Communist Revolution, just over fifty years old. In the words of a man who sat next to me at the barbershop, it's all about a crisis of faith (*xinyang weiji*).

The rhetoric of the revolution promised to deliver more than just a new political order; it preached an orthodoxy that would emancipate and transform the way people believed and behaved. Mao Zedong, who had particular scorn for Confucius and religious "superstition," propagated a new faith that directly confronted the past.

During a month-long 1927 trip to Hunan Province's countryside, for example, during which he investigated a nascent peasant movement, Mao poked fun at the farmers' traditional beliefs: "The gods and goddesses are indeed pitiful; worshipped for hundreds of years, they have not knocked down for you a single local bully or a single one of the bad gentry! Now you want to have your rent reduced. I would like to ask: How will you go about it? Believe in the gods, or believe in the peasant association?"[5]

The "reactionary cultures" of tradition and religion, Mao argued, had to be thoroughly swept away if a new order was to be established, capable of cultivating the "new man" that Communist ideology so vigorously promoted.

Post-1949 history offers a grim litany of the havoc wreaked by Mao's Communist dream. Revolution and waves of antisuperstition campaigns gutted traditional religious and philosophical systems, but in the pursuit of the perfect society—itself, mind you, a very traditional theme—the ideal went awry. The people's revolution became a Mao-centered personality cult, complete with the high-pitched fervor of all extreme religions.

Mao may have made a first-class revolutionary, but he was a deity of the poorest order. Anarchy and the millions of deaths that resulted during the Cultural Revolution showed what happens when rulers play god. Heights of exuberance, followed by depths of crushing tragedy and disillusionment, left many people burned so badly they could no longer put their faith in anything or anyone. Recalling that period and her life since, one woman, a student and loyal follower of Mao during the 1960s, described her heart to me as a rock—unable to feel anything or trust anyone.

With the erosion of communism as a belief system, Chinese pragmatism—despite the window dressing of Marxism, Leninism, and Mao Zedong Thought—revived under Deng Xiaoping. "Black cat or white cat, a good cat is one that catches mice," Deng preached, as he introduced reform and opening.[6] Since the 1980s, economic growth, not revolutionary ideology, has become the people's hope and the ticket to the Communist Party's legitimacy. Most Chinese began to sing from a new page in their hymnbooks: "To Get Rich Is Glorious."

While Deng-led reforms resulted in remarkable economic advances for hundreds of millions of people, another reality has become abundantly clear: wealth alone cannot fulfill the human heart, neither can it substitute for the core values of a nation. With tradition destroyed (or at least suppressed), communism as a value system discredited, and the pursuit of wealth incomplete or unattainable, a vacuum of belief has become pervasive. Frenetic social change and dislocation have exacerbated it. One Guizhou Province government official recently described the present situation to me in broken English as "a lost heart."

Matters of the soul are never easy to quantify, and their interplay with social, economic, and political forces is both subtle and complex. But the links can be seen. Spiritual search and a self-described moral crisis provide the clearest evidence of China's dilemma. The closer one lives to the country's grassroots realities and the more intently one listens to people speak on the streets and in the mountains, the more apparent the predicament becomes. Dishonesty, disregard for the law, abuse of power, irrelevance of means to achieve desired ends, and a general frailty of community relations have reached troubling proportions, locals tell me. Where I lived, these problems have become the norm, not the exception. Their most extreme forms are expressed in prostitution (both supply and demand), gambling, and every imaginable form of corruption.

The most egregious anecdote came during a trip to a rural county to report on

an education project. Just after arriving at the county seat, my travel companion
and I ran into one of his boyhood friends. They hadn't seen each other for years.
This friend, now apparently a rising star in the county police (public security)
department, was thrilled to see his boyhood friend. Proud to show off his power,
he insisted that we have dinner together. When the time came, he picked us up at
the county guesthouse in an old black car, with no license or markings. Even
though one could easily walk the length and breadth of the county seat, we drove.
When we arrived at the best restaurant in town, other "friends" were there waiting: several local lawyers and businessmen. Over much good food and many toasts,
the dinner participants celebrated their relationships and how they protected each
other's interests. After a few hours, I was the only sober one left. Someone settled
the bill and we stumbled out of the restaurant, now walking, not riding. I was
relieved that the dinner was over, though fascinated to have gotten an inside glance
at how local police, businessmen, and lawyers cooperate. I could now get some rest.
But we were not done. The bumbling policeman suggested that we have a cup of
tea and eat some sunflowers seeds before turning it in. The teahouse was just next
to the guesthouse where I was staying, he said. We could still get to bed early.

After climbing a few flights of stairs, we entered through a nondescript door and
passed a reception desk, where greetings were exchanged and we were shown into
a large room with dimmed lights. The music pulsated. A large open area, presum-
ably a dance floor, was lined on each side with tables surrounded by chairs. Most
of the light in the room came from an extra-large screen on the wall, which pro-
jected DVD images of American women dancing and bobbing in a wet T-shirt
contest, apparently in Hawaii. In the room's shadows lurked dozens of teenage
girls, grouped in clusters that seemed to move in unison like schools of tropical
fish. In a minute, at the policeman's command, two or three attractive but awk-
ward junior high school girls gathered around each of us. "Hold their hands! Sit in
their laps!" the policeman barked. Naturally, the young women hesitated. "*Xiagang!* [the term used for laid-off state-owned enterprise workers] Get out of here!
Next group!" the drunken police sergeant roared.

At about that time, an older gentleman strolled in. I was told that he was the
county head of the politics and law department. Celebration erupted among the
men. Apparently, this was the county club, the place to be seen, to hang out, and
to get what you want.

The policeman's now-drunken partner came over and said to me, "My colleague told me not to tell you because he said you may be a journalist, but I think
it is okay to say. Do you know how much it costs to come in here?"

"I have no idea," I replied.

"Five hundred yuan [U.S. $60] for the night. But you can have anything that
you want until the sun comes up." Before long, I was out of there and safely
locked into my little room at the county guesthouse.

The morning after, while visiting with the school principal I had come to
meet—just walking distance from the "county club"—I curiously asked him the

total cost for a young person to pay for his or her child to attend four years of high school. "Oh, about five hundred yuan," the principal replied, quite as a matter of fact. My stomach turned. In this county, whose annual per capita income averages around five hundred yuan, and whose precious few can afford to go to school, I had just been told that to get what I want in the county club house costs exactly that—but for one night.

Certainly, many of the problems described are inherent to any country in the midst of historic social and economic transition. Some even blame China's problems on Western influence. But as central as any of the causes given for today's moral muddle is the issue of belief. Epidemic-sized numbers of people are caught suspended somewhere in the vacuous space between collapsed tradition, discredited Communist ideology, and the elusive pursuit of wealth. This crisis of faith has eaten away the bedrock beneath ongoing efforts to construct the People's Republic of China.

SEARCH

During my two years living in Guizhou Province and subsequent return visits, it has been fascinating to observe and listen to people describe a widespread quest for belief—efforts to find a meaningful worldview, peace, satisfying human relationships, moral guidance, and a basis for social justice. In fact, people tell me, the very breadth of the search verifies the depth of the need.

In both urban and rural areas, there has been a rampant revival of all forms of orthodox religion practiced before the Communist Revolution of 1949. A *China Daily* article stated that China's five major religions (Buddhism, Taoism, Islam, Catholicism, and Protestantism) are thriving. For example, 30,000 mosques dot China's northwest; 200,000 monks and nuns serve 13,000 Buddhist temples; and 12,000 churches (75 percent of which have been built since the Cultural Revolution) provide a home for Christians. And those figures report only government sanctioned activities.[7]

Outside the pales of orthodoxy—the place where most people live—the spiritual search is eclectic and unfocused. On the train one day between Guiyang and our home in Duyun, a stylish, twenty-something woman sat across from me. A jade Buddha hung from her neck.

"Do you believe in Buddha?" I asked.

"I guess so."

"What do you mean?"

"My friends and I think this brings us good luck."

"All her friends go to the temple and burn incense when they need something or have a problem," her boyfriend said, jumping into the conversation, "but they don't know who Buddha is. They couldn't pass a test on even the basics of Buddhism."

"And you? What do you believe in?"

"I am not sure. But none of my friends believe in nothing. We all believe that there is something out there. Hey, by the way, have you ever heard of UFOs?"

In the countryside, the revival of religion came earlier than in China's urban areas. Although there are followers of orthodox faiths, most rural residents I have spoken with believe in folk religion: "a belief in a host of benevolent and baleful gods and spirits, and the prevalence of numerous practices such as the makings of offerings to win their aid or the observance of taboos to escape their wrath."[8] During travels across Guizhou's countryside, I have encountered widespread faith in astrology, dream interpretation, witchcraft, palmistry, fortune telling, and other forms of charms and magic, most of which are tied to ancestor worship.[9]

An elderly woman in a village in Guizhou's Zunyi District has two grown sons, now in their late forties, who were not able to marry because of a horrible skin condition. The culprit? They believe that improper burial of their ancestors has left their sons cursed. No cures have worked. In another village, family problems led to a woman's mental illness. The witchdoctor who was consulted told the family members that if they erected a shrine and installed a Buddha, she would recover. The family took up a village-wide collection and built the altar. That was ten years ago; the woman is still ill.

In yet another rural area, "demon fire" (*gui huo*) that the locals described to me was seen hovering around a village home several nights before the couple that lived there was tragically killed by a downed electrical wire.

Though relaxed government policy (relative to the era of Mao Zedong) has created a degree of space for religion's revival, continued marginalization of religion, combined with rapid social change and spiritual hunger, has created fertile ground for the emergence of extreme belief systems. Falun Gong is the best example of a quasireligious movement that has swept the nation. And it is not the only one that fits no religious category but its own.[10]

THE STONE THRESHOLD

The question of belief is also part of the reason two friends and I traveled to a remote township, accessible only by Jeep, in Guizhou's most northwestern corner, known as the Stone Threshold (*Shimenkan*). At an elevation of over six thousand feet, the mountain region that surrounds Shimenkan, Wumeng Shan, is one of the most rugged and poor areas in the province.

The most numerous ethnic group in the region is the Big Flowery Miao (*Da Hua Miao*), one of a dozen or so Miao subgroupings. The Miao have long been a despised people. In fact, several Chinese told me of a Western scholar who suggested that the two most oppressed peoples in the world have been the Jews and the Miao. Even today, prejudiced Chinese use the word *Miao* the way racists in the United States use the term *nigger*.

Of all the Miao subgroups, the Big Flowery Miao have been the most oppressed. Just over one hundred years ago, for example, their ethnic neighbors in northwest Guizhou, the Yi people, though in the minority, enslaved many of them. Treated as less than human, the Big Flowery Miao were housed with the animals and forced to eat out of the same stone troughs the animals used.[11]

Previously unknown and isolated, Shimenkan was put on the map by a foreigner: Samuel Pollard (1864–1915), a British missionary with the United Methodist Church, who moved to Shimenkan in 1904. Even to Pollard, an experienced missionary, Shimenkan was the most wretched place he had seen in China.

After relocating to Shimenkan, at the time a village of a dozen families, Pollard lived the lifestyle of the Big Flowery Miao. He wore the same clothes as the Miao, refused to ride on horseback or in sedan chairs as other privileged people did, did not carry weapons, used the Miao language to communicate, ate potatoes and wheat porridge with the common folk, and initially lived in a thatched-roof hut like everyone else.[12] Pollard's lifestyle authenticated his message of God made flesh in Christ.

To Pollard's amazement, many of the Miao ancestral legends and children's rhymes were consistent with biblical themes: a creation story, a flood myth, and even Noah's ark.[13] For many Miao, the rest of the Bible filled in their gaps. In less than two decades, Pollard and his coworkers saw the conversion of more than ten thousand people. Churches, schools, medical clinics, a soccer field, and even a swimming pool, followed. Mountainous and remote Shimenkan became known as "Heaven from Abroad" (*haiwai tianguo*). Over time, locals who previously feared doctors were studying medicine. Two of their own later went on to win doctorates. Pollard and his Miao coworkers even developed a written language for the Miao and translated the New Testament and other literature into the language. Even today, Shimenkan's Big Flowery Miao continue to use the Pollard script.

According to China scholar Zhang Tan's thorough examination of Pollard's life and the history of Shimenkan, there are no believers left.[14] The primary reason Zhang gives for this abrupt change is that the liberation that the Miao's savior had given them was a freedom of the soul, not of politics and the flesh. When another savior appeared—the Chinese Communist Party—that could provide economic and political liberation, people began turning to socialism. Faith in Christ, Zhang concludes, expired without a whimper.

Based on Zhang Tan's conclusions, I expected to find Shimenkan a fascinating piece of prerevolution, foreign-missionary history. Nothing more. Even so, I could not help but wonder, given the crisis of belief I have observed in other areas of Guizhou Province, whether the faith of ten thousand believers had in fact simply disappeared like a lost tribe.

Seven hours from Weining's county town, over dirt-packed gravel and sometimes-sloppy mud roads, we finally arrived in Shimenkan. Constant rain and thick fog made the trip seem longer than it actually was. Then there it was, just like the picture in Zhang Tan's book: Samuel Pollard's former home, now used as the Shimenkan township government offices.

Market day was just wrapping up when we pulled in the driveway, so we had many observers. The Big Flowery Miao I had read so much about circled around us. We exchanged the curious stares of distant strangers.

We were then led on a tour of Shimenkan's remnants of the past. Though a large earthquake shook the area in 1948 and destroyed many of the buildings, the original teacher-student dormitory, parts of the school, a leprosy clinic, Pollard's home, the soccer field, and the swimming pool remain.

An enthusiastic band of locals followed us, including five women who were never far behind, enjoying the excitement. Having read the history of the Big Flowery Miao and Shimenkan, we found it indeed remarkable to observe firsthand all that had been accomplished in an area that until 1958 was accessible only by narrow walking paths.

As daylight turned to dusk, light rain and a blanket of fog created an almost eerie atmosphere. The last stop of the tour was Samuel Pollard's tomb. Pollard died of typhoid in 1915 while tending to locals with the same disease. He and another missionary who followed him, Herbert Goldsworthy, are both buried on the top of a hill that overlooks Shimenkan. Our entourage, now about twenty strong, slowly worked its way up through waist-high brush in the heavy fog. A local official led the single-file line, thrashing rainwater off the bushes.

Pollard's and Goldsworthy's tombs, originally built by the Miao churches, were badly damaged during the Cultural Revolution but later reconstructed by the Weining County government. Three languages on the tombs—English, Mandarin, and Miao—commemorate their lives and contribution. Our group milled around the tombs for about twenty minutes, reflecting on Shimenkan, the Big Flowery Miao people, and Samuel Pollard.

As we tracked back down the hill toward the road, I walked behind several of the Miao women, my mind full of thoughts of their past and questions about their present.

"Do you believe in Jesus?" I quietly asked the woman who walked in front of me, eager to know for myself if they or others in the area had carried on their prerevolution faith.

"Yes, I believe," the woman replied, turning her head with a smile.

"I am a believer, as well," I replied, "That means we are one family." I sensed that she was not the only one.

As we continued to walk, one of my travel companions asked the women if there were only elderly women in their church. No, they said, there are men as well, and young people and middle-aged people. Their church is their community.

"Are there many churches in Shimenkan?" I followed.

"*Duo de hen!*" (Very many!), she replied with a sparkle in her eye.

It was almost dark and time for dinner. The tour was over. We did not know if we would see the Miao women again, so we said good-bye. An older woman came up to me and, with strong hands that had obviously farmed for many years, firmly grasped mine. With a penetrating look I will not forget, she said, "We will meet again in heaven. Pray for us, we will pray for you."

The Big Flowery Miao women, dressed in traditional hemp skirts, blue blazers, and muddy rain boots, stood quietly at the turn in the road as we walked off. As their figures began to disappear in the mist, they began to sing. We stopped, turned, and listened.

The first song sounded like a Miao melody. It was beautiful, but I could not understand it. Then they began to sing a chorus in Mandarin, well known among believers of Christ around China: *"Zai Yesuli woman shi yi jiaren"* ("In Jesus we are one family"). As they sang, I could see through the fog that several of them were wiping tears from their eyes with aprons that hung from their Miao skirts. They had met family; we had met living history—and vice versa.

With that taste of faith, I realized that Zhang Tan was wrong, or at least his information was incomplete. Religion, after all, appeared to be alive and well in Shimenkan. When we went for breakfast the following morning, there they were: the same women from the previous evening, standing patiently down the road, now accompanied by several men. They walked up to us and presented us with a few dozen hard-boiled eggs and then returned to wait for us at their distant post.

With a bit of arm twisting, we were able to convince our hosts to allow us to visit a Miao village. Our tour the previous day had been around the immediate vicinity of the township headquarters. We wanted more. The most convenient village for us to visit, it turned out, was the home of the women who had sung to us.

Within an hour we were off to their village, our urban hosts appearing less than enthusiastic about having to visit a poor Big Flowery Miao village. We slipped and slid down a mud path, as shepherds, wearing thick wool capes to protect them from the cool and rain, tended their sheep and goats on the lush shrub-covered mountains that surrounded us. Animals dotted the expansive landscape. The air was moist and clear. Before long, our entourage had arrived at their village of hovels made of thick earthen walls and thatch roofs. Pigs moved in slow motion as chickens dashed through the inch-thick muck that covered the village grounds. Big Flowery Miao began to gather as we mingled, standing around one of their homes.

We remained in the village just a few hours, chatting and even singing. My companions and I were struck by the sense of dignity among the people. Yes, they were very poor. But compared to dozens of other villages I have visited in Guizhou, there was an absence of apology for their backwardness (I am usually overwhelmed upon arrival with self-deprecating excuses for the people's poverty). These villagers made no excuses. In fact, *Moxi* (Moses), who appeared to be the local leader, stated confidently, "We are poor, but we are rich."

Moses, as the village spokesman, said that forty out of the fifty families in the village were Christians. With the easing of government restrictions on religion after Deng Xiaoping came to power, a significant number of them had begun to follow Christ in the 1980s. The villagers gather weekly to worship. "What difference does your faith make to you?" I asked Moses as we stood around, county and township government officials included.

Moses replied that under the government's policy to protect freedom of religion, their community was strong. Then, calibrating his response, he added that they did not smoke, did not drink, and did not carouse. His facial expressions communicated that there was a lot more he could have shared, indicating that perhaps freedom of religion has only gone so far.

Coming full circle from the rhetoric of the revolution, I have thought how fascinating and noteworthy it is that during this transitional period in China's history, the search for meaning and community continues as it does: from shrines that dot Guizhou's countryside, to overflowing state-approved places of worship, to young women wearing jade Buddhas, to the Big Flowery Miao of Shimenkan, and the members of Falun Gong. The heart of the matter is that the people's quest will play an essential, albeit subtle, role in determining the nation's evolving future.

SUGGESTIONS FOR FURTHER READING

Aikman, David. "China's Search for Its Soul." *American Spectator* 33, no. 2 (March 2000): 22–25.

Eastman, Lloyd E. "Gods, Ghosts, and Ancestors: The Popular Religion." Pp. 41–61, in *Family, Field, and Ancestors: Constancy and Change in China's Social and Economic History, 1550–1949*. New York: Oxford University Press, 1988.

Florcruz, Jaime A., Joshua Cooper Ramo, Mia Turner, and Edward Barnes. "Inside China's Search for Its Soul." *Time* 154, no. 14 (October 4, 1999): 68–72.

Kendall, R. Elliott. *Beyond the Clouds: The Story of Samuel Pollard*. London: Cargate, 1947.

Lambert, Tony. *The Resurrection of the Chinese Church*. Weaton, Ill.: OMF, 1994.

"Popular Religion and Secret Societies." Pp. 285–314, in *Sources of Chinese Tradition*, Vol. 2, edited by Wm. Theodore De Bary, Wing Tsit Chan, and Chester Tan. New York: Columbia University Press, 1960.

Xiao, Hongyan. "Falun Gong and the Ideological Crisis of the Chinese Communist Party: Marxist Atheism vs. Vulgar Theism." *East Asia: An International Quarterly* 19 (2001): 123–44.

Yang, C. K. *Religion in Chinese Society: A Study of Contemporary Social Functions of Religion and Some of Their Historical Factors*. Berkeley: University of California Press, 1961.

18
The Revolution at Fifty Years

This image, like the one on the book's cover, was painted by Long Kanghua, a local painter from a rural county in southern Guizhou Province who paints from "the people's perspective." Entitled Old Grindstone (Lao Mo, *136 x 136 cm, 1998), this painting intends to represent the lives of many Guizhou farmers. Long Kanghua says that many farmers' lives in Guizhou have slowly gone round and round, like a heavy old grindstone, yet have produced precious little for their efforts.*

In the spring of 1999, the fiftieth anniversary year of the People's Republic of China, large-scale riots paralyzed two cities in Guizhou Province for days. One took place in Liuzhi, to the west, where laid-off coal miners threatened to clog a major railway by sitting on the tracks—human shields—until they were paid long-overdue severance allowances. The other occurred in Zunyi, to the north, where "thousands," according to eyewitnesses, clashed with security forces. Ironically, the conflict in Zunyi occurred within walking distance of the Long March site, where in 1935 Mao Zedong was made de facto leader of the Communist movement and chief architect of the revolution.

Neither story made it into the Western or Chinese press, but according to those who were at the scene in Zunyi, a few dozen neighbors had been protesting around a noodle shop after a teenage woman from the countryside who had been working there suddenly died. The neighbors believed that the shop owner had murdered her. The shop owner said she had died from a sudden illness. Unconvinced and angry, the neighbors set the eatery on fire. The authorities moved in, roughing up the demonstrators in the process.

Like a lit match dropped into a pool of gasoline, the conflict erupted, thousands coming out to protest what they believed to be unfair treatment by government security forces. What began as a call for justice by a small circle exploded into a full-scale outcry against the city government. The disturbance continued for several days, the mayor eventually talking down the crowds through a bullhorn and explaining that an autopsy showed that the woman had indeed been sick. And all of this in Zunyi—a landmark of the revolution.

More recently, a Hong Kong newspaper reported protesting workers in Guizhou's capital, Guiyang, on Labor Day, May 1, 2002: "They shouted 'Down with Corruption! We Want to Live,' and other slogans, demanding that the authorities face squarely the hardships faced by laid-off and unemployed workers."[1]

Dramatic progress and staggering challenges, now coupled with an increasing willingness of people to act on their grievances, illustrate China's paradox today. Though protests are on the rise in cities across China, especially in the decaying factory towns that speckle the map with orange, state-owned rust marks, dissatisfaction is not limited to the country's urban centers. Farmers as well, in growing numbers, have been more actively speaking out against injustice.

Anecdotes abound. In Long Branch village in Zunyi, farmer Wang explained one evening why his friend had snatched the camera of a township government official. And stomped it into the sodden earth. The previous year the township civil affairs official had come to inspect their flood-damaged village, said Lao Wang, his face a picture of a brown, sun-dried tomato. The official had had his picture taken with the farmer in front of his flooded field, promising to show the photo to the county government to secure funding assistance for his misfortune. Not one penny arrived, though the farmers had heard that funds had been dispersed from the county to the township government. One year later, heavy rain again damaged the farmer's field. Once again, the township bureaucrat came, pledging anew his commitment to serve the people and to help the farmer secure assistance. This time, when the official asked the farmer to take a photo with him, the farmer refused, complaining that last year's photo yielded nothing. Brushing off the peasant's rejection, the official told one of his colleagues to stand in while the third traveling companion snapped the shot. Outraged, the man rushed over, grabbed the camera, threw it on the ground, and promptly crushed it under foot. I asked these farmers if this would have happened ten years ago. "Oh, no," came the reply. "But times are changing."

Before moving to Guizhou, I had thought that regional economic disparity was the hot issue in China's hinterland, the flashpoint of present complaints and potential instability. The visible differences between coast and interior certainly make clear that it is an important theme. I had imagined the country to be like a large flat surface, slanted downward from the interior toward the coast—resources, labor, and talent sliding east. Indeed, viewed from Beijing, Shanghai, or the United States, regional disparities dominate one's perspective.

At the aggregate level, provincial economic growth figures confirm the imbalance. In two decades China has gone from one of the world's most egalitarian societies to one of the most unequal, in terms of distribution of wealth, income, and opportunity.[2] In fact, measured by human development indicators, the difference between China's most developed and least-developed provinces is comparable to that between the Western industrial countries and the poorest countries in the world.[3]

Not as obvious, however, are the inequalities within provinces that distance and more general regional data conceal. With the passage of time, firsthand observation revealed that the most fundamental standard-of-living inequality in China exists between the country's rural and urban areas. Though significant and widening, the coast–interior divide, in relative terms, is less dramatic than the gaping "two-caste" split between the countryside and cities, particularly in China's hinterland.[4] The World Bank says that in other countries, the ratio of urban to rural incomes is normally below 1.5 and rarely exceeds 2.0, but in China, real urban incomes are as much as 4.0 times real rural incomes, if urban residents' welfare benefits of various kinds are included.[5] When combined, urban–rural and coast–interior disparities leave western farmers, like Shui Jianhua in Splendid Village, as China's poorest of the poor.

So are the farmers of western China ready to revolt, to take up hoes, bricks, and steel pipes and overwhelm the cities? My observations and interviews do not support this. In fact, most of the hundreds of people I spoke with in smalltown and rural Guizhou do not resent the disparity. Rather, they view the differential as an opportunity, a chance to travel to and work in the country's urban centers, both those in nearby cities within Guizhou and those in distant economic powerhouses like Shanghai, Guangzhou, and Shenzhen. What the people of Guizhou—not only the rural poor, but also the urbanites—communicated consistently was that the hot issue in China's hinterland, the engine of present complaint and potential hostility, is not economic disparity. It is the corrosive corruption that monopolizes opportunity and resources.

From Guizhou I traveled to Beijing to meet a former vice minister who had been involved in the economic reforms of the 1980s. During the course of our private conversation, this man told me that corruption in China now surpasses pre-1949 levels, which, during the Nationalist regime, was credited as a chief cause of Chiang Kai-shek's defeat. Actual or perceived, the observation from someone of such high rank caught my attention. The next day, while meeting with a Chinese scholar, I referred to the retired official's statement. "Oh, there's nothing new about that," the professor replied. "That's what we all say." I gulped and returned to Guizhou.

Chinese economist Hu Angang calls corruption China's largest "social pollution" (*shehui wuran*), accounting for between 13 and 16 percent of China's GDP.[6] That would make China, in dollar value, among the most corrupt countries in the world. The people detest corruption because it serves to unfairly dominate resources that would otherwise benefit them, particularly in the area of social services like public health, education, and infrastructure improvements. The common person sees corruption as rot in the system—a failure of the revolution, a wrong that directly affects them.

Corruption often has a human face: that of a factory manager, a township official, a village chief, or a local policeman. How many farmers during my travels pointed to their pitiful dirt roads, for example, and said to me, "The money was sent down to fix our road, but it went to local officials' pockets instead." A village elementary school teacher told me how a full one-third of their school's meager annual budget was spent on *one* banquet, wining and dining visiting government officials—"on inspection"—who never asked once about how the school was doing, while they feasted on local village specialties and drink. Or consider the factory manager who lives like a king, while workers file out the door, unable to collect their wages.

Dishonesty is at the heart of the problem. A 2001 *Far Eastern Economic Review* article cited officially published figures to illustrate the extent of the quandary:

- Tax evasion accounts for 50 percent of taxes due in the private economy, while total losses from tax evasion are 100 billion yuan (U.S. $12 billion) a year.
- Counterfeit goods and substandard goods account for 40 percent of all products made in China, with losses running at 200 billion yuan a year.
- Two-thirds of the biggest state firms produce false accounts.
- The underground economy is the equivalent of 20 percent of GDP (actually twice that, say independent estimates).
- On an average infrastructure or building project, 15–20 percent of the spending is lost to bribery, fraud, and poor-quality work.[7]

While the government must continue to try to tackle the far-reaching problem of corruption—which Jiang Zemin has called a "matter of life and death for the party and the state"—it has simultaneously stepped up its efforts to address regional disparities.[8] Primary among these initiatives is the Develop the West campaign (*xibu dakaifa*), a high-profile initiative launched by the central government in 2000 to invest more resources in the country's western regions. In its first year, Beijing invested $3.6 billion in seventy-eight medium-sized and large infrastructure projects.[9] I am encouraged by the program, but I am also concerned. On the one hand, efforts to address the people and regions of China's hinterland—those who were not among those "certain groups of people and certain regions to prosper first" during Deng Xiaoping's outward-looking economic growth strategy—are long overdue. And the money is flowing. New expressways, state-of-the-art telecommunications projects, and water conservation initiatives are being built, designed to create the macroeconomic conditions for an improved western economy.

On the other hand, corruption's impact leaves so many "holes in the bucket" that one must wonder about the percentage of assistance that actually arrives at the intended destination. Locals call them "tofu projects": jobs that look good but, because of the skimming of resources during the construction process, end up as "porous" and shoddy products, like fancy highways that develop gaping potholes just months after completion.

A related concern about the Develop the West campaign is based on the reality that the country's economic divide is first and foremost an urban–rural split, not coast–interior. Factoring in the effects of corruption, unless great care is given to the design and implementation of these investments, the campaign may end up strengthening hinterland cities like Guiyang and Duyun, while leaving the rural poor further and further behind—islands of wealth in a sea of poverty.

My emphasis on social justice is not meant to downplay the importance of government initiatives to address widening inequalities among the Chinese people. Rather, it is meant to reflect the gravity of attitudes among ordinary Chinese toward what have become endemic levels of decay in the system. To fully comprehend China's current predicament, however, corruption, inequality, and poverty need to be considered and understood as all of one piece. Taken together, they form a combustible mixture, particularly in China, where the material conditions of the political and economic elite are improving, while the masses, urban and rural—by whom the revolution was championed, fought, and won—are often left observing and sometimes suffering the abuse of the system.[10]

More and more, despite the widespread economic and social advances, people across China are standing up and expressing their dissatisfaction. The trend is clear. During the 1990s, collective protests grew fourfold, increasing from 8,700 in 1993 to 32,000 in 1999.[11] Not surprisingly, among the reasons for complaint and action by the people, corruption regularly tops the list of people queried in polls.[12]

Rapidly rising resistance—like the events in Zunyi and Liuzhi—is not necessarily an immediate threat to the regime itself. The majority of protests are localized, unorganized, and isolated. They are typically specific efforts to redress injustices for which local government officials are responsible, like unpaid wages and financial scams.[13]

The increase in public protests is due to a greater willingness by the government—beginning in the 1990s—to tolerate sporadic unrest as a price of progress and a cost of reform. The government appears to allow such opposition for at least three reasons. First, the authorities realize that limited acceptance of resistance helps make up for what are otherwise few formal mechanisms—like labor unions—through which the people's interests can be formally expressed and pressures relieved.[14] Second, the government continues to possess significant strength and sufficient self-confidence in its ability to keep protests largely isolated and localized.[15] And third, the government believes that such activity brings some degree of accountability—consequence—to the corrupt behavior of local officials.

While the rise in incidences of protest is significant, and widespread dissatisfaction with corruption and inequality is noteworthy, it is important not to overstate the case. Most of Guizhou's inhabitants—rural and urban—are fully engaged in their lives' common pursuits: Lao Tang labors with his pushcart in downtown Duyun, Li Fangfang delivers her 2,000 bags of milk each day, Chen Dongfang struggles upstream to educate his village's children, and the fertilizer executive works on his golf game. The challenge for the China observer is to hold together the paradox and contradictions of *both* the people's fulfillment and their struggle. To do otherwise would be to miss China's complex reality.

The alarm, however, has sounded. While one hopes that nationwide instability is unlikely, one cannot say it is impossible. Things could get worse. A recent survey of social trends by the Chinese Academy of Social Sciences reports that China has entered a period of "recurring crisis."[16] Kang Xiaoguang adds that events of profound political, economic, or social crisis could touch off general and lasting turbulence. "Factors such as a financial crisis, unfairness (especially corruption), inequality (and especially poverty), and population flow, are all 'tinder,' and what ignites the crisis could be economic decline, bank runs, a Taiwan crisis, etc."[17]

An irony of the post-Mao era is that a rapidly expanding economy has undermined the authority of the political leaders and the government system that made it all possible. With Deng Xiaoping advocating "economics in command," rather than "politics in command," a more decentralized political-economic structure has arisen. Individuals and groups can now voice their own views and pursue their own interests, thereby setting in motion processes in society, politics, and culture that no one could have anticipated.[18] This dynamic has resulted in the emergence of social forces that both balance and destabilize.

Mao Zedong's legitimacy, just as the movement he led, was rooted in the longings of the Chinese people and the promises of the revolution. Early declarations were based on a vision of liberation, equality, justice, and national power. Richard Baum, who describes Mao as a "peasant, revolutionary, philosopher-king," explains that his life was "deeply paradoxical and self-contradictory. His millenarian vision of a world without egotism and greed, without mandarins, landlords, or bureaucrats, had inspired legendary feats of revolutionary heroism and endurance. Yet the very radicalism of Mao's vision, and the draconian means used to implement it, had visited great suffering upon the Chinese people."[19]

Mao's new-society vision and the ideological means by which he mobilized the people to pursue it, created the basis for the Communist Party's legitimacy for the first three decades after "liberation" in 1949. The result, however, was destruction and poverty. The disastrous Great Leap Famine and the Cultural Revolution represent the twin towers of this calamity. China's independence and self-sufficiency came at great cost.

When Deng Xiaoping rose to power in 1978, he inherited a tired mandate. By opening China to the outside world and implementing pragmatic policies that stimulated economic production, Deng helped the country turn a corner. As standards of living began to improve, rapid economic growth became the engine of the Communist Party's legitimacy. Ideology continued to play a role, but more to define the fault lines of the political struggles in the 1980s than to stir the people to revolutionary loyalty and action. The stresses of reform resulted in the Tiananmen tragedy of 1989.

Despite Deng Xiaoping's pragmatism of the 1980s, a fundamental recognition of a market economy—China's "socialist market economy"—did not fully take place until the Fourteenth Party Congress in November 1992, following Deng's landmark trip to southern China earlier in the year. With it, economic growth became firmly established as the basis for the legitimacy of the Communist Party. In so doing, Deng Xiaoping saved the revolution by redefining it. While pitching the platitudes of his predecessors, he rationalized the revolution in ways that supported continued material gains for the people, while accepting the unavoidable inequalities.

With Jiang Zemin's ascent, representing the rise of a third generation of leadership, the trajectory of economic reform has continued. So have the inequalities and contradictions. Yet while the economy has continued to grow, the ever-evolving rhetoric of the revolution has become increasingly hollow. Furthermore, the relative status of political groupings has also taken a dramatic shift. During Mao's rule, the masses—urban workers and peasants—provided the social foundation of the Communist Party and served as the vanguard of the revolution. With Deng's rise and the reforms he initiated, elite classes began to emerge.[20] During the 1980s everyone won, elites and masses alike. But in the 1990s, it was a decade of "winner takes all," in which the position of the masses declined relative to that of the political, economic, and even intellectual elites. This signified a great reversal in the status of China's social classes, effectively turning on its head the original social structure and political ideals of the revolution.

As Jiang Zemin consolidated power throughout the 1990s, he, like leaders from every previous generation, was left to face the legitimacy issue, but now with the levers of ideology and economic growth diminished in their utility. Under Jiang's watch, corruption, growing inequalities, and the increasingly advantageous positions of the elite have led to the decline of the Communist Party in the eyes of the masses. And this despite the historic material gains most of them have experienced—even in Guizhou Province—during the last twenty years. Indeed, it is staggering to think that between 1978 and 1996 China's gross national product quadrupled. Jiang Zemin and the new generation to follow must address the issue of how the people—masses and elite alike—view the Communist Party. How and why do they or do they not invest the regime with a stamp of approval? The Communist Party must regain the people's trust.

Jiang Zemin appears to be aware of this. In February 2000, like Deng Xiaoping nearly ten years earlier, Jiang traveled south to launch what has become a critically important initiative. Jiang gave a speech in Guangdong Province, at which he introduced his "Three Represents" (*sange daibiao*) theory. In summing up the Party's history, Jiang claimed that it has always represented the most advanced productive forces, the most advanced culture, and the fundamental interests of the broad masses of the Chinese people.[21] The "Three Represents" campaign has become an effort to provide a framework that bridges the revolutionary rhetoric of the past with both contemporary culture and traditional Chinese civilization, while attempting to shore up support from key constituencies in the present. The Central

Party School's newspaper described Jiang's "Three Represents" theory as "the basis of our party, its foundation for governing and the source of its strength."[22]

In appealing to the economic elite—"the most advanced productive forces"— while still reaching out to the broad masses—"the fundamental interests of the broad masses of the Chinese people"—Jiang appears to be trying to address the "winner takes all" (read: elite takes all) predicament of the 1990s. Either that, or he is rationalizing the supreme position of the elite while continuing to pay lip service to the masses. Kang Xiaoguang says,

> By controlling and implementing policies slanted toward benefiting elites, the govern- ment has effectively won the political support of society's elites. At the same time, in controlling the policy process, the government is listening more and more to the voices of society by way of "consultations." As the most important object of consulta- tion, the intellectual and economic elites have gained more and more opportunities to express their interests. I believe that the "Three Represents" is a political declaration of elite alliance. This declaration indicates that the alliance between the political elite, the economic elite, and the intellectual elite is moving toward institutionalization.[23]

The trend toward convergence among elite groups often comes at the expense of the masses. Because effective mechanisms for the enforcement of social justice or the distribution of resources are few, and because the interests of the privileged are well entrenched, the masses may very well be left further and further behind.

So what about the masses, like those who live along the Long March trail, the elder country-girl-turned-mayor Meng Shihua and farmer Chen Meixian in Big Nest Village? Do they feel reassured by Jiang Zemin's pronouncement that their fundamental interests will now be cared for in ways these have not been before? Are their opinions sought after? Do people listen to Beijing? Do they care? In my experience, the answer is no. One of the government's greatest challenges is that the successive campaigns of the last five decades have left people tired. They have turned a deaf ear to the rhetoric.

With ideology all but bankrupt and the cure-all of rapid economic growth less and less potent, how will the Communist Party overcome the legitimacy gap between itself and the people it rules? And how will the Party manage the relation- ship between the masses and the elites? These are the tasks that face the fourth generation of China's political leadership. The question is as relevant in Beijing as it is in rural Guizhou. How to redefine, yet again, the promises of the revolution— and reform—in a way that attracts the people's trust, while deepening government capacities to better represent and regulate the interests of the majority of its peo- ple?[24] The beginning of the answer lies in a more authentic understanding of the peoples' perspective.

Many of the fourth-generation leaders are familiar with China's grassroots per- spective, having experienced the harsh realities of rural life firsthand in years past. Some lived with the peasants as "sent-down youth" during the 1960s and 1970s.[25]

A significant number of others have spent time in responsible provincial positions of power as part of government leadership-training programs.[26]

Hu Jintao, the emerging principal of the fourth-generation leadership, did both. During the Cultural Revolution, shortly after graduating college, he was sent to backward Gansu Province to work, emerging later as the local leader of the Communist Youth League there and then as the organization's national leader in the early 1980s. Like other "rising stars" before and after him, Hu was then sent to "practice" his skills in Guizhou Province, famous in Beijing for having a high concentration of all of the country's most stubborn problems within its mountainous borders.[27]

While in Guizhou Province as party secretary (1985 to 1988), Hu demonstrated a sincere interest in understanding local perspective.[28] And this at a time when many leaders had little idea of how ordinary people lived. When in Guizhou Province, Hu Jintao would frequently visit people's homes. Shortly after arriving in Guizhou, he dropped by the apartment of a Qinghua University classmate. Finding his friend not there, he stayed for two hours chatting with his friend's parents. Only after he left did the friend's parents slowly realize that he was the new party secretary.

Guizhou also provided Hu Jintao's most severe test.[29] Students across China, encouraged by Hu Yaobang's political reform movement, began pro democracy demonstrations in late 1986. Students at Guizhou University suddenly occupied the main lecture hall. As a sense of crisis gripped the leadership in Beijing, Hu personally visited the campus and persuaded the students to leave. Hu "did a beautiful job winning over the students by treating them as equals," says Ge Shiru, a Guizhou-based writer who followed the events. Now in Beijing and helping to lead the country, Hu Jintao and others like him are challenged to continue to connect with the masses.

Of more importance to the common person in Guizhou Province than the quality of central government leaders is whether or not local bureaucrats listen to Beijing and govern well. Or will the rhetoric continue to be the distant garble of an emperor who is as far away as the sky is high, divorced from the peoples' reality? If the government officials and the people I got to know in Guizhou are any indication, society has moved beyond the promises of the revolution, however defined. Local government officials parrot the words—"that the Communist Party has always represented the most advanced productive forces, the most advanced culture, and the fundamental interests of the broad masses of the Chinese people"—but their actual motivation and methods of governance operate at a different level, sometimes consistent with the interests of the people, but often not.

And how do central government leaders act when increasingly powerful local leaders are no longer as motivated to action by Beijing's slogans, but rather behave more and more in their own self-interests? David M. Lampton once compared the phenomenon to the captain of a ship, seemingly firmly in control, but not realizing that his steering wheel was not connected to the rudder.[30] The challenges of effective local governance in China are enormous.

Perhaps the greatest opportunity for the fourth generation to regain legitimacy for the Communist Party in the eyes of the people would be through creating the conditions for widespread social reform.[31] Whether private school initiatives like Principal Bi's computer school in Duyun, Project Hope's care for poor children, the growth of religion, or other "social strength" initiatives, the Party's ability, both at the central government level and at the local level, to cultivate strong social foundations is critical to the country's future. A rapid empowerment of civil society would yield great payoff for the Party and simultaneously benefit the people. A policy environment created by top-down legislation and support, met by a bottom-up response of increased civic participation by the people, could combine to create an atmosphere that enables society—the people—to better meet its own needs.

At issue is the government's ability to deepen its own capacities through institution building, as well as its resolve to strengthen the role of social organizations that constitute civil society.[32] This would best be done through the development of a more robust society, brought about by rationalizing and liberalizing the regulations for nongovernmental and nonprofit organizations. This would unleash social creativity. Grassroots cooperation can solve problems that government and business cannot address. Moreover, as Robert Putnam points out, successful collaborative efforts build a "trusting society" and are self-reinforcing and cumulative, as they establish a "cultural template" that facilitates future collaboration.[33] Progress in social reform would help build back the social capital deficit that has plagued China since the 1950s, just after the promises of the revolution were made.[34]

"Whether China can accumulate this type of social capital rapidly and successfully, as it has with business capital, bears directly on the sustainability of all China has accomplished," says Carol Lee Hamrin. "It would appear that 'social cohesion,' not 'social stability,' is what matters most. Economic productivity without social cohesion is a house built on sand."[35]

Positively stated, greater social cohesion—healthy cooperation among the state, business, and nonprofit actors in win–win–win combinations—could undergird a new phase of economic growth for the country.[36] It would also create the conditions for meaningful and sustainable political reform. As China's new generation of leadership evolves, a government-enabled social revolution could potentially be as important as any of those Mao or Deng orchestrated.

However, the obstacles to success in this direction are enormous. In particular, the "class struggle" mentality and the once-much-touted concept of "continuous revolution" that characterized the first several decades of the regime, which at the time led to a fundamental breakdown of trust in society, continue to cast their long shadows on the ability of people to cooperate.[37]

It will take strong and effective leadership to implement needed changes, particularly because local interests are becoming deeply entrenched and because many believe that the more difficult decisions of reform have yet to be faced. And these efforts will need to be effective not only in Beijing, where Hu Jintao now sits, but also as far as Big Nest Village in northern Guizhou Province.

Meanwhile, the stories of fulfillment and struggle in Guizhou will continue, full of contradictions, complexities, and, most of all, the paradox of the revolution. Together, Guizhou's 36 million people, like all of China's population, will continue along a challenging, painful, and yet hopeful search for modernity. It is a human drama that, when viewed from the bottom looking up and from the hinterland looking back to the coast, reminds us that for all the dramatic advances and monumental challenges, China is still in search of itself.

SUGGESTIONS FOR FURTHER READING

Fewsmith, Joseph. *China since Tiananmen: The Politics of Transition.* Cambridge, U.K.: Cambridge University Press, 2001.

Fukuyama, Francis. *Trust: The Social Virtues and the Creation of Prosperity.* New York: Free Press, 1995.

Goldman, Merle, and Roderick MacFarquhar, eds. *The Paradox of Post-Mao Reforms.* Cambridge, Mass.: Harvard University Press, 1999.

Grindle, Marilee S. *Getting Good Government: Capacity Building in Public Sectors of Developing Countries.* Cambridge, Mass.: Harvard University Press, 1997.

Jensen, Lionel M. "Everyone's a Player, but the Nation's a Loser: Corruption in Contemporary China." Pp. 37–67, in *China Beyond the Headlines,* edited by Timothy B. Weston and Lionel M. Jensen. Lanham, Md.: Rowman & Littlefield, 2000.

Li, Cheng. *China's Leaders: The New Generation.* Lanham, Md.: Rowman & Littlefield, 2001.

Pei, Minxin. "China's Governance Crisis." *Foreign Affairs* 81, no. 5 (September–October 2002): 96–111.

Perry, Elizabeth J., and Mark Selden, eds. *Chinese Society: Change, Conflict and Resistance.* New York: Routledge, 2000.

Pye, Lucian W. *The Spirit of Chinese Politics.* Cambridge, Mass.: MIT Press, 1968.

Wang, Shaoguang. "The Social and Political Implications of China's WTO Membership." *Journal of Contemporary China* 9, no. 25 (November 2000): 373–405.

Notes

FOREWORD

1. For the provincial income figure for Guizhou in 2000, see *Shehui Lan Pishu, 2000* (Blue Book of Chinese Society) (Beijing: Social Sciences Documentation Publishing House, 2002), 146.

INTRODUCTION

1. Harrison E. Salisbury, *The Long March: The Untold Story* (New York: Harper & Row, 1985), 107.

2. For an earlier bookmark in time, written at the time of the Communist Revolution, see A. Doak Barnett, *China on the Eve of Communist Takeover* (New York: Praeger, 1963), which documents Barnett's observations of grassroots China from 1947 to 1949.

3. The other ICWA China fellows include C. Walter Young (1931–1933), Albert Ravenholt (1947–1949), Anthony Dickes (1962–1968), Geoffrey Oldham (1962–1965), Joseph Battat (1975–1979), and Cheng Li (1993–1995). Barnett's and Li's ICWA reports were subsequently published as books: see A. Doak Barnett, *China on the Eve of Communist Takeover* (New York: Praeger, 1963), and Cheng Li, *Rediscovering China* (Lanham, Md.: Rowman & Littlefield, 1997).

4. A. Doak Barnett, *China's Far West: Four Decades of Change* (Boulder, Colo.: Westview Press, 1993), Preface.

5. Cheng Li, *Rediscovering China* (Lanham, Md.: Rowman & Littlefield, 1997), 6.

CHAPTER 1

1. The per capita GNP difference between Guizhou and Shanghai grew from 7.3 times in 1990 to 12 times in 2000. See Cheng Li, *China's Leaders* (Lanham, Md.: Rowman & Littlefield, 2001), 190.

2. Edward A. McCord, "Local Military Power and Elite Formation: The Liu Family of Xingyi County, Guizhou," in *Chinese Local Elites and Patterns of Dominance,* ed. Joseph W.

Esherick and Mary Bachus Rankin (Berkeley: University of California Press, 1990), 162–88.

3. Harrison E. Salisbury, *The Long March: The Untold Story* (New York: Harper & Row, 1985), 106–7.

4. For a literary perspective on the difficult realities of life during the 1930s in Guizhou Province, see Jian Xian'ai, "The Salt Calamity," *Short Story International* 21, no. 116 (February 1997): 18–40. Jian Xian'ai was a contemporary of Lu Xun. I translated this story for China's Foreign Language Bureau in 1992.

5. Theodore H. White and Annalee Jacob, "War," in *The China Reader: Republican China*, ed. Franz Schurmann and Orville Schell (New York: Random House, 1967), 258.

6. Sandu County is the only autonomous Shui county in China; over half of all 380,000 Shui people live in Sandu County.

7. Dali L. Yang, *Calamity and Reform in China: State, Rural Society, and Institutional Change since the Great Leap Famine* (Stanford, Calif.: Stanford University Press, 1996), vii.

8. The Great Leap Forward (1958–1961) was an attempt launched by Mao Zedong to raise economic productivity dramatically through mass mobilization, rapid expansion, and revolutionary fervor. For an extensive study of the Great Leap Forward, the subsequent famine, and the effect it had on peasant and leadership attitudes, see Dali L. Yang, *Calamity and Reform in China* (Stanford, Calif.: Stanford University Press, 1996), and Jasper Becker, *Hungry Ghosts: Mao's Secret Famine* (New York: Henry Holt, 1998).

9. Yang, *Calamity*, 38.

10. For an in-depth discussion of China's Third Front construction, see Barry Naughton, "The Third Front: Defence Industrialization in the Chinese Interior," *The China Quarterly* 115 (September 1988): 351–86.

11. Naughton, "Third Front," 365.

12. Ezra F. Vogel, *One Step Ahead in China: Guangdong under Reform* (Cambridge, Mass.: Harvard University Press, 1989), 125–60.

CHAPTER 2

1. My travel companion was a young Chinese man, a good friend who grew up in Guizhou's mountains.

2. Lucien Bianco, *Origins of the Chinese Revolution, 1915–1949*, trans. Muriel Bell (Stanford, Calif.: Stanford University Press, 1971), 67.

3. Edgar Snow, *Red Star over China* (New York: Grove, 1961), 215–16.

4. Even for those who survived the Long March, the personal cost was staggering. Mao Zedong, for example, and his second wife reportedly left three of their children with peasant families along the way (and this in addition to the hardship of his wife giving birth en route). "The Long March was a searing experience in the lives of the survivors. The going was so difficult that many of the survivors suffered stomach ailments and insomnia for the rest of their lives." Kenneth Lieberthal, *Governing China* (New York: Norton, 1995), 47.

5. Tibor Mende, *The Chinese Revolution* (Worcester: Thames & Hudson, 1961), 111.

6. The home they met in (now a museum marking the site of the Zunyi Conference) belonged to a wealthy Nationalist military official. The six rooms on each floor provided living space for Red Army leaders, as well as a large meeting room. Among the twenty

people present at the meeting were Mao Zedong, Zhu De, Chen Yun, Zhou Enlai, Bo Gu, Deng Xiaoping, Liu Shaoqi, Li De, and Comintern representative Otto Braun.

7. Retold as fiction by Anthony Grey, *In Peking* (London: Pan Books, 1989). See also the missionary's autobiography, Alfred and England Bosshardt, *The Guiding Hand* (London: Hodder & Stoughton, 1973).

8. China's post-Deng era (Deng Xiaoping died in February 1997) marked the transition to a generation of leaders who did not experience the Long March firsthand. Whereas Long March veterans led by an implicit appeal to revolutionary history, today's leaders must seek and consolidate legitimacy—both their own and that of the Communist Party—from economic and policy success. Furthermore, whereas shared experience among Long March veterans established camaraderie, it is school ties, family backgrounds, and patron networks that now serve as binding forces among the political elite. Today's leaders, however, continue to claim the legacy of the Long March as part of their movement's epic story, even though it is not something they experienced firsthand. For a detailed discussion of China's changing political elite, see Cheng Li, *China's Leaders: The New Generation* (Lanham, Md.: Rowman & Littlefield, 2001).

9. Tibor Mende, *The Chinese Revolution* (Worcester: Thames & Hudson, 1961), 224.

10. Harrison E. Salisbury, *The Long March: The Untold Story* (New York: Harper & Row, 1985), 107.

11. The first fifty years of the twentieth century were a period of fluid politics and ever-shifting loyalties. People's allegiance often depended on who had the upper hand for the day. Guizhou had been a stronghold of Nationalist control, with varying degrees of cooperation with area warlords. For more on warlords at that time, see A. Doak Barnett, *China on the Eve of Communist Takeover* (New York: Praeger, 1963), 157–80.

12. Information from China Kweichow Moutai Distillery (Group) Co. Ltd. home page at www.cbw.com/company/moutai/1.html (August 1, 2002).

CHAPTER 3

1. Martin King Whyte, "City versus Countryside in China's Development," *Problems of Post-Communism* 43, no. 1 (January–February 1996): 9.

2. Sheryl WuDunn, "China's Rush to Riches," *New York Times,* September 4, 1994, 38.

3. Cheng Li, *Rediscovering China* (Lanham, Md.: Rowman & Littlefield, 1997), 111.

4. See Kam Wing Chan, "Recent Migration in China: Patterns, Trends, and Policies," *Asian Perspective* 25, no. 4 (2001): 131. More recent figures, based on the China National Rural Survey conducted in fall 2000, estimate that by 2000 almost as many of China's 200 million off-farm workers were living away from home as in the village. See Alan de Brauw, Jikuan Huang, Scott Rozelle, Linxiu Zhang, and Yigang Zhang, "China's Rural Labor Markets," *The China Business Review* 29, no. 2 (March-April 2002): 20.

5. Chan, "Recent Migration," 141–51. See also Dorothy J. Solinger, "China's Floating Population," in *The Paradox of China's Post-Mao Reforms,* edited by Merle Goldman and Roderick Macfarquhar (Cambridge, Mass.: Harvard University Press, 1999), 223–25.

6. Chan, "Recent Migration," 141–51.

7. Ezra F. Vogel, *One Step Ahead in China: Guangdong under Reform* (Cambridge, Mass.: Harvard University Press, 1989), 125–60.

8. *Guizhou jingji ribao* (Guizhou Economic Daily), February 5, 1998.

CHAPTER 4

1. From 1991 to 1996, 88,000 women who had been kidnapped for marriage were released by the police and 143,000 kidnappers were caught and prosecuted (*Sunday Telegraph,* November 22, 1998). But if that is how many were freed, imagine how many women are yet to be discovered.

2. Indeed, approximately two-thirds of all migrant labor in China stay within the same province. Kam Wing Chan, "Recent Migration in China: Patterns, Trends, and Policies," *Asian Perspective* 25, no. 4 (2001): 139.

3. Making charcoal in the countryside and selling it in the city is another cash-generating activity for rural residents living on the outskirts of the city. This woman had walked three hours from her village home to sell the stacks of homemade charcoal for 35 yuan (U.S. $4). The result, however, has been devastating deforestation. Note that this book's cover depicts migrant laborers who have brought charcoal into an urban area on their bicycles.

4. Princelings, or *gaogan zidi,* are children of high-ranking cadres. They sometimes function as a privileged clique.

5. For a thorough discussion of the urban–rural divide as a two-caste system, see Martin King Whyte, "City versus Countryside in China's Development," *Problems of Post-Communism* 43, no. 1 (January–February 1996).

6. He Qinglian, *Xiandaihua de xianjin: Zhonguo wenti baogao (The Pitfalls of Modernization: China's Problems Series)* (Beijing: Today's China Press, 1998), 251.

7. Wei Houkai, "Zhongguo xiangzhenqiye fazhan yu quyu chayi" (The Development of China's Township and Village Enterprises and Regional Disparities), *Zhongguo nongcun jingji (China Rural Economics)* (May 1997): 56–60.

8. China's Ministry of Agriculture reported a decreasing trend in net farm income growth: 5.6 percent in 1996, 4.6 percent in 1997, and an estimated 3.0 percent in 1998. *South China Morning Post,* December 24, 1998.

CHAPTER 5

1. The first paragraph is quoted from "Let the Facts Speak for Themselves," *The Selected Works of Deng Xiaoping, Volume Three* (Beijing: People's Daily Press), March 28, 1986. Second paragraph from "Seize the Opportunity to Develop the Economy," *The Selected Works of Deng Xiaoping, Volume Three* (Beijing: People's Daily Press), December 24, 1990.

2. The ratio of per capita government investment (total fixed-asset investment) strongly favored China's richest regions. Between 1978 and 1995, for example, the distribution of per capita investment in China's coast increased 19 percentage points (from 45 percent to 64 percent), while it decreased 11 percentage points in central China and 7 percentage points in western China during the same period. Instead of government investment promoting and balancing development, it served only to exacerbate disparity. Between 1993 and 1995, the

ratio of central government funding for basic construction projects (e.g., transportation, power, telecommunications) increasingly moved in favor of the coast. In 1993, the ratio was 1.44: 0.98: 1.0 (coast: central: western); in 1995, the ratio shifted to 1.6: 1.12: 1.0. Source: Zhou Piping, "Guanyu zhongxibu liyong waizi zhengci de jidian sikao" (Points to Consider Regarding Central and Western China's Foreign Investment Policies), *State Council Development Research Center Report,* no. 59 (August 10, 1997).

3. At the Fourteenth Party Congress (1992) four provincial leaders from China's high-income regions (Shanghai, Beijing, Tianjin, and Guangdong) and one provincial leader from upper-middle income regions (Shandong) were recruited into the Politburo of the Party's Central Committee. No provincial leader from the interior, low-income regions participated in the central government elite. Hu Angang, Wang Shaoguang, and Kang Xiaoguang, *Zhongguo diqu chabie baogao* (China Regional Disparity Report) (Shenyang: Liaoning renmin chubanshe, 1995), 82.

4. Hu, *Zhongguo diqu,* 82.

5. Hu, *Zhongguo diqu,* 288.

6. Hu, *Zhongguo diqu,* 290.

7. The book by Hu Angang, Wang Shaoguang, and Kang Xiaoguang, *Zhongguo diqu chabie baogao* (China Regional Disparity Report) (Shenyang: Liaoning renmin chubanshe, 1995), (now translated by M. E. Sharpe, *The Political Economy of Uneven Development: Case of China* [Armonk, N.Y.: M. E. Sharpe, 1999]), was specifically aimed at influencing the drafting of the Ninth Five-Year Plan. Hu Angang, who based his pleas on the use of surveys of government officials who feared the disparity would lead to social instability, called for the abolishing of the Special Economic Zones, saying they had played their role and were no longer necessary. The result was a very public and ugly—but interesting—debate with the mayor of Shenzhen.

8. Hu, *Zhongguo diqu,* 285.

9. Hu, *Zhongguo diqu,* 284.

10. These figures and commentary come from an interview with a Beijing scholar in 1998.

11. Ma Jun, *The Chinese Economy in the 1990s* (New York: St. Martin's, 2000), 149.

12. *Xinhua News Agency,* February 5, 2000.

13. Hu Angang, *Xibu kaifa xinzhanlue* (New Strategy for Developing the West) (Beijing: Zhonguo jihua chubanshe, 2001).

CHAPTER 6

1. For a more thorough introduction to the Chen family, see chapter 8.

2. Add to that, one of every four illiterate people in the world is Chinese and two hundred million Chinese cannot read or write. Kang Xiaoguang, *Chuangzao xiwang* (Creating Hope) (Guilin: Guangxi Normal University Press, 1997), 101.

3. The central government reports that 98.8 percent of all primary school–age children were enrolled in school in 1996. These annual enrollment surveys are typically conducted at the beginning of the school year and do not reflect actual rates of attendance or the nonattendance of dropouts during the school year.

4. *China 2020* (Washington, D.C.: World Bank, 1997), 48.

5. World Bank, Staff Appraisal Report (1995): China Southwest Poverty Reduction Project (Report No.13968-CHA).

6. Visits I have made to remote mountain villages like Big Nest Village in northern and Splendid Village in southern Guizhou Province reflect similar levels.

7. The contents of this section are based on interviews with Xu Yongguang and Kang Xiaoguang, a scholar at Qinghua University, in Beijing on February 13, 1998.

8. Kang, *Chuangzao xiwang,* 137.

9. In the spring of 2002, a flurry of newspaper articles reported accusations by former Project Hope employees, alleging that more than 100 million yuan (U.S. $12 million) of donations had been used in unsanctioned, highly speculative investments. China Youth Development Foundation officials dismissed the allegations, saying that all of its investments were profitable and "completely abide by China's relevant laws." In April 2002, the foundation opened its books to auditors and an international accounting firm. "Fund for Chinese Children Accused of Misusing Money," *The Straits Times (Singapore),* March 2, 2002; Elizabeth Rosenthal, "Under Pressure, Chinese Newspaper Pulls Expose on a Charity," *New York Times,* March 24, 2002.

10. Kang, *Chuangzao xiwang,* 135.

11. For a brief, well-written introduction to China's "third sector" and civil society related issues, see Nick Young, "Searching for Civil Society" at China Development Brief, www.chinadevelopmentbrief.com (August 9, 2002).

CHAPTER 7

1. Rice seedlings are grown to a height of six inches in a nursery paddy (they look like grass because they are planted so close together), then are bundled and transferred to open paddies where seedlings are placed six inches apart in rows. Before the seedlings are transplanted, the open paddies are plowed.

2. Although tuition is theoretically free, "miscellaneous fees" add up to make education a luxury item. Splendid Village's elementary-school students are about 70 percent male. Village illiteracy surpasses 65 percent.

3. On its six *mu* of land the Shui family has a fifty-year lease, which began in 1980 when the land was divided among the villagers. I asked Jianhua's uncles what it was like when the land was distributed. They said it was a very tense time—no one wanted to get the short end of the deal. In an effort to satisfy everyone, the land was divided by general categories of soil quality and then parceled out to families in shares of approximately one *mu* per person (six members of Jianhua's immediate family lived together at the time). As a result, Jianhua's twenty-one plots of land are not in one place; they are scattered throughout areas of varying soil quality.

4. In 1987, the China's National People's Congress passed a law establishing the structure and functions of village committees. According to the law, these committees are to be directly elected bodies, consisting of three to seven members that oversee village administrative and economic affairs. International organizations like the International Republican Institute have observed that since village elections were instituted, the process has, generally speaking, become increasingly democratic. Since 1987, the Ministry of Civil Affairs has provided guidelines and training in open nomination procedures, multicandidate election,

secret-ballot voting, transparent vote tabulation, and immediate transfer of power. The case of Splendid Village, however, demonstrates that some areas of China's countryside are yet to join this hopeful process. For a thorough discussion of village elections in China, see Anne F. Thurston, "Muddling toward Democracy: Political Change in Grassroots China," *Peaceworks* 23 (August 1998).

5. Township government officials are the lowest strata of administration in China to receive government salaries. Village-level officials (e.g., village party secretary, village head, and village accountant) are not on the government payroll. This reality has interesting implications for local politics, especially for the widespread problem of corruption.

CHAPTER 8

1. For a discussion on the status of rural women in China, see Patricia D. Beaver and Hou Lihui, "Rural Chinese Women," *Modern China* 21, no. 2 (April 1995): 205–33. See also Paul G. Pickowicz and Liping Wang, "Village Voices, Urban Activists: Women, Violence, and Gender Inequality in Rural China," in *Popular China: Unofficial Culture in a Globalizing Society,* ed. Perry Link, Richard P. Madsen, and Paul G. Pickowicz (Lanham, Md.: Rowman & Littlefield, 2002), 57–87.

2. Such trauma, though fortunately not in this case, sometimes leads to suicide. China is the only country in the world whose reported suicide rates for women outnumber those for men. China accounts for 56 percent of all female suicides worldwide. For an in-depth discussion of female suicides in China, see Sing Lee and Arthur Kleinman, "Suicide As Resistance in Chinese Society," in *Chinese Society: Change, Conflict and Resistance,* ed. Elizabeth J. Perry and Mark Selden (New York: Routledge, 2000), 221–40.

3. Chen Dongfang is currently studying at an education college in Guizhou far from home. He continues to draw his 200-yuan-per-month salary, even as a student living away from Big Nest Village. He taught at Big Nest Elementary for four years before beginning the current two-year program.

4. A short story I translated for China's Foreign Language Bureau in 1992 tells in story form the chaos of the 1930s in northern Guizhou when warlords controlled the salt trade. See Jian Xian'ai, "The Salt Calamity," *Short Story International* 21, no. 116 (February 1997): 18–40.

5. A. Doak Barnett, *China on the Eve of Communist Takeover* (New York: Praeger, 1963), 157–204.

6. See Andrew De Brauw, Jikun Huang, Scott Rozelle, Linxiu Zhang, and Yigang Zhang, "China's Rural Labor Markets," *China Business Review* 29, no. 2 (March–April 2002): 18–24.

CHAPTER 9

1. Tse-Tung Mao, *Selected Works of Mao Tse-Tung,* vol. 1 (Peking: Foreign Language Press, 1965), 21–57.

CHAPTER 10

1. At the same time, many do value education. Migrant laborers, when they come home, strongly encourage village children to study and improve themselves. The trend is increasing.

CHAPTER 11

Chapter opener image used by permission of the IISH Stefan R. Landsberger Collection: www.iisg.nl/~landsberger/lf.html.

1. Seminar participants represented five of Qiannan Prefecture's seven "impoverished" counties: Changshun, Dushan, Huishui, Libo, and Sandu (Luodian and Pingtang not included). Qiannan Prefecture has a total of ten counties and two cities. The poverty line is based on an average annual rural per capita income of 650 yuan (U.S. $79) and an average annual per capita grain production of 650 kg.

2. Since such statistics were revived in the early 1980s, Guizhou Province each year has had the lowest gross domestic product (GDP) figures in China.

3. With Deng Xiaoping's rise to power in late 1978 and official permission to criticize the Mao era, Dazhai commune was publicly discredited by a *People's Daily* article in 1980. Chen Yonggui had overreported production figures, underreported available land, and exaggerated grain sales. Chen Yonggui lost his Politburo seat in 1981.

4. Dawn Einwalter, "Selflessness and Self-Interest: Public Morality and the Xu Hong-fang Campaign," *Journal of Contemporary China* 7, no. 18 (July 1998): 257–70.

5. Karst describes rocky geological configurations characterized by irregular limestone formations. In karst mountain regions, the barren mountains are completely rock-covered, with little soil. Rainfall drains off immediately; cultivation and irrigation are practically impossible.

6. At that time, 60 yuan equaled less than U.S. $20. 60 *mu* = approximately 10 acres (1 *mu* = 0.0667 hectares = 0.10 acres).

7. *China: Overcoming Rural Poverty* (Washington, D.C.: World Bank, 2001), xiii.

CHAPTER 12

1. China has 56 ethnic nationality groupings. Han make up 92 percent of the population; the 55 other national minorities comprise the remaining 8 percent of the population. China's ethnic minority nationalities live predominantly in the country's northwest, southwest, and northeast regions. Guizhou Province is one of China's most colorful and ethnically diverse provinces.

2. Relative economic vitality fills only the areas where transportation is convenient. On another day, we climbed a steep but simple mountain one hour from the county seat to discover a Miao village mired in poverty and at least twenty years behind the county seat.

3. China has more than 100,000 beekeepers who have followed seasonal migratory trails around the country for centuries. The Ministry of Agriculture encourages the migrant beekeepers because their bees contribute to increased crop yields through pollination. For

the full story, see Sheila Melvin, "Nomads: China's Itinerant Honey Farmers," *Asia Wall Street Journal,* July 4, 1997.

4. See Andrew Morris, "'I Believe You Can Fly': Basketball Culture in Postsocialist China," in *Popular China: Unofficial Culture in a Globalizing Society,* ed. Perry Link, Richard P. Madsen, and Paul G. Pickowicz (Lanham, Md.: Rowman & Littlefield, 2002), 9–38.

5. From a policy perspective, the "autonomous" category provides affirmative action–like measures for the area, such as the requirement that a certain percentage of government positions is filled by ethnic-minority representatives. The designation also results in preferential treatment in government aid and taxes.

6. For the fundamental role of Confucianism in Han culture and religion, see C. K. Yang, *Religion in Chinese Society: A Study of Contemporary Social Functions of Religion and Some of Their Historical Factors* (Berkeley: University of California Press, 1961), 244–77.

7. There are regions of China where indigenous cultures are ambivalent toward Han modernizing culture—regions like Xinjiang and Tibet.

CHAPTER 13

1. The "Mao era" ended with Mao Zedong's death in 1976. Deng formally rose to power in 1978. He immediately advocated the Four Modernizations and Special Economic Zones.

2. For a thorough discussion of China's Third Front construction, see Barry Naughton, "The Third Front: Defence Industrialization in the Chinese Interior," *China Quarterly,* no. 115 (September 1988): 351–86.

3. Naughton, "Third Front," 351.

4. Ezra F. Vogel, "Special Economic Zones: Experiment in New Systems," in *One Step Ahead in China: Guangdong under Reform* (Cambridge, Mass.: Harvard University Press, 1989), 125–60.

5. "Off-post" (*xiagang*), often translated as "laid-off," refers to state-owned enterprise workers who have been asked not to come to work due to factory shutdowns, lack of production, or insufficient funds to pay salaries. They are, however, usually due a basic compensation package.

6. Before the Third Front construction started, Guizhou Province had only 377 miles of railroad track. Between 1965 and 1972, an additional 1,144 miles of track were completed. Naughton, "Third Front," 351.

7. Nicholas R. Lardy, *Integrating China into the Global Economy* (Washington, D.C.: Brookings Institution, 2002), 20. China's accession to the World Trade Organization is a historic breakthrough that signals consensus among China's top leadership that there is no viable alternative to economic globalization.

8. Lardy, *Integrating China,* 23.

9. Marquand, Robert, "China Airs Its Dirty Laundry, a Bit," *Christian Science Monitor,* June 8, 2001, 6.

10. *Guowuyuan fazhan yanjiu zhongxin jingji gongzuozhe xuexi ziliao* (State Council Development Research Center Economists' Study Material), no. 59 (1997): 44.

11. *Guowuyuan,* 44.

12. A prefecture-government official told me that more than half of Duyun's factories are not providing basic compensation for their laid-off workers.

13. The age distribution of laid-off workers is 11 percent between the ages of 16 and 24; 70.5 percent between the ages of 25 and 44; and 18.5 percent over the age of 45. See Yang Yiyong, ed., *Shiye chongji bo: zhongguo jiuye fazhan baogao* (The Lashing Waves of Unemployment: China Employment Development Report) (Beijing: Today's China Press, 1997), 328.

14. Chinese police reports estimate that there are four million prostitutes in China. See Bates Gill, Jennifer Chang, and Sarah Palmer, "China's HIV Crisis," *Foreign Affairs* 81, no. 2 (March/April 2002): 100. In addition, Guizhou Province is becoming a significant drug-trafficking hub in China. Narcotics come from Southeast Asian countries like Burma, cross into China through Yunnan Province, then move on from Guizhou to other regions of China and the world. Cooperation on narcotics control is becoming an important area of common interest for the United States and China.

15. For more information on the urban unemployed entering China's migrant labor force, see chapter 3.

16. *Guizhou jingji ribao* (Guizhou Economic Daily), May 3, 1998.

17. Zhihong Qian and Tai-Chee Wong, "The Rising Urban Poverty: A Dilemma of Market Reforms in China," *Journal of Contemporary China* 9, no. 23 (2000): 113–25.

18. Qian and Wong, "Rising Urban Poverty," 120.

19. Matt Forney, "We Want to Eat," *Far Eastern Economic Review,* June 26, 1997, 14–16.

20. *Guizhou jingji ribao* (Guizhou Economic Daily), April 19, 1998.

21. *Guangming ribao* (Guangming Daily), May 19, 1998.

22. Pamela Yatsko and Matt Forney, "Demand Crunch," *Far Eastern Economic Review,* January 15, 1998, 44.

CHAPTER 14

1. According to the second article of *Shehui liliang banxue tiaoli* (Regulations for Schools Established by Social Forces) "schools established by social forces" are defined as "educational institutions established by businesses, social organizations, or individual citizens and financed by nongovernment sources." *Renmin ribao* (People's Daily), August 12, 1997. This is no different than the *American Heritage Dictionary*'s definition of private schools: "A secondary or elementary school run and supported by private individuals or a corporation rather than by a government or public agency."

2. Students choose this type of school through one of two channels: through a standardized test that is given prior to graduation from middle school or, personally, through the school's advertisements or hearing about the school by word of mouth. More than half of the students at Qiannan Computer Vo-Tech enrolled because someone they knew recommended the school. Tuition is competitive with that of public schools, which also charge fees.

3. Students progress through China's education system as follows: After nine years of compulsory education (six years in primary school, three years in middle school), students, if they continue to study, proceed to high school (which puts them on a college-prep track) or one of two kinds of two-year vocational/technical schools: a *zhongzhuan* that trains local

government cadres (bureaucrats, teachers, medical workers, etc.), or a *jishu xuexiao* to prepare workers with specific skills, like computer technicians. If the student enters high school
but then does not test successfully for college, he or she may test into yet another type of
two-year vocational school (*dazhuan*), also designed to train government cadres. Because
fewer than 5 percent of Chinese middle-school graduates move on to higher education,
there is a tremendous need to train middle-school graduates in skills that enable them to be
productive members of the country's workforce. Private schools like Qiannan Computer
Vo-Tech help meet this need.

4. For a more thorough introduction to the Third Front Construction period, see chapter 13.

5. Jing Lin, "Private Education in China: Its Development and Dynamics," *Harvard
China Review* 3, no. 2 (2002): 21–26.

6. Principal Bi was included as a participant in an exchange program sponsored by the
National Committee on U.S.–China Relations that joined him with other private educators
in Guizhou and the United States.

7. Jing Lin, "Private Education in China," 21.

8. He Qizong and Zhang Yizhong, "Some Thoughts about Current Private Education
in China," *Chinese Education and Society* 30, no. 1 (1997): 38.

9. Private schools in Guiyang are not just for rich kids, though some do cater to the
better-off. A private educator in Guiyang told me that more than half of the twenty private
primary schools in the provincial capital are filled with children of China's "floating population." "Floating population" refers to all people children, elderly, working age, urban,
and rural—who have left their place of official household registration (*hukou*), either tempo-
rarily or permanently, to reside in another part of the country. Much of the "floating population" in Guiyang consists of people from other parts of the province who have traveled to
the provincial capital to look for work.

10. Private education remains primarily an urban phenomenon in China's interior,
although there is tremendous need and potential for rural areas. Friends I know in Guizhou's countryside are aware that central-government policy permits them to establish private schools or revive traditional education methods (*sishu*), where an educated villager
teaches a group of students. Because of problems brought on by decentralized education
financing, these methods would also provide education more cheaply than current government-run elementary schools. Local-level policy, however, requires passing through so
many hoops (each involving a fee) that it effectively prohibits villagers from setting up their
own schools.

11. "Outline for China's Education Reform and Development" was issued by the Chinese Communist Party Central Committee and the State Council on February 13, 1993.
Zhongguo Jiaoyu bao (China Education News), February 27, 1997.

12. *Renmin ribao* (People's Daily), September 7, 1998.

13. *Renmin ribao* (People's Daily), April 11, 1998.

CHAPTER 15

1. *Zhongyang qiannan zhouwei bangongshi, zhou ban fa* (General Office of Guizhou Province Qiannan Buyi and Miao Autonomous Prefecture Communist Party), document no. 17
(1996).

2. In 1993, Guizhou introduced its version of a nationwide law that called for two-day weekends. Prior to that, six-day workweeks were the standard practice.

3. *Guizhou dushi bao* (Guizhou All-City Newspaper), June 7, 1998, has an entire spread on the Magenuojie Grasslands.

4. Our guests were a U.S. energy company executive and the director of the Shanghai office of the U.S.–China Business Council, both good friends from graduate school.

5. In addition, the prefecture tourism bureau has a squabble going with the county: County officials have set up tollbooths at either end of the road leading into the grasslands. Even our provincial-government vehicle had to hand over the appropriate fees (8 yuan— about U.S. $1—per person) before being permitted to pass. One frustrated official told me: "You could be the emperor and they wouldn't let you past without paying. This problem must be solved."

6. The horses, which are much larger than the local work ponies, are advertised as "Japanese thoroughbreds." "Actually," Director Liu later mentioned in private, "the horses are Chinese, we got them for free when an illegal race track in Guiyang was shut down. Chinese like things that are 'imported,' so we say they are Japanese."

7. The ten Miao performers receive 200 yuan (U.S. $24) per night for their hour's performance and a free meal. They make in one month what most villagers in that area make in one year.

8. *Survey on China's Domestic Traveling, China Tourist News,* October 9, 1997.

9. *Mai xiang xin shiji: qiannan gaige kaifang jishi* (Striding toward the New Century: A Record of Reform and Opening in Qiannan Prefecture) (Beijing: Xinhua Publishing House, 1998), 252.

10. Guizhou Province is 87 percent mountainous.

11. *Guizhou ribao* (Guizhou Daily), May 27, 1998.

12. The problem was especially acute in the 1960s and 1970s when the central government directed a national defense–motivated strategy in western provinces like Guizhou— called the Third Front— that emphasized the construction of steel, armaments, machinery, electronics, and petroleum industries.

13. *Gua zhi,* the practice of sending talented young central-government officials to a remote province to work for a few years, is a fascinating method of cultivating future leaders. These officials usually return to promoted positions in the central government after learning, through hands-on involvement, about regions of China quite different than Beijing. It should be noted that *gua zhi* is practiced on more local levels of government as well. For example, a promising young prefecture-level official may be sent to work for a time as a county-level official. Guo Shuqing's arrival was part of this leadership-training arrangement. In 2000, Guo returned to Beijing, where he is now deputy governor of the People's Bank of China and director of China's Foreign Exchange Administration. Note that Hu Jintao, China's future president, spent three similar years in Guizhou in the 1980s under a similar arrangement.

14. *Guo shuqing fu shengzhang tingqu luyou gongzuo huibaohou de jianghua* (Vice Governor Guo Shuqing Remarks after Hearing Tourism Work Reports), October 20, 1998.

15. Universal Films (1989), starring Kevin Costner.

CHAPTER 16

1. Someone told me that these county officials would have probably been given "honorary" club memberships. Such an arrangement would probably go a long way in preserving healthy club–county relations.

CHAPTER 17

1. Jaime A. Florcruz, Joshua Cooper Ramo, Mia Turner, and Edward Barnes, "Inside China's Search for Its Soul," *Time* 154, no. 14 (October 4, 1999): 69.

2. Falun Gong, a quasireligious movement that combines a range of breathing, healing, and meditation techniques, was established in 1992. Li Hongzhi, its leader, a forty-eight-year-old former grain official from northeast China, now based in New York, claims a higher authority than Buddha, Mohammed, and Jesus. Only he knows the "way," he says. Falun Gong claims 100 million followers worldwide.

3. *New York Times,* July 26, 1999, 1.

4. *New York Times,* April 5, 2002, 4.

5. Wm. Theodore de Bary, *Sources of Chinese Tradition,* vol. 2 (New York: Columbia University Press, 1960), 213.

6. Note that Deng Xiaoping's phrase "Black cat or white cat, a good cat is one that catches mice" dates from the early 1960s at which time he also emphasized a pragmatic approach to China's development. Though he got in trouble for this saying during the Cultural Revolution, history shows that Deng remained realistic in his advocacy of China's economic development.

7. *China Daily,* June 7, 1999, 4.

8. De Bary, *Sources,* 285.

9. The revival of ancestor worship in China's countryside, because it is so closely tied to clan relations, has interesting implications for rural politics. This is so because local, rural organization traditionally revolved around clan association. With the veneration of ancestors, loyalties that surpass government influence can easily develop. Clan influence in some areas has also been galvanized as a response to extreme levels of local corruption.

10. David Aikman, "China's Search for Its Soul," *American Spectator* 33, no. 2 (March 2000): 22–25.

11. Zhang Tan, *'Zhai men' qian de shimenkan* (The Stone Threshold in Front of the Narrow Gate) (Kunming: Yunnan Education Press, 1992), 25.

12. Tan, *Zhai men,* 122.

13. Tan, *Zhai men,* 57.

14. Tan, *Zhai men,* 228.

CHAPTER 18

1. *Hong Kong Ming Pao,* May 2, 2002.

2. *China: National Human Development Report. Human Development and Poverty Alleviation 1997* (Beijing: United Nations Development Programme, 1998).

3. Wang Shaoguang, "The Social and Political Implications of China's WTO Membership," *Journal of Contemporary China* 9, no. 25 (November 2000): 373–405.

4. Martin King Whyte, "City versus Countryside in China's Development," *Problems of Post-Communism* 43, no. 1 (January–February 1996): 9.

5. World Bank, *Sharing Rising Incomes: Disparities in China* (Washington, D.C.: World Bank, 1997), 7–8.

6. Hu Angang, ed., *Zhongguo: Tiaozhan fubai* (China: Fighting against Corruption) (Hangzhou: Zhejiang renmin chubanshe, 2000), 34.

7. Bruce Gilley, "People's Republic of Cheats," *Far Eastern Economic Review* 21 (June 2001): 60.

8. Susan V. Lawrence, "Excising the Cancer," *Far Eastern Economic Review* 20 (August 1998): 10.

9. "China to Focus on Western Development," *ChinaOnline,* 2000, at www.chinaonline.com/issues/econ—news/NewsArchive/cs-protected/2000/march/b100030706.asp (11 September 2002).

10. Kang Xiaoguang, "Weilai 3–5 nian zhongguo dalu zhengzhi wendingxing fenxi" (An Analysis of Political Stability in Mainland China in the Next Three to Five Years), *Beijing zhanlue yu guanli* (Beijing Strategy and Management), trans FBIS-CHI, June 1, 2002. I am grateful to Kang Xiaoguang for his analysis and use his understanding of the relationship between elites and masses throughout the rest of this chapter.

11. Minxin Pei, "China's Governance Crisis," *Foreign Affairs* 81, no. 5 (September–October 2002): 109.

12. John Pomfret, *Washington Post,* March 8, 2002.

13. Minxin Pei, "Rights and Resistance: The Changing Contexts of the Dissident Movement," in *Chinese Society: Change, Conflict and Resistance,* ed. Elizabeth J. Perry and Mark Selden (New York: Routledge, 2000), 20–40.

14. Because of the lack of more conventional avenues of expression, protests and riots often flare to the extreme, far beyond what may seem appropriate to the particular grievance. Such was the case with the Zunyi riot.

15. Elizabeth J. Perry and Mark Selden, eds., *Chinese Society: Change, Conflict and Resistance* (New York: Routledge, 2000), 14.

16. "Protests but No Bullets," *Economist,* April 6, 2002, 38.

17. Kang, "Weilai."

18. Merle Goldman and Roderick MacFarquhar, eds., *The Paradox of Post-Mao Reforms* (Cambridge, Mass.: Harvard University Press, 1999), 6.

19. Richard Baum, *Burying Mao: Chinese Politics in the Age of Deng Xiaoping* (Princeton, N.J.: Princeton University Press, 1996), 3.

20. For analysis of the emergence of China's economic elite, see Margaret M. Pearson, *China's New Business Elite: The Political Consequences of Economic Reform* (Berkeley: University of California Press, 1997), and Kellee S. Tsai, *Back-Alley Banking: Private Entrepreneurs in China* (Ithaca, N.Y.: Cornell University Press, 2002).

21. Joseph Fewsmith, *China since Tiananmen: The Politics of Transition* (Cambridge: Cambridge University Press, 2001), 229.

22. Erik Eckholm, "China's President May Be Reluctant to Cede His Power," *New York Times,* July 13, 2002.

23. Kang, "Weilai."

24. Francis Fukuyama, *Trust: The Social Virtues and the Creation of Prosperity* (New York: Free Press, 1995).

25. Cheng Li, *China's Leaders: The New Generation* (Lanham, Md.: Rowman & Littlefield, 2001), 56. The full name of the "sent-down" movement is "Up to the Mountain and Down to the Village Movement."

26. Cheng Li, "Inland Hu and Coastal Zeng?" *Woodrow Wilson International Center for Scholars, Asia Program Special Report,* no. 105 (September 2002): 31.

27. Other national figures who have risen through the ranks in Guizhou are Zhu Houze

(minister of propaganda in the 1980s), Lou Jiwei (current executive vice minister of finance), and Guo Shuqing (current deputy governor of the People's Bank of China and director of the Foreign Exchange Commission). ,

28. Matthew Forney, "Taking the Helm," Timeasia.com at www.time.com/time/asia/features/hu—jintao/cover.html (September 7, 2002).

29. Matthew Forney, "Taking the Helm," Timeasia.com at www.time.com/time/asia/features/hu—jintao/cover.html (September 7, 2002).

30. David M. Lampton, *Policy Implementation in Post-Mao China* (Berkeley: University of California Press, 1987), 3.

31. Carol Lee Hamrin and Wang Zheng, "China's Social Capital Deficit" (unpublished paper, 2002). I am grateful to Carol Lee Hamrin for her analysis of social capital as it relates to China's situation.

32. Marilee S. Grindle, *Getting Good Government: Capacity Building in Public Sectors of Developing Countries*. (Cambridge, Mass.: Harvard University Press, 1997).

33. Cited in Peter Schirmer, Ryan Atkinson, and Jeff Carroll, "Introduction," *Civil Society in Kentucky* (1998), 1–4.

34. The concept of "social capital" was developed by Pierre Bourdieu and James Coleman and popularized by Robert Putnam and Francis Fukuyama. In Fukuyama's book *Trust*, he refers to social capital as the informal values and habits that enable people to work together for common purposes in groups and organizations. In chapter 1 of his book, Fukuyama discusses many aspects of the definition of social capital, using "habits" to combine values and resulting behavior. A government that could facilitate these developments would regain legitimacy because it would be seen as fostering between the people and the government and among the people themselves one of China's more rare assets. trust.

35. Hamrin and Wang, "Social Capital."

36. Hamrin and Wang, "Social Capital."

37. For further commentary on China's winner-take-all tradition of political contestation, see Joseph Fewsmith, *China since Tiananmen: The Politics of Transition* (Cambridge, Mass.: Cambridge University Press, 2001), 5.

Index

About the Author

Daniel B. Wright is the executive director of the Hopkins-Nanjing Program at the Johns Hopkins University Paul H. Nitze School of Advanced International Studies (SAIS). Prior to living in China's Guizhou Province as a fellow of the Institute of Current World Affairs (1997–1999), Wright was manager of Asian affairs for the Washington, D.C., consulting firm Andreae, Vick & Associates and translator at the Foreign Language Bureau Chinese Literature Press in Beijing. He is also the author of *Wo kan zhongguo* (China through My Eyes), published in Chinese by Guangxi Education Publishing House (2000).